Music and Urban Geography

Music and Urban Geography

ADAM KRIMS
University of Nottingham

Routledge is an imprint of the
Taylor & Francis Group, an informa business

Routledge
Taylor & Francis Group
270 Madison Avenue
New York, NY 10016

Routledge
Taylor & Francis Group
2 Park Square
Milton Park, Abingdon
Oxon OX14 4RN

Routledge is an imprint of Taylor & Francis Group, an Informa business

Printed in the United States of America on acid-free paper
10 9 8 7 6 5 4 3 2 1

International Standard Book Number-10: 0-415-97012-1 (Softcover) 0-415-97011-3 (Hardcover)
International Standard Book Number-13: 978-0-415-97012-9 (Softcover) 978-0-415-97011-2 (Hardcover)

Library of Congress Cataloging-in-Publication Data

Krims, Adam.
Music and urban geography / Adam Krims.
p. cm.
Includes bibliographical references (p.) and index.
ISBN 0-415-97011-3 -- ISBN 0-415-97012-1
1. Music--Social aspects--History. 2. Urban geography. 3. Social history. I. Title.

ML3916.K75 2007
780.9173'2--dc22 2006031347

Visit the Taylor & Francis Web site at
http://www.taylorandfrancis.com

and the Routledge Web site at
http://www.routledge.com

To Dr. Marvin B. Krims, with love and admiration

Contents

Preface

This book brings together the two disciplines named in its title. My own disciplinary training has been in music theory and musicology, whereas urban geography is a discipline that I adopted by necessity along the way. (I first published an article on classical recordings and urban geography in 2001.) Initially, I pursued academic research in urban geography because I found that it answered a lot of questions that musicologists and music theorists were asking about music, both classical and popular; and since it approached those questions from a totally new perspective, I found that the answers were uniquely convincing and coherent. With so many central American, Canadian, and European universities located in major cities, and with so much of the intelligentsia also publishing and broadcasting from those same cities, most music scholars seemed nonetheless little, if at all, interested in how the character of those cities may be shaping how we hear and think about music. Once the urban context of music making, distribution, and consumption is restored, many hoary debates suddenly sport new profiles. This book draws those profiles and synthesizes them into a theoretical framework; it addresses both popular and classical music because (as I found in the course of researching the book) many of the changes happening in the musical world transcend the boundaries that presumably divide the two.

In the course of presenting some of the work in this book to geographers, I was initially surprised to find that my approach, coming from music theory, actually addressed a number of the questions that *they* were asking, also in a new light. Although many geographers had studied and published on issues of culture, including expressive culture, a theoretical approach from somebody trained to treat music as a certain kind of object (or activity) actually threw music and space into a new light for many of them. Progressive music scholars such as I are so used to thinking of a "discipline" as a potential pitfall that we sometimes forget that in constructing things, disciplines also enable. Michel Foucault told us this, of course, a long time ago.

So this book addresses all these people, and others, as well. It should have something to offer not only music scholars (music theorists, musicologists, and ethnomusicologists) and geographers, but also students and scholars in other disciplines to which music and social aspects of space bear some relevance. This would include people in film (which is particularly addressed in Chapter 3, but also in Chapter 1), cultural studies, critical theory, sociology of culture, literature, drama, art history, and regional studies. The book assumes no background in urban geography but rather introduces most of that pertinent information in its Introduction (and more specifics within the chapters). For teaching purposes, the Introduction and Chapter 1, Chapter 3, and Chapter 5 may be used for advanced undergraduates; Chapter 2 and Chapter 4 are best left for graduate students. Those without a formal music background will have some difficulty understanding parts of Chapter 1, Chapter 2, and Chapter 4, although much even in these chapters will still be accessible.

The contributions of my extraordinary friends, colleagues, and relatives to this book are such that their presence hides behind many moments of which the reader could hardly be aware.

The former music editor at Routledge, Richard Carlin, offered not only infinite wisdom, but, probably more crucially, infinite patience as due dates flew by. Many thanks to him for nonetheless believing that the book would arrive one fine day. Thanks also to his successor, Constance Ditzel, and to Devon Sherman.

Some of the research for this book was funded by a major grant from the Social Sciences and Humanities Research Council of Canada.

Other research support was provided by various research funds at the universities of Nottingham and Alberta. In addition, the University of Alberta provided a research leave that proved critical to writing the bulk of the manuscript. Katarzyna Borkowska provided invaluable assistance with fieldwork in later stages of the research.

A great number of colleagues have offered crucial input throughout the years that have steered me away from overt errors. I owe an enormous debt to Henry Klumpenhouwer, without whom I very much doubt Chapter 2 of this book would exist. Bonnie Blackburn performed a helpful copy edit on an early draft. Along the way, I received crucial theoretical feedback from such extraordinary minds as Robert Adlington, Ian Biddle, Evan Bonds, Jim Buhler, Tim Carter, Andrew Dell'Antonio, Robert Fink, Dan Grimley, Tim Hughes, Brian Hyer, Jean-Marie Jacono, Anahid Kassabian, Henry Klumpenhouwer, Larry Kramer, Andrew Leyshon, David Matless, Allan Moore, Jocelyn Neal, Severine Neff, Max Paddison, Erkki Pekkilä, Patricia Schmidt, Allen Scott, Michael Spitzer, Robert Walser, Alastair Williams, and countless others. The remaining faults stem, no doubt, from my obstinacy.

My wife, Kasia, and my son, Stéphane, not only gave me constant emotional support throughout the process of writing the manuscript, but they also provided the inspiration and incentive to finish it. My father, Dr. Marvin Krims, lent emotional and moral support without which I would never have had the opportunity to do anything so exotic as to write an academic book. He has also provided constant intellectual and personal companionship; most important, he has served as an inspiration. It is to him that this book is lovingly and gratefully dedicated.

Parts of Chapter 4 were previously published as "Marxist Music Analysis Without Adorno: Popular Music and Urban Geography," in Allan Moore, ed., *Analyzing Popular Music* (Cambridge: Cambridge University Press, 2003). (Reprinted with permission.)

Parts of Chapter 5 were previously published as "Marxism, Urban Geography, and Classical Recordings: An Alternative to Cultural Studies," *Music Analysis* 20.3 (2001). (Reprinted with permission.)

Introduction

Changing Cities and the Music Studies of the Present

The phonogram and video store Fame lies in the central district (*Centrum*) of Amsterdam, on the Kalverstraat, just across from the Damrak. The Kalverstraat resembles similar centrally located pedestrian shopping streets in most major Dutch (and other Western European) cities. The storefronts are dominated by retail goods and concentrate on consumer products: clothing stores, bookstores, and sellers of souvenirs and trinkets predominate, along with cosmetics and, of course, music and video recordings. Many of the shops represent chains, some Dutch (e.g., Bart Smit, a toy and video game store chain, or De Slegte, a chain of bookstores selling used and discounted new books); others are international, especially American-owned shops (e.g., Foot Locker footwear and two Levis Centers selling casual clothing). The Kalverstraat does not host the most unusual or innovative stores in Amsterdam (by quite a margin), and I have heard both locals and tourists complain about both its predictability and the massive pedestrian crowds that often render movement difficult, slow, and unpleasant. Nevertheless, probably because of its location and the sheer concentration of businesses, the Kalverstraat remains a hub of retail business in the center of Amsterdam.

Fame stands toward the northern end of the street. By far the largest retailer of music there, they advertise the largest selection of CDs in the Netherlands, also offering movie DVDs, video games, and common accessories for music and video playback (e.g., iPod cases). Organized like many similar stores selling music and visual media all over the advanced capitalist world and especially in its cities, Fame consists of departments spatially divided by floors and partial or full walls. Some departments are identified by medium, such as a DVD department that carries a selection of films that would be familiar to many buyers all over the industrialized world, in addition to some Dutch titles and selected films and music video compilations from elsewhere in Western Europe. Smaller selections of books, music- or movie-themed gifts, board games, and T-shirts benefit from cross-marketing with the movies and, especially, music. Indeed, phonograms predominate within the inventory of Fame, especially compact discs, and accordingly, most departments are identified by musical genre. "World music" constitutes one such genre, for instance, and the store's corresponding department both proffers internationally distributed titles and projects the specific history of the Netherlands (such as a substantial selection of recordings from the Netherlands Antilles, a region discussed in Chapter 2). Most of the music-generic departments stand at certain points contiguous to another, via an open entrance, or even share one room with other genres within a large open space; however, the classical department and its smaller subsidiary jazz section, exceptionally, are separated from the rest of the store, completely closed off via a single entrance with a glass door. Its physical isolation serves at least one practical purpose: to some extent it soundproofs the space, allowing the department to play featured titles with minimum interference from neighboring departments, which often play music at far higher volumes. But the isolation of the classical department also constitutes a symbolic act, reproduced at many other record stores worldwide, namely, marking off classical music (and sometimes its fellow 'high' music, jazz, along with it) as a specialized genre, one whose marketing, consumption, and appreciation require special conditions and an impermeable separation from other music. In Fame, that special status receives reinforcement from some properties unique to the classical department, including a resident baby grand piano and a sitting/listening area for customers to preview reflectively the recordings offered for sale.

The status of classical music therefore finds its spatialization in Fame—and, of course, in many other similar large phonogram retailers—and the experience of shopping at Fame thus projects classical music's generic status into a geographical fact. At the same time, the store's location in a retail district of a city whose economy depends largely on entertainment and tourism bespeaks layered practices of cultural consumption. Classical music, in this case, becomes not just something one hears, and not only a set of discourses; it also becomes a way of experiencing space. And music's social functions loom all the larger in an entertainment- and tourism-oriented district like that of central Amsterdam. Music can spatialize, in this case, only in a context in which it has already been spatialized.

In the case of Fame, classical music is specifically a manner of experiencing urban geography. This is not only for the possibly trivial reason that the shop is located in a major city; it also has to do with the overall relation of the store to the city of Amsterdam and the character of Amsterdam in the larger structure of world cities and states. The Kalverstraat itself constitutes a particular route with a particular role in Amsterdam, a city whose high reliance on service and informational industries, including (but by no means limited to) tourism, necessitates a supportive infrastructure of commodities and entertainment. Not just the existence but also the location and design of the shop find their significance only in that context, and one of the key arguments of this book (especially this introduction and Chapter 5) will be that the deployment of music as a spatializing practice also finds its significance in the particular *kind* of city that Amsterdam has become. The classical department at Fame, therefore, forms an experience of urban geography not only in the obvious sense that it occurs in a certain city location, but also in the much profounder sense that it produces a certain socializing experience for a very particular kind of urban resident or visitor, one appropriate to Amsterdam at a certain point in its history. All that need not detract from the extent to which a visit to that room also forms a musical experience, one that deploys strategies of musical notes, musical pleasure, and the great variety of melodies, rhythms, harmonies, and timbers more often discussed in strictly musicological and music-theoretical contexts (and which will always remain central to this book). On the contrary, the psychological investment in such aspects of music, the quick and often deeply felt attribution of musical affect to "the body" or ineffable depths of subjectivity, most likely assign music a particular and lamentably underexplored role in mapping the contemporary city. This book will also advance another key argument that some of the particular strategies of such investment themselves develop in tandem with the changing urban environment, in ways that are far from random.

A trip to the classical music department thus constitutes both a voyage through urban geography and a musical voyage, inseparably and through an integrated gesture, rather than through two separate processes. So not only the layout of Fame and its classical department, but also the kinds of music played and sold there, serve to socialize listeners and consumers for both a certain conception of music and also for the rapidly changing city. In the case of the music itself—and it is important to underline that the conception of "music itself" is not, as some contemporary musicology would have it, a mystification but rather a crucial, highly planned, and controlled social object—the poetic strategy increases in significance as music increasingly acquires a central role in characterizing spaces. The present book will serve to elaborate and demonstrate these processes; understanding them will not only shed some light on current debates in musicology and cultural studies, it will also introduce a new perspective with which to understand life in the major cities that exercise a growing influence on economic and cultural life in the world.

The Population Reference Bureau reports that 47 percent of the world's population lived in cities in 2000; it projects that by 2030, 60 percent of the world's population will be urban.[1] But a concentration of population constitutes only one aspect of the overall cultural significance of urbanization and city life; a strong argument could be advanced that cities began dominating cultural production, distribution, and consumption long before the projected point when most of the world's people will happen to live in them. After all, the bulk of professional concerts, record labels, and movie and television production—in short, the commercial life of music production, if not always its consumption—occurs in the developed world within cities, and often within a small number of specific cities.[2] The statistics about urban populations, therefore, might offer only symbolic significance, rather than a nuanced and theoretically sound index of the cultural significance of urbanization in the contemporary world. They do suggest, however, a process that will also gain visibility in many of the theoretical discussions that follow, namely the agglomeration of activity and labor around the world's cities as their role in global economic and cultural life develops and expands. Those changes have been widely theorized over the past thirty years or so, and they constitute much of the background behind the discussions in this book. As they have been discussed at length elsewhere, in findings and debates that far outdistance the scope of this book, here I will only summarize those aspects of recent discussions of urban geography that are necessary to comprehending the findings of this book.

Major changes have taken place in cities of the world, especially larger cities in the developed world, over the past few decades; although debates have certainly raged concerning the character and scope of those changes, no researcher in economics or urban studies, to my knowledge, has seriously suggested that no such changes have taken place. Whereas the development of urban spaces sometimes receives the tag "postindustrial," perhaps boosted by the 1970s North American popular description of "deindustrialization," the notion of postindustrial cities at best references a half-truth, a symptom more than an entire process, and not an entirely accurate description even of the symptom. More usefully, one can posit that a number of heavy, labor-intensive manufacturing industries, at various points during the early 1970s and afterwards, left cities like Chicago and Detroit, but they have not necessarily left urban areas entirely—nor have the affected cities in all cases lost industry so much as hosted differing kinds of industry. As evidence for the latter, one might note that a good number of cities that were spoken of as "deindustrialized" in the 1970s and 1980s underwent revitalization sometime afterwards, such as Manchester, Leeds, and Pittsburgh. In some cases, large-scale manufacturing was replaced by service industries and business services, in other cases by culture-based regeneration,[4] and in yet other cases by differently organized industries of the type sometimes pegged as "flexible" (about which Scott Lash and John Urry, on one hand, and David Harvey, on the other, offer sharply contrasting theoretical explanations); in many instances, cities that succeeded in maintaining their economic vitality combined these strategies.

And there have been, of course, many cities, such as Gary, Indiana, or Vigo, Spain, that have yet to recover from their loss of heavy, labor-intensive manufacturing. Even attempts to emulate successful strategies have never met with guaranteed success; one need only think of the tragicomic scene from Michael Moore's classic *Roger and Me* (1989), in which Flint, Michigan, attempts recovery from the shattering of its auto industry through tourism and convention hosting, only to fail through lack of consumer interest. Whereas most studies concentrate on the successes rather than the failures, the latter invite counterstudies that remain all too rare.

The processes affecting the major cities with advanced economies, therefore, have constituted not so much deindustrialization as a series of shifts in activities and scales, both internally and in terms of their relations to the rest of the world. It will not be difficult to imagine that a change in the function of metropolitan economies will entail profound shifts throughout virtually every register of life: after all, urban regions arguably exist precisely as lynchpins of production, places where goods and services are combined with a qualified workforce, such that their very infrastructure hinges on capital accumulation. Thus, if a city supports a different economic activity, then multiple registers will also shift. One will observe mutations in the character of its spaces, its buildings, its retail storefronts, its residential stock and, just as important, the kinds of people that will inhabit it. Along with the latter come changes of more direct interest to those who study expressive culture: different workers, when attracted to the metropolis, will support different restaurants, clothing stores, films, musical productions and recordings, and so on. So it is not at all far-fetched to imagine that a transformation in the economic functioning of major cities may correspond to some concomitant developments in musical life in those same places.

But one need not restrict the link between shifts in cities overall and shifts in musical culture to a matter of displaced human populations.

On the contrary, anybody interested in understanding contemporary music production and reception may take at least one cue from so-called cultural musicology, seeing music as a socializing agent with its own complex channeling from, and back into, the organization of society as a whole. Such a characterization admittedly projects a more sociological framework than has generally been fashionable in cultural musicology, which traditionally has tended to underline either music's hermeneutic value or, more commonly, its contribution to discourses, either conformant or resistant.[6] Nevertheless, the notion coexists among all these approaches that music retains a specific agency, relying crucially on, and sometimes acting on, its specificity as sound that is organized and continually reproduced in a developing social context. What is more, the transformations of the physical space, flows, and pace of life in the city cannot help but inflect expressive culture as well (as will be argued in Chapter 1, Chapter 4, and Chapter 5).

The theoretical approach of this book, therefore, will take as a premise the dramatic changes in world metropolises over the past few decades, using them as instances for explaining changes in musical culture, and looking toward how the two processes may find a connection in a larger unity, including contributions from music back toward urban form. That unity will not subsume one process in the other: that is to say, music will not be the ultimate determinant of urban change nor will the changing city propel musical developments as in a caricature of Second International Marxism (about which more will be said presently). Rather, neither register will cause each other, in the sense of an Aristotelian efficient cause, so much as they will participate in each other as different moments in a larger unity.

As Derek Sayer has argued, Marx, despite many who have theorized in his name, did not conceive of economics and culture (or other registers of society) as separate realms with inherent logics, which may then inflect other, separately constituted logics causally.[7] Instead, Sayer corrects a long-standing (and in his view fallacious) interpretation of Marx's views of culture and economy via an interpretation, drawing on most of the major texts, of just what Marx means by "relations of production" in his preface to *A Contribution to the Critique of Political Economy*.[8] That very text, of course, has often served as the foundation of what Sayer calls "traditional historical materialism" (by which he means to signal those interpretations that separate off material as "base" and ideas as "superstructure," producing the kind of mechanistic "materialism" represented, in his view, by Gerald Allen Cohen).[9] But in Sayer's view, the economically driven determinism, as well as the separation of human thought and culture from the realm of "relations of production," misreads Marx's intentions, both in this text and in the many other key classic texts that Sayer examines. At one point, opening with Marx's own statement (not from the *Contribution to the Critique of Political Economy*, but rather from the *Grundrisse*) that "human life has from time immemorial rested on production, and, in one way or another, on *social* production, whose relations we call, precisely, economic relations,"[10] Sayer observes:

> What Marx is doing here is so devastatingly simple, and at the same time so genuinely revolutionary, that generations of commentators have somehow managed to overlook it. He is not, as with "traditional historical materialism," reducing social relations to economic relations as conventionally conceived, or explaining the former in terms of the latter. He is precisely redefining "economic" relations ... as comprising the totality of social relations, whatever these may be, which make particular forms of production, and thus of property, possible. ... As he wrote in 1846, introducing the notion of a "mode of production," his mode "must not be considered simply as being the reproduction of the physical existence of ... individuals. Rather it is a definite form of activity of these individuals, a definite form of expressing their life, a definite *mode of life* on their part. (*Violence*, 76–77; emphasis Sayer's)[11]

The relations of production, then, that form the bedrock of the mechanistic historical materialism sometimes practiced, turn out, in Marx's original conception, to embrace the production of the whole social body, not simply factories and burlap bags. Any aspect of what one traditionally calls "culture" may therefore (and in fact must, insofar as it is "social") participate in the relations of production, so long as it enables the particular form of production. The latter requirement, interestingly, can be taken as an opportunity to turn the stereotyped economic determinism of Second International Marxism on its head and to investigate how aspects of our society often taken as purely cultural (or "superstructural" in some versions) may, in fact, play key roles in the very heart of developing strategies of accumulation—and quite consistently with Marx's own approach. Indeed, a central premise of this book (most explicitly in the final chapter but, in fact, throughout) is that music, as a shaper of subjectivity, does indeed participate in building us as listeners within a historical context shaped by the overall contours of production (here defined, of course, with precisely the breadth indicated by Sayer). Strategies of musical poetics do not gear us as good workers, in a simplistic conception of socialization, but they do form a complex subjective unity with the spaces that societies build in their continuous self-production.

Neither production (narrowly defined, unlike in Marx's writings) nor musical culture (again, narrowly defined) evinces either a self-sufficiency or a primacy that could be isolated or treated as determinative of the other; both find unity in the context of a *totality*, and only a fetishized approach would look for some instance such as "culture" or "economic production" to take precedence that could then be called upon for explanatory privilege.[12] Conceiving of urban change and musical change as mutual conditions of possibility also enables one to avoid some of the sharper rocks on which so many theories of culture seem to be shipwrecked, namely, the debilitating and often mystifying debates concerning determination versus freedom. Just about nobody disputes that music creates structures of feeling for listeners; urban residents, workers, and those affected by their creative choices and preferences cannot help be affected by profound changes in their environments (including, but not limited to, the latter's determining just what kinds of people will live in cities). Thus, choices are indubitably made by actors in any situation, but it is the structure of the situation itself that will engage the perspective of this book, along with the structure of the new situation resulting from the actor's previous choices. Insofar as one conceives of an element of freedom in those choices, by the very definition of freedom, one cannot model that element—nor does one need to slide toward epistemological abjection on that account.

Music and urban geography will illuminate each other in this book within a framework that is fundamentally Marxist in the way just outlined. That is to say, the studies presented here will treat both broader urban change and specifically musical practices as particular locations in a single mode of production (capitalism), at a certain point in history. In keeping with what Derek Sayer maintains are the actual contours of Marx's argument, "culture" will not be separated off from the "economic" and treated as epiphenomenal. Rather, the two, as conventionally (and too narrowly) conceived, will be taken as proper both to the mode of production and to the mode of accumulation in which they fully participate. In order to finish laying the foundation for that approach, the remainder of this introduction will outline some of the relevant scholarship on recent urban geography and will render explicit the kind of Marxist approach common to the discussions in the book.

The following section supplies some of the historical and scholarly background concerning the notion of post-Fordism and changes in cities (especially of the developed world) over the past few decades. It is necessarily sketchy and, furthermore, highly selective; it emphasizes only those aspects of urban development that will turn out to be crucial to the principal arguments of this book. Those readers familiar with post-Fordism and recent urban geography may wish to skip the following section and proceed to Chapter 1.

Post-Fordist Cities

The debates on so-called post-Fordism and cities date back almost as far as the earliest use of the term.[13] *Post-Fordism* as a term falls far short of being adequate, for at least two reasons. First, like the (thankfully) now little-used term *new musicology*, it defines itself mainly negatively, not offering a unique characterization of that which it claims to describe. And second, and more damagingly, it implies a clean break from Fordism, when in fact, as John Tomaney (1994) and others have suggested, many if not most of the aspects of Fordism continue, even in some respects predominate, in the period of so-called post-Fordism.[14] Thus, the relation of post-Fordism to Fordism may more resemble what in recent years has increasingly been modeled as the relation of postmodernism to modernism (e.g., Harvey, *Condition*, 39–65), namely a significant transformation within continuity, rather than a clean break followed by a new epoch.

Some of the characteristics most commonly associated with the term post-Fordism in recent geographic and sociological literature are the following:

1. Limited, small-production runs (rather than mass production)
2. Fragmented niche markets (rather than mass markets)
3. Flexibility in production runs, with quicker innovation
4. Flexibility in labor (both job description and worker affiliation)
5. Outsourcing of noncore functions (vertical disintegration)
6. Spatial agglomeration of disintegrated functions
7. Weakened labor power in a segmented work force
8. Growth of the tertiary sector
9. Growth of the information sector
10. Growth of the service sector, especially business services
11. Centrality of information in production
12. Increased informational and symbolic participation in value
13. Increased independence of private actors from state regulation and control ("liberalization")
14. Increased transnational flow of materials, information, and labor ("globalization")
15. Increased significance of regional and urban specialization

This is a selective, not comprehensive, list, and it emphasizes factors that will turn out to be crucial to the arguments of this book. These characteristics are culled from a great number of different discussions, most of which emphasize some over others; in addition, many, although listed discretely, are clearly inseparable from others (for example, 5 and 6).

As well as disagreeing in their descriptions of post-Fordism (indeed, in some cases, about whether the term even describes something real), commentators also differ concerning exactly what time it characterizes. Many commentators (e.g., Harvey, *Condition*) see in it processes that began just after the recession and financial crisis of 1973; certainly, any description of post-Fordism sees it in full swing by the early 1980s, usually earlier.[15] Certain items in the above list are clearly related to the rise of computers and, especially, to inexpensive, powerful, and compact computing (for example, items 3, 9, 11, and 12); however, most descriptions of post-Fordism date its beginnings, if not its full blossoming, well before the rise of the desktop computer, and most are careful to avoid any technological determinism that would suggest that computers 'caused' post-Fordism.

Most important, many aspects of post-Fordism bear an intimate relation to urban geography, including the form of cities, their economic function, the kinds of people, buildings, businesses, activities they host—in short, nearly every aspect of life in the metropolis around much, perhaps most, of the world (especially the developed world). The ascendance of small, flexible production runs and the internationalization of labor and capital, for instance, came together to form the "deindustrialization" mentioned earlier in this introduction, beginning most likely sometime in the early 1970s. The flight of mass production from a good number of American cities during that period enacted powerful changes in many of them, documented in artifacts as diverse as Michael Moore's documentary *Roger and Me* (1989) and Bruce Springsteen's song "Youngstown."[16] The changes were not limited to sheer economic slowdown or a vague sense of economic doom: large numbers of formerly working-class neighborhoods became impoverished, with displaced and unemployed workers and their families increasingly turning to crime that threatened large sections of major cities.[17]

The plight of North American (especially United States) cities during the end of the 1970s and much of the 1980s achieved notoriety through intensive media coverage. Spectacular events like the near-default of New York City in 1975 fascinated and horrified Western readers and television viewers worldwide, as did media events like then-President Jimmy Carter's 1977 presidential campaign stop in the South Bronx, which appeared to television viewers like a bombed-out war zone. During this period and just after it, the development of so-called impacted ghettoes accelerated, not only increasing crime rates (though mainly within those ghettoes) but also, through often one-sided media coverage, projecting even more strongly than before the notion that cities, at least in the United States, were dangerous places.[18] Tax revenues of cities diminished, decreasing their abilities to deal with the mounting social problems, as federal support for social programs plunged with the political swing in the United States to the Right.

Cities in capitalism have always served as foci for certain strategies of accumulation, however, and so, as some aspects of post-Fordism listed above developed, so did many cities, inside and outside North America, increasingly come to host those strategies most amenable to urbanization and development under the new conditions. Information-based businesses, spurred by developing computer technology and the need to coordinate increasingly disintegrated services, came to occupy parts of many cities, as did a number of business services and control operations geographically separated from manufacturing (Sassen, *Global City*). Some of them were new operations, others disintegrated from larger companies.[19] Some located in the central business districts (CBDs), taking advantage of their compact operations and the centrality of the location; others agglomerated on the edge of cities, where real estate was less expensive, or close to universities that helped sustain their innovation and labor force.[20] Financial and business services, particularly those located in CBDs, to some extent filled in the vacuum of the deindustrialized urban landscape, becoming media-cultivated icons of North American urban life. The term "*yuppie*" was coined to describe many of the workers attracted to the inner city to own, run, and staff such operations.

Yuppies do not simply work for information providers and business services; they also live in cities and transform their character, consuming and producing culture. Indeed, yuppies, in the 1980s and afterwards, were mainly discussed in the print and electronic media as a cultural rather than economic phenomenon, despite having clearly been both, simultaneously. Changes in food habits and food-related services (e.g., high-end pasta and sushi delivery services) marked upscale urban districts, as did changes in residential (along with commercial) real estate and housing prices, and a proliferation in personal businesses and services—including, of course, music recordings and live music clubs.[21] In fact, priorities of cities, from small business owners to public officials, adjust to the influx of moneyed populations, as one would expect in a capitalist society, with disproportionate zeal. Sharon Zukin (*Loft Living*), for instance, has demonstrated how the priorities of developers in SoHo, at the end of the 1970s, dictated the renovation of formerly commercial properties to create a (then) new urban social phenomenon that came to be known as "loft living." As new workers and owners moved into cities to found and operate information businesses and service operations, property values shifted, driving out former residents and transforming the character of many inner cities. With other areas still stung from the departure of the formerly urban heavy industries, intraurban polarization increased sharply, spurring more policing of some urban subjects.[22] Thus, one of the basic realities of the so-called post-Fordist city became a profound polarization by district (with the borders of those districts, of course, constantly shifting). Although class polarization has always been a famous reality of cities in the capitalist world, the changes induced by post-Fordist production have intensified it to levels previously unseen in many places.

Not only have the departure of heavy manufacturing and the influx of information and business services transformed cities, so has the increasing reliance of urban economies on other kinds of personal services, in particular entertainment and tourism. Not every city has been able to rely on tourism for revenues, but those with the natural, cultural, or historic attributes that enable tourism have turned to it with increasing vigor and sometimes with major transformations in the built environment and economic structure.[23] Although the enhancement of cities for tourism has sometimes been denounced in the popular media as "Disneyfication" and has raised issues of authenticity, moral denunciation promises less benefit than a consideration of exactly *how* tourism affects areas. Within that rubric, the question of tourism rejoins another widely discussed aspect of post-Fordist urban geography, so-called cultural regeneration. This term refers to the increasingly common tendency to transform urban areas for cultural consumption, including sports arenas, multiplex cinemas, historic promenades, and arts and music districts.[24] Cultural regeneration is widely and consciously adopted by a good number of cities whose economic base has become shaky or perpetually insufficient. In many cases, it has been remarkably effective (e.g., Manchester, United Kingdom, and Bilbao, Spain) in achieving some of its intended goals. That is to say, although culture-based economic development clearly has its limits, it may be effective for certain central districts; among many other advantages, it may enhance tourism and attract to the city young, single, and educated labor with relatively high amounts of disposable income.[25]

Furthermore, central-city districts with a high concentration of artistic industries and public spaces lend municipalities a coveted image of being "lively" and "creative." Such an image not only enhances property values, it also helps to attract the labor needed to operate the information and business-service sector described above.

Both tourism and cultural regeneration develop certain specific aspects of the cities in which they are cultivated. Personal services are conveyed by businesses such as hotels and hairdressers, many of whose workers cannot afford to live in the relevant areas. Young, single, educated, and well-paid workers are particularly valued for these developmental strategies, just as they are for business services.[26] Retail development thus tends to cater to such a constituency, emphasizing cosmopolitanism, fashion, leisure, and novelty in design (just as the housing market does when property values rise). At the same time, in cities with older zones of historical development, like Philadelphia or Barcelona, the preservation and enhancement of those areas may coexist with new facilities that benefit from their value. Attracting cultural workers to the city, in particular, requires development of communities in which artists and others involved in creative industries can agglomerate, collaborate on projects, and exchange ideas (Scott, *Cultural Economy*, 16-39).

In point of fact, the agglomeration of certain kinds of urban workers in geographic proximity far transcends the realm of cultural production or tourism. The vertical disintegration of large corporations, earlier mentioned as a hallmark of post-Fordism, itself tends to encourage spatial agglomeration of certain kinds of businesses and the growth of districts.[27] Such concentrations of specialty stem from, among other things, the intensity of knowledge in much of post-Fordist production. Thus, not only physical objects, but also ideas and information that at one point moved through vertically integrated large firms now move among smaller, vertically disintegrated firms in many urban areas. Among the smaller detached firms, exchanges of goods and information are externalized (e.g., discussed in informal socializing within bars and restaurants), and thus the character of the environment, including physical proximity, becomes crucial to their success. Some agglomerations of information-based firms have gained international fame, such as California's Silicon Valley, whereas some lesser-known business service areas, such as a concentration of credit-card accounting businesses in Wilmington, Delaware, have also contributed to forming characteristic urban environments. Thus, the formation of focused zones of educated workers characterizes both tourism/culture-based development and zones of concentrated business services and information-based firms. And most important, such specialized workers bring along with them their own cultural preferences and "lifestyle" choices, including particular musical preferences. Not coincidentally, the musical tastes of educated bourgeoisie tend to dominate such regions, with eclecticism and the "omnivore" tendencies predominating.[28]

The final institutional factor of post-Fordist cities relevant to the discussions in this book is *privatization*, whose increasing grip on central cities has drastically reshaped them. Certainly inseparable from the liberalization mentioned as characteristic of post-Fordism, privatization has profoundly shaped the practice of urban planning, such that the very spatial form of advanced economies' downtowns may express, and further, the interests of the heavily capitalized transnational corporations that often settle in those districts.[29] Whereas in the past municipalities have often (though by no means always) exercised significant control and oversight—sometimes direct control—over the planning and building of cities, even those traditionally quite strenuous in resisting such efforts (such as Amsterdam) have, in recent decades, been privatizing and/or relaxing such control. Rather than publicly guided development, inner cities have therefore been subject to private development, dictated by the priorities of capital accumulation. Thus, large-scale projects of public access such as Frederick Law Olmsted's Central Park in New York City represent less and less the norm in urban development; instead, such development more and more resembles projects such as Baltimore's Inner Harbor Project (Harvey, *Condition*, 88–96) and Boston's Quincy Market, in which the basis for public assembly is retail consumption, and the public targeted to populate such districts is consciously limited by class.[30] Design then tends to reflect such priorities, in which "heritage" sites (like Quincy Market) add value to upscale consumption of food, leisure activities, and souvenirs. Urban residents ensconced in districts dominated by such development cannot avoid spatial sensibilities that foreground *design* in specific ways (and Chapter 5 will elaborate some musical consequences). Similarly, large swathes of cities are simply developed as office space, even with elaborately designed lobbies closely resembling the public spaces of Fordist and prior urbanization (e.g., the Sony/AT&T Building in New York City), but, again, with restricted access. The privatization of urban spaces and their restriction to only certain desired populations, in turn, receives its practical reinforcement from increased urban surveillance (e.g., London's ubiquitous closed-circuit cameras), architecture, and policing (Davis, *City of Quartz*, 221–264). Thus, the polarization of cities by class, mentioned above, finds its spatial equivalent in neighborhoods and districts sharply characterized by concentrations of class and, often, ethnicity. Although, of course, cities in the capitalist world (and elsewhere) have always enacted such segregation to some extent, the trend in recent decades has been toward a qualitative change and a sharp curtailing of commingling public spaces. The bounded, intensively designed sense of space finds its musical complement in design-intensive musical commodities that will be discussed in Chapter 5. Further discussion of post-Fordism and cities can be found in the initial discussion of Adorno and mass culture theory in Chapter 4.

Design-Intensive Production and the Integrated Aesthetic Space

By (perhaps ideologically useful) contrast, those privileged areas of the now privatized and segregated city enjoy and, significantly, concentrate an aspect of advanced economies most famously described by sociologists Scott Lash and John Urry (*Economies*, 15, 193), namely *design intensity*. The term refers to the tendency in advanced societies for products and services to owe much of their value to aspects of design and informational content, and for design and informational aspects of products and services to develop rapidly. Design has, of course, always figured as a characteristic of commodities, but only with the development of certain kinds of computerization and small-batch production has it assumed the prominence it now has in our object world: if a thought experiment would help, one might think of how many functionally identical but differently designed coffeepots, computer tables, or desk lamps one could buy in various regions of London or any other major city. Flexibility also adjusts design to demand: one now routinely designs one's own CD at a website, customizes a bag from Lands' End, or plans a computer system component by component. The amount of information involved in such transactions was prohibitive before some point in the 1980s; earlier, such products were subject to either small-scale, specialized artisan production or standardized mass production. Similarly, the development of new automobile styles relies far less on technological or demographic change (as during the 1950s and 1960s) than it does on changes in stylistic preferences (which is not to say that such preferences are purely aesthetic). Apart from consumer tastes, design and informational innovation powers entire industries such as software and increasingly propels certain marketing innovations. As with many aspects of the post-Fordist city described here, design intensity represents not so much a clean break with the past—of course, design and information have always played roles in goods and services—as an intensification of certain tendencies.

Design intensity in the post-Fordist city, in the present context, is significant insofar as the development of the metropolis increasingly depends on design elements (including, but not limited to, aesthetic elements). Such dependence inscribes design on the literal spaces in which one lives the city: thus, for example, many apartments and condominiums, especially in cities, may have been built, in the early- to mid-twentieth century, in such a way that units varied little, except in their size and amenities (and hence the much-maligned "International Style"). By the late twentieth and early twenty-first century, however, the design content of residences came to carry a far greater weight in their valuation, ranging from renovated industrial spaces and lofts (Zukin, *Loft Living*, 58-81) to highly stylized units sold according to their uniqueness. And, perhaps equally important to the design of retail spaces, design intensity also inflects many of those domestic interiors in which one might listen to music recordings. Of course, the return of ornament to architecture has long been one of the points identified as properly postmodern, providing one of many possible contact points between the post-Fordist city and more common academic discussions of postmodernism. But as important as the overall architectural layout may be to city structure and social character, design intensity pervades the metropolis in many other respects. For instance, the design of certain kinds of retail spaces increasingly governs their character, such that city boutiques and large branded stores take on the character of totally planned and themed environments; Prada's flagship Manhattan store, located in SoHo and designed by Rem Koolhaas, provides only one recent prominent example. Such destinations, which project urban shopping as spatial experience, rely as much on spectacle and the shopping environment as on the wares and prices on display. Design intensity may be, in many cases, difficult to separate from other aspects of the post-Fordist city described in this section; for example, the orientation of many cities toward tourism and entertainment involves careful attention to, and manipulation of, the design of buildings, shops, streets, hotels, restaurants, public walkways, and so on. Similarly, attracting artists and related workers for cultural regeneration may well involve designing residences, retail stores, restaurants, streets, and so on, that will prove attractive and promise a high quality of life for them. Music then acquires a significance in such places and for those socialized in them, insofar as it, too, can come to characterize space.

One aspect of design intensity and urban life that seems implicit in many discussions but is not often discussed as such should be underlined here and will prove crucial to many of the following discussions. It lies, in fact, at the intersection of the aspects of post-Fordist cities already outlined here. It unites not only the design intensity but also the tourism, cultural regeneration, privatization, personal services, and even the agglomeration of workers in information-dependent production districts. Such factors often combine to render many urban districts regions of *integrated aestheticized space*. I use such a term to denote tendencies to coordinate aspects of urban spaces to unified, or complementary, aestheticized purposes; of course, as the preceding discussion has outlined, such aesthetics serves less the purpose of a Kantian free play of the imagination than the accumulation of capital. Such coordination has always existed for less aesthetically driven goals: the designs of CBDs, for instances, often successfully integrate convenient grid-pattern streets, street-level shops servicing local employees, electronic and data networks, and so on. However, the idea of an integrated aestheticized space, in the present context, centers precisely on the aestheticizing of that space and thus gravitates more readily to retail, consumption, and tourism. It is in those areas that recent changes in urban geography achieve visibility to most urban residents and workers. Remaking the design of advanced cities for tourism and consumption—their partial transformation into spectacles of sight, smell, taste, and sound—arguably translates more directly into the proper context for the cultural developments described in this book. It is crucial to underline that the present study does not rejoin earlier discussions that represent urban life as somehow fundamentally a matter of spectacle and voluntarist play, in the manner of Raban's *Soft City* (1974).[31] Rather, the argument here historicizes, proposing that the integration of different kinds of design to create a highly controlled, aestheticized, and isolated urban environment is a relatively recent development, representing a specific strategy of capital accumulation. That strategy not only comprises entertainment and retail consumption of highly stylized goods and services, but, more basically, it requires a fundamental and thoroughgoing design and aestheticizing of life in the city. Similarly, although the control of access by populations has long existed (and one may invoke certain suburban shopping malls to demonstrate that the practice is neither extremely new nor specifically urban), the argument here, as before, is that such tendencies have been concentrated recently in urban areas of (mainly) developed societies.

The overlap of such developments with classic descriptions of postmodernism has already been remarked above, and one more remark on that overlap will be useful for the present discussion. Fredric Jameson's famous analysis of the Westin Bonaventure Hotel in Los Angeles underlines that building's internal spatial incommensurability, its resistance to the possibility of cognitive mapping standing in for late capitalism's generalized ability to disable totalization while saturating culture ever more thoroughly.[32] But when one considers the urban developments discussed above as a background, such places take on a slightly different, though not incompatible, hue. Its enclosure and total remaking of space reproduce more generalized processes in the contemporary metropolis, whereas the saturation with design elements (sometimes described, in architecture, as the "return of ornament") models a significant emphasis in capital accumulation, recognizable throughout advanced economies but concentrated in their cities. However, despite the partial convergence of many descriptions of postmodernism with the urban transformations just outlined, "postmodern" will not suffice as the preferred description of the economic/cultural processes theorized in this book. Although that term certainly captures some important developments in the cultural realm, the notion of postmodernism simply does not adequately address the mediations that shape urban life, nor does it convey the specificity of the urban experience and its radiating influence throughout our culture.[33]

One paradox (among others) emerges from the processes just outlined, namely, the simultaneous expansiveness and closure of the city. On the one hand, the post-Fordist metropolis enacts closure on multiple levels: public barriers go up separating 'undesirable' citizens from those whose presence fuels the economy of the city, while policing effectively segregates certain neighborhoods,[34] security systems and gated communities insulate privileged citizens,[35] and retail spaces and entertainment centers create environments that are elaborate, highly designed, self-contained, and closed off to their exterior (Hannigan, *Fantasy City*, 67–80). Edge retail developments, replete with box stores and massive cineplexes, establish zones of consumption and entertainment isolated from the rest of the city's structure, accessible only to those equipped with automobiles. Thus, the recent metropolis relies on exclusion, control, and closure. But on the other hand, cities of the advanced world on a certain level have opened up: migrating workers from around the earth bring with them cultures and artifacts; retail shops and restaurants offer commodities and cuisines from far-flung places, ranging from gift shops offering "exotic" Tibetan clothing to Cambodian eateries, and images and sounds from virtually everywhere on earth flood urban televisions, radios, newspapers, and magazines, not to mention the Internet. Simultaneously more open and more closed than ever, the contemporary city presents a series of often interlocked, highly controlled and designed patterns and experiences. In a sense, urban experiences thus approach some conception of concentrated virtuality, except that they unfold in real space and select by class. Although it seems to draw from the entire world as a potential source of delight, consumption, finance, and labor, the metropolis locks such dizzyingly varied experiences into tight, highly controlled, and intensively structured packets.

The intensively designed and controlled metropolis also projects images, including its own, worldwide through its centrality in the production and distribution of images. Not only are the world's major producers of images—electronic and print media, as well as fashion—largely concentrated in the kinds of spaces described here, but also the workers who produce and disseminate those images often spend the majority of their time in precisely such environments. Thus, images of newer city configurations not only announce themselves as originating spaces, but they are also shaped and contextualized by subjects who may have naturalized those same surroundings as core experiences. Although one might argue that the advent of the Internet may, or will in the future, democratize control over images, it is difficult to recognize, in the contemporary mediascape, any deemphasis of urban images. On the contrary, the city continues to dominate a good deal of media content, sometimes as explicit focus (e.g., the television series *Sex and the City*, which will be discussed in Chapter 1) and sometimes as indispensable context (e.g., the *New York Times*, the music of Beck or Philip Glass). Thus, the role of such places as centers of media production includes the role of reproducing themselves, announcing themselves, and setting themselves as the focus of culture in the developed world. The significance of urban change in this way far transcends the scope of the city itself, saturating the visible iconography of media culture and imprinting ideas of "the city" on listeners (and viewers) throughout the inhabited world, urban and rural alike. Much of this process will be discussed in Chapter 1.

Music in Urban Geography (Arguments and Layout of this Book)

Such media production, reproduction, and dissemination has always crucially included, and relied on, music for its shape, characterization, and some new central functions that will be described in the following chapters. One relatively blunt but still notable respect in which music projects the new urban form involves its lyrical and musical characterization of cities, i.e., involves *representation*. Representing the metropolis affords the observer one way to observe changes in cultural feel for the city, as cities are described and projected throughout great swathes of musical history, across numerous genres. Music has long figured in representation generally—one of the most valuable contributions of cultural musicology has been precisely to underline that—and its role in disseminating senses of city life, in particular, has been curiously underestimated in scholarship on popular music. As media increasingly saturates everyday life for many subjects worldwide, crossing borders of nearly all sorts, such processes may well constitute a neglected formation of collective senses of social possibility. But treating musical representation requires exquisite care, since it always threatens to collapse into a closed system (or a looser set of forces nevertheless closed) that treats representation as a bottom line, the fetishized premature totalization of some cultural studies, an idealization disowned by pronouncements of "worldliness." By contrast, the goal of describing musical representation here will be to outline a process that is fully integrated to culture most generally, including but not limited to the momentous changes to production and everyday socioeconomic life throughout cities of the developed world, already described above. The most systematic discussion of musical representation of cities can be found in Chapter 1, although the topic recurs prominently in later chapters as well. As cultural studies and representation, most generally, already form a major stream of music scholarship, the first chapter of this book will probably bear the closest resemblance, methodologically, to other recent studies of musical culture. It will, however, present and describe in some depth a notion, the *urban ethos*, not yet described in the scholarly literature and crucial, as the chapter will argue, to understanding much about both popular music and urban life. The urban ethos, in fact, extends far beyond music as a medium, encompassing much expressive culture and design.

But as has already been signaled, music's participation in urban geography extends far beyond the confines of representation, as musical structures and characteristics interact with other realms of human activity. Such far-ranging, and more difficult to analyze, aspects of music and urban geography preoccupy the majority of the present study. The musical changes traced in the more wide-ranging discussions occupy the same totality as the transformations discussed above that characterize cities generally. Thus, for example, the shopping/entertainment complexes that cater to new kinds of urban workers/visitors deploy music in ways that are substantially novel—music there not only becomes subject to more intensive cross-marketing than previously, but it also becomes implicated in elaborately designed ways of characterizing spaces.[36] Anybody who has encountered, in gift shops or other retailers, a self-standing display of themed compact discs (and sometimes analog cassettes) for domestic use, will recognize such novel configurations of music: there, the music is both cross-marketed with other items in the store and also projected as a way of decorating or characterizing a (usually domestic) environment.[37] Often, as well, the particular selection of CDs will to some extent coordinate with the theme of the store carrying the display, so that a "Celtic"-themed gift shop may offer a particularly large selection of "Irish," "Welsh," or indeed more vaguely "Celtic" titles. Cross-marketing music represents no novelty in itself, but the prominence of such music displays in retail spaces *does* constitute a recent phenomenon, in which music *characterizes highly designed spaces*. That development points back to the more generalized proliferation of design as an aspect of value in production, not necessarily as effect points to its cause, but rather as a lively and culturally saturated corner of a more widespread phenomenon. By this example, as well as others that will appear in the pages of this book, one can see how music is presented differently, correlated to other aspects of urban life differently, in changing urban environments.

But the argument of this book extends even further, to claim that the transformation of the metropolis, in the advanced world over the past few decades, interacts powerfully with musical structure, both the changing sounds and the way the sounds are processed commercially and culturally. That argument sees music both as mediated and as itself a level of mediation, a crucial channel through which social relations are formed and reproduced, an aspect of overall human production fully as much as (for example) securities regulation, nanotechnology, or commercial cinema. To those versed in cultural musicology, music's representational powers may present an obvious case of mediation (although the latter word is rarely invoked in the more postmodern theoretical climate of musicology): when Ice Cube, for example, offers a normative (and to some extent counternormative) model of contemporary masculinity, both supporters and opponents of rap music do not doubt his cultural power.[38] And furthermore, musical structure and processes have been recognized in cultural musicology as key elements in social formation. Lawrence Kramer, for instance, has outlined in a number of intriguing publications the extent to which music has participated in the construction (and sometimes undoing) of subjectivities that circulate widely in Western societies.[39] And while Kramer may not tag music as mediation, given the less sociological or systematic bent of his approach, in the context of the present study, mediation would indeed be an appropriate term for music's presence in a larger system of production and everyday life. Some musicologists and theorists have even traced musical sound through intimate recesses of the social world of what many non-Marxists would deem "production" (i.e., the more narrowly defined world of corporate and/or industrial culture). Robert Fink, for example, offers a provocative glimpse into the world of "production music," the prepackaged, mass-produced music that is marketed for use in business environments such as presentations, commercials, websites, and so on;[40] through a discussion of the tagged and categorized tiny music compositions, Fink concludes that they form a "system of music objects" (in the sense of Baudrillard) rather than a full-fledged semiosis.[41] Although Fink's primary interest turns out to be a certain formation of masculinity, a skewed glance at his study suggests a broader picture, in which music forms cultural environments for socioeconomic activity, shapes subjectivities that drive and fashion development, and contributes to the structure of work life. That it does so with elaborate (and often incoherent) cues to attitudes and business goals suggests continuities and intimate feedback between the emotive stimulus of musical sound and the cultural practices of economic production, even if (as is almost certainly the case) the musical production company exaggerates the force and specificity of the tags. In short, Fink's study not only suggests the point outlined earlier in this introduction concerning the error of separating production and culture as separate and complete realms; it also signals music's centrality in mediating aspects of daily life not normally conceived as "musical."

But to hang one's hat on the music of corporate culture for a view of music and production relies on a damagingly constrained view of just what constitutes production in a society.[42] For production, in a Marxist sense, does not simply occur at the workplace, or even simply in some sort of life cycle consisting of work, sustenance, and reproduction; rather, it can be taken as a sum of human activity, all of which, of course, has to be produced, and reproduced, at all times.

So music both represents the city under changing regimes of accumulation and also functions within the developing spatial practices of new urban working populations. Thus an adequate approach to music and urban geography must be partially hermeneutic and partially music-analytical, in the latter being flexible enough to capture what it is about music that may be symptomatic (which may or may not involve pitch). Chapter 1 begins the hermeneutic task, theorizing the *urban ethos* as a set of possible representations of cities within Anglophone music of the developed world (focusing on the United States). It posits an intimate relationship between the characteristics of that range and certain key developments in American cities and their mediated character. Several particular songs and music videos provide, through their musical and visual poetics, clues to the expressive contours of urban ethoi, past and present.

Chapter 2 turns from the US south to Curaçao, and from a notion of cities in general to a particular one, namely Willemstad, the island's capital and only city. That far more marginal urban context provides the occasion, however, for a meditation on a much more general phenomenon, namely the valorization of locality and place (especially the latter) in popular music studies. The chapter lays out an argument that such valorizations rely on outdated concepts of capital and geographic development; post-Fordist urban development has taken forms that undermine precisely those qualities that scholars value in place, its presumably "resistant" characteristics and humane appeal. Through a detailed discussion of Willemstad, a local Curaçao musical genre called *tumba*, and a particular song from that genre, it becomes apparent that place and the spatial regimes that it presumably resists cannot be so easily disentangled in a post-Fordist environment.

Chapter 1 and Chapter 2 show that changes in urban accumulation bear profound significance for, respectively, representations of cities and theoretical evaluations of their music. Chapter 3, by contrast, looks at a staging of urban change itself, namely the film *Boogie Nights* (1997), a film from the late 1990s that lays out the landscape of the late-1970s and early-1980s in California in the San Fernando Valley. Through that most particular of urban spaces, *Boogie Nights* thematizes a far more generally felt historical change, in which libidinal freedoms and investments gradually lose their possibility through changes in urban object worlds. The film presents the transition from the late 1970s to the 1980s starkly as the onset of that loss, and since the film views that transition from the end of the twentieth century, the sense of loss associated with urban change turns out to be suffused with ambiguity. In particular, the musical treatment of the film's soundtrack, a much-touted and discussed aspect of the film,[43] frames *Boogie Nights*'s libidinal investments as impossible, forever removed from our full apprehension in the urban environment of the end of the twentieth century.

Chapter 4 revisits the urban ethos and develops it more explicitly with Marxist themes. For better or worse, any music theoretical study of the early twenty-first century that investigates music through the lens of capital must encounter the spectre of Theodor Adorno, or at least those ideas attributed to him (correctly or not) nowadays. The chapter investigates in detail how a certain construal of Adorno's seminal writings continues to shape debates about popular music, including the positions of those who most vehemently disown him. Changes in capital accumulation since the time of his writing, however, greatly undermine the relevance of his views to discussions of contemporary popular music. Chapter 4 therefore outlines a non-Adornan Marxist way to discuss the urban ethos and popular music more generally. Some songs and videos from rap music—in popular parlance, of course, the quintessentially "urban" music—provide an opportunity to demonstrate that urban geography and the urban ethos may offer more fruitful ways of analyzing music.

Chapter 5 concludes by foregrounding a recent trend that suffuses the worlds of both popular and classical music recordings, namely the music-poetic strategy of characterizing playback spaces and delineating their limits. The creation of such virtual listening environments, together with certain common themes such as that of the "angelic" in classical recordings, suggest an intimate parallel to the urban changes discussed above, namely the erection of urban barriers and their design-intensive development. Thus, the cultural and economic practices central to the urban accumulation of capital that bear the more pressing relevance to music studies are, in fact, also central to understanding the sound and cultural practices of music itself. The contours of musical culture and overall urban development draw together most conspicuously in such processes, suggesting that understanding both the sounds and the social significance of music—not two different tasks, but rather two ways of conceiving of the same thing—requires, after all, a theoretical knowledge of urban geography, and (perhaps more surprisingly) vice versa.

The reader will notice that questions of individual agency, despite their currency in cultural studies and (by extension) ethnomusicology, do not figure at all prominently in this book. That is not because they hold no significance; of course, what actors in any situation intend and decide to do can figure prominently in the course of events and in the shape of a society. But what forms the central focus of this book will not be the agency of individuals so much as the historical situations in which those agencies are exerted. In other words, those situations form the constraints of those agencies, the ensemble of relationships that unites them. Those can often be inferred from the shape of agents' actions, of course, and as every act, every product of expressive culture, forms a unique and concrete thing, ultimately the actions of agents are all that we have with which to describe historical situations. In that sense, one analyzes simultaneously historical situation and agency. However, the explicit interest of this book lies in the 'big picture,' the great currents and sweeping unfoldings that abut our present time. Some who champion moralistic approaches and the allied concept of agency will find this approach distasteful; it can only be hoped that even such readers might profit by setting such a framework aside provisionally in order to conceptualize the grander scheme. For just as a historical situation can only be inferred from many acts and products of agency, so does any given agency take its shape, force, and meaning only from the historical situation in which it is conceived and executed. There is probably no single adequate approach, only a dimly imaginable dialectical simultaneity of situation and agency. This book openly embraces the former, while remaining agnostic about the latter, which delves too deeply into questions of free will and morality to be of interest to the present approach.

Above all, this book represents an aspect of what I would like to call a *music studies of the present* (with music studies embracing music theory, musicology, and ethnomusicology). Although painting an accurate and informative picture of the past remains a most valuable project, my own interest ranges more toward measuring the contours of the world that surround us right now. Even though scholars certainly lack the distanced perspective on that world that we might be able to achieve concerning, say, eighteenth-century Berlin, on the other hand we do have immediate sensory access to our own time. I would, at a minimum, maintain that we evade a theoretical grasp on the world around us at our own risk; a music studies of the present simply represents an attempt to achieve that grasp concerning music. The hope is that armed with such an elaborated music studies, one might wander the streets of Amsterdam to Fame, and purchase there a CD of Curaçao music and another one of J. S. Bach violin and harpsichord sonatas, with a somewhat better understanding of the musical world through which one passes, and perhaps even a better understanding of how to change it.

1

Defining the Urban Ethos

This book's first approach to music and urban geography will concern representation, not because the study will end there, but precisely because of the need, at some point, to transcend the limits of representation as a problematic and see it, instead, as part of a totality enveloping other aspects of social life. The urban change outlined in the Introduction will turn out not just to frame the aspects of representation described as the "urban ethos," but also to form a necessary continuity with them. Some selected slices of musical history will help to elucidate just how the changing face of popular music may prove a powerful symptom of basic social conditions.

Petula Clark's hit "Downtown" was released in 1964.[1] Clark had been well known in her native England literally since childhood and had already been a star in France, though her career in the UK by then was on the wane. The song initially was released in Europe in four different languages late in the year, and it scored immediate success in several countries. When an executive of Warner Brothers heard the song on a visit to Clark's record company in France, he acquired the rights to distribute the song in the United States. Subsequently, the song reached number one status in January 1965, ultimately selling more than three million copies there alone and winning a Grammy award. "Downtown" thus became, perhaps unintentionally, Petula Clark's vehicle of entry to the lucrative US market. So, while the song enjoyed European origins, its ultimate life breathed freely on both sides of the Atlantic, and, in fact, it had contact with an important American city before it even existed: the composer and arranger, Tony Hatch, had been inspired to write the song by a trip to New York City and initially intended to write it for the Drifters. It can be signaled right now, in fact, that many of the artists discussed in this chapter are non-US artists breaking into the American market and thus

"American" not so much in national origin as in national destination and representation. The song's successful crossing into the US market, in fact, speaks significantly, because it indicates that this song projects a representation of cities that was at least recognizable to American consumers at that time, on a large scale.

In the lyrics, taken for the moment in isolation from their musical settings, the downtown district is cathected as a locus of excitement, adventure, and even cheerful escape. Not only do all the lyrical descriptions offer the unnamed city as a solution to all personal problems, but Tony Hatch's musical arrangements, harmonies, and production also underline the point. The approach to the refrain (starting with "The lights are much brighter there") happens chromatically through B-flat and then B-natural to a bass C that supports a dominant 6/4 chord, which in turn sets most of the refrain; the string parts crescendo in great climactic upwards scales over that tense 6/4 chord; the thickening of the orchestration there increases the textural energy as the resolution is delayed, and then the final line of each refrain arrives as a glorious conclusion, with the force of a slogan: "Everything's waiting for you," or "You're gonna be allright now." The musical strategies—chromatic bass approach to a climactic dominant chord, thickening of texture to emphasize an emotional climax, sustaining of an unstable chord to build suspense and underline the following musical event—are all, of course, standard with quite a bit of popular music compositions from that era, and they would have been most accessible to audiences. Such structural ploys open up a musical space of ecstatic pleasure that not even the gushing lyrics manage to convey. By the time that the listener has passed through the gentle, supportive encounters with strangers (!) in the fragmentary third verse, the music and lyrics in tandem have projected the city as a destination of diversion, fun, and humane encounters. The joyous urban image closes with a pseudo-jazz-style muted trumpet solo, reiterating a well-known musical semiosis of exciting city nightlife, adventure, and sophistication. It would be difficult to imagine an image of urban life more brimming with optimism, enthusiasm, and energetic embrace.

Representations of the city in popular music during this period, however, did not always match the sheer ebullience of "Downtown."

Just two years later, in fact, Petula Clark herself enjoyed another US hit with "Who Am I?", which projects the city as a locus of alienation and anxiety.[2] One could find, in fact, a range of constructions of "the urban" in the American popular music charts of 1965, correlated at least loosely to music genre, public identities of performers, and other aspects of the industry. From the unifying celebrations of Martha and the Vandellas's "Dancing in the Streets" to the ominous silliness of Jan and Dean's "Dead Man's Curve,"[3] music audiences in the United States embraced a large range of representations of urban life in a great number of different contexts. "Downtown" represented just one extreme, and, as will be seen, a telling one.

But there were limits to the range of city representations at that time, too, and the most effective way to feel out those limits is to look at another point in music history and find an image of the city that would have been inconceivable at the time of greatest popularity for "Downtown." For contrast, and also because it falls within the period that constitutes the principal focus of this book, one can look at a song from the first decade of the twenty-first century, 50 Cent's "In My Hood" from his (officially) second album *The Massacre* (2005).[4] Aside from the question of his real talents, 50 Cent may legitimately claim to have resonated, for whatever reason, with mass audiences: his first album, *Get Rich or Die Tryin'*,[5] had become the highest-selling debut album in history, selling more than 870,000 copies in its first week and shooting to the head spot on the album charts. It then went on to sell more than 7,000,000 copies in 2003 alone. This second album, as of the time of this writing, seems to have followed up with comparable sales, already having gone quadruple platinum. "In My Hood" serves as the lead song of the album (after the near-ubiquitous spoken introduction). It also addresses unusually explicitly the urban surroundings by the standards of 50 Cent, who more normally focuses (in nonsexual contexts) on alternating bragging and threatening, with only passing references to the city surroundings. Not surprisingly, both the musical beats and 50 Cent's flow seem to accentuate the rather old-fashioned (by rap music standards) focus on the "'hood." 50 Cent's flow comes far closer here to what in my rap book I described as a "speech effusive" flow, whereas Dr. Dre's beat veers away from his usual consonant and highly accessible g-funk style to produce something much closer to (if not fully) what I, in the same book, define as the "hip-hop sublime": the layers are detuned, the alternation of the C-minor and E-flat-minor chords (the latter appearing near the end of verses and refrains) produces a jarring close-relation, and Dr. Dre also mixes in the vinyl-style "surface noise" that formerly (especially in the early to mid-1990s) lent a "hard" edge to hip-hop soundscapes.[6] The semantic aspects of the lyrics present unusually (for him) detailed and focused representations of his origins: "I'm from Southside / Motherfucker, where them gats explode, If you feel like / You're on fire, boy, drop and roll, Niggaz'll / Eat yo' ass up, 'cause they heart turned cold, Now you can / Be a victim or you can lock and load."[7] As the song (like so many of 50 Cent's) begins with some singing, the above lines constitute the first lyrics actually rapped; immediately, 50 Cent establishes the speech-effusive (again, by his standards) style with his delivery, as the first four words arrive in spoken style before he gradually settles more into something between his usual simple sing-song style and speech-effusive MCing. All these features combine to mark "In My Hood" as something of a "retro" song, perhaps more at home stylistically some ten years before its release. At the same time, such a "ghettocentric" urban landscape lies, of course, behind the construction of 50 Cent's authenticity, every bit as much as his fabled near-fatal shooting, his history as a crack dealer, or the menacing glare that he seems to manage for every album cover.

And more important for the present content, such a relentlessly bleak and nightmarish conjuring of city life would simply be unimaginable to contemporary audiences of Petula Clark's "Downtown." Of course, illicit drugs existed in 1964–1965, as did gun violence and urban underclasses. What was lacking, however, was a widespread, shared sense, on the part of Anglophone Western popular music audiences, that such things somehow constituted a fundamental and essential aspect of urban existence. And, likewise, to the analogous audiences at the turn of the twenty-first century, something like the vision of a worry-free, hospitable city life had disappeared (Downtown")—or, at the very least, had to be framed and modified.

To see that necessary framing, one might look at a recent attempt to project just such a carefree urban existence, like that of Elvis Costello and Burt Bacharach in their famous 1998 collaboration *Painted from*

Memory.[8] The song "Such Unlikely Lovers" from that recording stages its urban setting as a backdrop for the drama of an interpersonal encounter, a chance meeting between strangers who end up, as the song title implies, lovers: "On a hot city day when your white shirt turns to grey / That's when she'll arrive / When you look how you feel, someone steps upon your heel / That's when she will come." The city's dangers here are projected as trivial—some dirt and perspiration on the clothing, a trampled shoe. Juxtaposed with such a trifle, the appearance of the future paramour stands out as the incident in question; the city, in other words, stands as a (relatively) harmless stage for interpersonal encounters. The resemblance to the final verse of "Downtown" ("And you may find somebody kind to help and understand you / Someone who is just like you and needs a gentle hand to / Guide them along") implies a common theme of the urban locus as background for romance. Indeed, in "Such Unlikely Lovers" the city seems to function as the occasion for serendipity: "Listen now, I'm not saying that there will be violins / But don't be surprised if they appear—playing in some doorway." The accidents of urban environments, then, can provide an unexpected romance. Nor does the anonymity of urban crowds prove an obstacle to human intimacy: "Though no one seems to notice as they hurry by." The inconveniences of the environment—blaring heat and a foot-treading accident—are dispensed with at the very beginning of the song, immediately becoming a foil to the central focus, which is the personal situation. The city here structures the encounter through its exciting potential for accident, while its pitfalls adopt the status of charming nuisance. And the musico-poetic climaxes project the same emphases within the specifically urban imagery. The strings wind into their dynamic climax and bring the harmony back to the tonic for the rhythmically staggered line "playing in some doorway"; sweeping conjunct melodic lines of increasing intensity set the rest of the urban imagery after the opening line, climaxing with the second iteration of "Though no one seems to notice as they hurry by." So although in an obvious semantic sense the city provides only the setting for the encounter, in another sense it is projected musically as the true locus of ecstasy—or at least it fully absorbs the emotional investment. Here the urban setting is not only livable but also a place through which one lives, and in which one invests, with a certain romantic intensity. The city becomes both urban and urbane, all the more elegant for its accidental magic.

But the musical poetics of the song also provide another crucial clue about how "Such Unlikely Lovers" projects urban experience, features that differentiate the song from "Downtown" and announce its origin in a different historical moment. The genre of the music and identity of the performers (especially, of course, Burt Bacharach) indicate how such a view of city life comes to be possible in 1998; the album, after all, presents a collection of retro-styled songs. The pop jazz harmonies, orchestration, and Costello's crooning all contribute to form the stylistic context of the urban jazz lounge. Indeed, not just the music but also the portrait of the city carries the frame of historical relic; the song presents a vision of urban life every bit as "retro" as Bacharach's pianistic style. The example of a song like "Such Unlikely Lovers" suggests that the portrait of the city as a locus for romantic adventure and charming serendipity may still have been possible for Anglophone Western popular music audiences in 1998—but it required a certain framing, as an outdated vision, rather than the wholesale, bubbling enthusiasm of 1964's "Downtown."

The three songs examined so far here, and the differences among them (both contemporaneously and across time), already can go some way toward suggesting some contours of musical representations of urban environments, and the historical mutations of those representations. Something that quickly becomes apparent is that there seems to be, at any given time, both positive and negative cathexes of the urban environment in Western Anglophone popular music. That, in itself, should not be surprising, given the broad range, at any moment, of experiences and ideologies of American cities by varying classes, ethnicities, genders, and so forth; a given person's or group's response could not simply be determined or read off the changing urban environment.[9] Thus, if one views songs such as those discussed here as responses to an urban environment (or better, a range of urban environments), it becomes clear that the responses may highlight different aspects and thus embrace or critique the city in different ways. A second implication, however, is that the character of both affirmative and critical representations of American cities seems to change drastically over time. Much more specifically than that, some kinds of urban representation seem not to appear at all at certain times, such as that projected by the 50 Cent song (absent in 1965) and, conversely, to appear uniquely at other times, such as that of "Downtown" (appearing only within a "retro" frame in 1998). Other kinds of expressive responses to urban life, such as "Such Unlikely Lovers," may appear at a certain time but with a necessary framing that modifies its force—whereas at some earlier time, a similar representation (like "Downtown") may have been able to appear without such careful qualification. One could also at least speculate on the likelihood that some kinds of city images predominate in some periods, yet occupy a marginal status in others—as that of "Such Unlikely Lovers" would seem marginal, compared with that of "In My Hood," around the turn of the twenty-first century.

All these observations seem to indicate that at any given time, there is a range of possible, and more or less likely, representations of the city in the corpus of American commercial popular music, and that certain representations call for framing at certain times. That range of possibility may often be distributed among certain genres (as rap seems to host the majority of the most nightmarish visions, at least since "The Message"), certain artists, and even particular songs.[10] It also would always have its limits. In the mid-1960s, there were certainly songs that addressed urban alienation and danger (like "Who Am I?"), but there were no visions as explicit and nightmarish as that of "In My Hood."

It is the scope of that range of urban representations and their possible modalities, in any given time span, that I call the *urban ethos*. The urban ethos is thus not a particular representation but rather a distribution of possibilities, always having discernable limits as well as common practices. It is not a picture of how life is in any particular city. Instead, it distills publicly disseminated notions of how cities are generally, even though it may be disproportionately shaped by the fate of certain particular cities, especially New York City and Los Angeles (just as "Downtown" paints a presumably anonymous place, inspired by Manhattan). Views of "cities" generally in Anglo-American media culture tend to be weighted disproportionately to American cities as well, as it is to a great extent the urban life of the United States against which much "international" popular music is imagined, even in the case of music produced outside the United States. (Of course, the exceptions are important, though they hardly outweigh the normal centrality of American examples.) The urban ethos certainly may shape the representations of certain particular cities, but it does so only as a background structure of feeling, usually unnamed; for example, the short-lived American popular infatuation for Seattle in the early 1990s seemed to measure out a exasperation with the decaying and increasingly dangerous metropolis of the East Coast and the drastic horrors of Los Angeles crack culture. The exasperation was not so much named as invested in an otherwise inexplicably vehement fascination with Seattle itself.

Now that the urban ethos has acquired at least a preliminary definition and a range of illustrations, it should be stipulated that it is not an autonomous characteristic of popular music; instead, it is a multimedia phenomenon developed among music, music video, films, television, newspapers and magazines, novels, theatre, and recently the Internet. Thus, for example, the Tom Wolfe's 1987 novel *Bonfire of the Vanities* participated in the same urban ethos as Madonna's "Open Your Heart," whereas the 1967 film *Barefoot in the Park* shared an urban ethos with The Association's "Windy."[11] In point of fact, it may be the case that much of the representational force of music in this context is built as much through television "star-texts," film soundtrack use, and media coverage as it is through the sonic properties of music and the semantic level of the texts that comprise my music-theoretical disciplinary focus.[12] But nevertheless, musical features then imbed aspects of the urban ethos that may function with at least temporary autonomy, much as images imbued with a semiotic value may then function as second-order signs.[13] In fact, precisely that process was audible at the end of "Downtown," in which the brief jazz-style muted-trumpet soloing signaled images of urban sophistication that would be familiar to 1965 listeners from exposure to film and television. In truth, this regime of representation always seems to ricochet back and forth among parameters of cultural production, in ways that are sometimes unpredictable but that as an aggregate can form some interesting and revealing patterns.

Historical Shifts (Diachronic)

Although it is a regime of representation, the urban ethos nevertheless interacts significantly with the structures of real cities, especially American ones. Not surprisingly, given the discussion in the Introduction, our present urban ethos seems to figure expressively those ways in which American cities, over the past twenty to thirty years, have had to change in order to host new strategies of capital accumulation. Such dramatic changes naturally have affected who lives in cities, who moves through them and in what ways, and how they experience urban space. The surprising development, in fact, would be if representations of cities in music (and other forms of expressive cultures) did *not* shift. One need not extrapolate far to see the spatial contours of the impacted ghetto behind the place-representations of early gangsta rap, the emergence of the "in the hood" genre of films like *Boyz 'N the Hood* (1991) or *Menace II Society* (1993), and related forms of expressive culture. But one does require a fair bit more theorizing to see more subtle but equally decisive ways in which the urban ethos has changed in tandem with some of the other dramatic restructurings described in the Introduction. To recognize the latter point, it would be most useful to begin with something rather foreign to our current-day ethos, like the video for Chaka Khan's 1984 cover of the Prince song "I Feel for You."[14] There, the ghetto is certainly figured by physical markers, but it still lies some distance from the kind of ghetto represented in hip-hop and R&B since roughly the end of the 1980s. Instead, the signifiers of early hip-hop culture—graffiti, popping-and-locking, break dancing, rapping, and DJing—mark out place, along with the more inclusive markers like obscure lighting, dry-ice "fog," and a chain-link fence. Equally important, Chaka Khan moves through the space freely and with self-possession, expressing the emotions she describes with her eyes and body, wandering calmly about the space, at one point even replacing the DJ; she is not determined by the character of the space but rather exercises her free desires within it. Such generic, even clichéd, constructions of the urban ghetto typify older representations of black inner-city areas, combined with the freely acting subjects within them, as they were imagined prior to the drastic remaking of cities for business (and other) service industries, entertainment, and consumption, and before the concomitant rise of the impacted ghetto. What one sees in the video "I Feel for You," in other words, is the ghetto of the older industrial city, little different from that of the television series *Fat Albert and the Cosby Kids* (1972–1979), which also deployed chain-link fences and graffiti (along with other markers, such as brownstones) to mark the inner-city black environment. Ironically, that industrial-city ghetto was already on its way toward extinction in 1984, when the video was produced; as William Julius Wilson has shown, the impacted ghetto had already begun its ascendance from the mid- to late 1970s.[15] But that social development and its consequences were not recognized as such until much later, and so their formation was not yet registered in the urban ethos of 1984. Instead, the impacted ghetto's emergence into the wider public consciousness, and thus its appearance in music video, had to await the rise of the crack economy and its spectacular violence, which Nelson George also identifies as the content of gangsta rap.[16] Such a "lag time" strongly suggests that the urban ethos does not track city morphology by any crude reflection, but rather imagines it in highly mediated and ideologically inflected forms. Put otherwise, the range and forms of representing urban life are shaped by those with access to the means of representation.

Just like "I Feel for You," older visions of cities often feature public spaces of dancing, playing, and singing, with a conspicuous mix of economic classes and ethnicities that American cities now segregate more aggressively; here one might think, for example, of the movie *Fame* (1980), or the 1984 Tina Turner video "What's Love Got to Do With It?".[17] Such antiquated ideas of public urban space, and their contrast with more recent city life, often find expression in "retro" visions of downtown society, much as the serendipitous, romantic city of "Such Unlikely Lovers" found an appropriate frame in old-fashioned musical poetics. Here one might take as an example one of the engagements of a 1970's city sensibility from a late-1990's perspective, like the video for Wyclef Jean's (1997) "We Trying to Stay Alive."[18] The visuals construct a hospitable urban setting, against which personal relationships, celebration, rivalry, and dancing become the visual and dramatic foci; in other words, here, as in "I Feel for You," the urban environment does not determine the fate of the characters, but rather they appear as free agents engaging in interpersonal struggle. The ending dance-duel, with echoes of Michael Jackson videos and *West Side Story*, not only choreographs the historical retrograde every bit as much as the BeeGees sample that serves as the basis for the song's beat (and title); it also stages personal freedom and expressive force within the inner-city environment, as the music overwrites disco with a celebratory and eclectic hip-hop. Such historically backward-looking music can prove especially informative if, as in this case, it involves a glimpse from one urban ethos into a city different from the one that shaped it. Of course, the urban ethos is not the only force shaping the video: one could certainly observe (in a manner more in line with mainstream music studies than the present study) that much of the character of both the song and the video forms an artistic identity for Wyclef Jean. After all, his generic eclecticism, "positivity" image, and "roots" cross-over with rap are built from adventurous musical blends (though more often with Caribbean music than one might think from this song) and the mixing of ethnic identities. One could certainly argue that Wyclef Jean's musical style already distances him from the more menacing view of black urban life more common in hip-hop videos of the mid- to late 1990s. But such an argument, which effectively sidelines the question of changing spaces in American cities, would effectively obscure how imagery of the 1970s can function in this late 1990s context—namely, by standing in for lost urban possibility and a feeling of community that would seem oddly quaint to a viewer of this video in the late 1990s. That quaintness, of course, serves as something of a historical match for the disco music and period clothing; but unlike the music and clothing, the quaintness of the group socialization is only explicable within the rubric of urban historical change: such public dancing and celebration simply do not fit comfortably into the current urban ethos. In other words, an understanding of how spatial restructuring of cities has imposed *limits of possibility* can lead to a historically informed view of how the social situation of this video signifies to its viewers.

A more temporally straightforward view from within the same urban ethos as that of "We Trying to Stay Alive" can be seen in the 1996 video for the Geto Boys' "Geto Fantasy."[19] As strongly marked as the landscape of "Geto Fantasy" is with inner-city location, it invites comparison with that of "I Feel for You," released twelve years earlier. Although both videos appear to situate themselves in some kind of ghetto environment, both the setting and the characters' relation to that setting could hardly be figured differently. In Khan's video, the ghetto setting is a true backdrop, stylized and sparse, with just enough detail so that one knows where it takes place. More important, the free and easy motion of the singer and the dancers through the environment, and the upbeat, synchronized dancing of the figures both project the notion of subjective freedom. The singing persona here moves unconstrained against a hospitable background; the surrounding inner-city embellishments, in fact, mainly serve in this video as anchors of authenticity, much like the DJ, pop-lockers, and break-dancers, for a brand of R&B energized by and associated with early hip-hop. In "Geto Fantasy," by contrast, the environment does not serve as a backdrop for the unconstrained expression of emotion and personal freedom; on the contrary, the environment acts very much as an agent, and a malevolent one at that—it imposes its conditions on the sad, inert figures that the viewer sees in slow, mournful pans of the camera. Whereas the ghetto arguably anchors the authenticity much as it does in Chaka Khan's video, here it far more importantly acquires the status of an active force. Its very structure assumes the form of an overwhelming presence, which is why an endless perusal of the area and its inhabitants constitutes, in a sense, the very plot of the video. The political commentary implicit in the scenes, as well as the song's lyrics, find their purported origins in Grandmaster Flash and the Furious Five's "The Message" but even here, the historical shift is worth noting: whereas "The Message" carried with it the spirit of political commentary and critique, "Geto Fantasy" assumes more the aura of classic tragedy, the very inevitability of the ghetto's effects feeling frighteningly like a terrible historical necessity.

In light of the three videos and three sound recordings discussed so far, it becomes tempting to conceive of an urban ethos as a set of representations detailing which subjects move through the urban landscape, which parts of that landscape they traverse, and the extent to which that landscape imposes its constraints on those subjects. This last and crucial element points to the fact that all the songs detailed seem to imply degrees of freedom, agency, and self-realization on the part of the people portrayed with respect to their surroundings. The urban ethos thus poses a set of basic stances concerning the relationship of subjects to their urban setting: who can go where and do what? Who is constrained by the city, and who is freed by it? The examples so far suggest an increasing sense of constraint on some urban subjects between 1964 and 1996, and even between 1984 and 1996, and it would seem impossible to ignore somewhere in that time period the rise of the "in the hood" genre of film and gangsta rap, both of them in turn figuring the rise in the cities themselves of the impacted ghetto. Certainly, other factors separate the Geto Boys from Chaka Khan; for instance, the relatively modest budgets of music videos in 1984 may be at least partially responsible for the sparse presence of the "ghetto" in "I Feel for You." But even with the larger budget, a similar subjective freedom could easily have been projected for the Geto Boys (much as it was in Wyclef's "retro" video). Such a notion, though, would clash not only with the kind of music being set, but also with a publicly circulated notion of what the impacted ghetto has become in the American city.

"Geto Fantasy," in fact, quite prominently situates its characters as singularly unfree, almost literally trapped by urban structure. The Fifth Ward of Houston, however romanticized by the camera's focus on its locality, remains a locus of constraint and material decay. More than simply a setting, it also imposes a set of firm physical boundaries: the clapboard houses and seedy, decaying neighborhood businesses might bespeak some notion of "home," but more dramatically they emphasize the spatial constraints on the people who live in the environment. If, as the lyrics say, "love don't live here anymore," and the musical beats situate the song solidly within the hardcore-lament subgenre,[20] then the visual component of the video elevates the departure of love almost to the status of metaphysical fact. What is more, the railroad tracks raise the geographic scale of the video to the level of complete urban structure. It is not just that one is so manifestly seeing the "wrong side of the tracks"; it is also that the railroad connotes the very infrastructure of a city. Like airports, highways, and other aspects of interurban transport, the railroad marks off the throwaway real estate; on its "wrong side" lie the habitations of people whose lives can be degraded and disrupted by proximity to noisy, dangerous, and polluting carriers of people and objects. But even more important than its immediate surroundings, the railroad tracks can be taken metonymically to relate this neighborhood to the infrastructure that supports the entire city's older regime of accumulation, the days of heavy urban industry and centralized inner-city production and transport. The setting for this video, then, not only lies too close to the undesirable infrastructure; it also relates the locality to the city as a whole only through a method of capital accumulation that has passed it by, the heavy manufacturing that largely abandoned American cities during the 1970s and 1980s. The railroad tracks, then—far from the romantic cathexis of railways one finds in, say, much Delta blues music—underline the seediness and decay of the impacted ghetto, its helpless abandonment among the debris of older production mechanisms. In the meantime, the imagery itself emphasizes the objective spatial relations in one more way worth noting: the video offers precisely two moments in which the viewer/listener sees just the eyes of the boy protagonist, looking over the built environment. The first is superimposed over the shot of the passing train; the second is superimposed over the only glimpse one gets outside the ghetto, namely the bridge and part of the skyline of Houston itself. The eyes serve to cue the subjective viewpoint of the young boy, the only cues to subjectivity the viewer/listener receives in the entire video. Crucially, it is not his immediate surroundings that he sees, but rather the contact points of his environment with the city as a whole. So ironically, although most of the visuals in the video suggest that one fetishize the ghetto itself in the fashion of much hip-hop music (especially from that period), the visuals cued to the standpoint of our protagonist encourage viewers to totalize the broader context of the city—and for that, the built environment becomes all the more suffocating. The ghetto winds up projected as an objectively and subjectively trapped space, with an objectively denigrated structural relation to the metropolis that is all too visible to the young boy. Outside the "retro" frame of songs like "We Trying to Stay Alive," the inner city becomes something quite different and quite a bit more shocking.

Internal Diffentiation (Synchronic): Range and Limits

Contrasting "I Feel for You" with "Geto Fantasy" quite clearly shows that the urban ethos figures changing cities diachronically, but the urban ethos also differentiates synchronically. Here, too, the urban ethos provides for distinctions among the kinds of subjects that exist in, and move through, urban space, and which parts of that space, and with what degree of freedom. To see that, one might simply choose to contrast "Geto Fantasy" with a roughly contemporary video that projects contrasting aspects, and interactions, of subjects and their city environment. Kylie Minogue's (2002) video "Can't Get You Out of My Head" presents an illustrative case, as it envisions its computer-generated city as something between a stage and a playground, a locus of pleasure and freedom.[21] Minogue's persona moves freely through a futuristic virtual downtown landscape, dancing as the city lies behind her, and dominating her dancers, who in turn serve as passive and decorative backdrops. Minogue thus appears as a subject in control of her destiny, for whom the city is a comfortable and hospitable place. It is perhaps for this kind of subject that the 2002 urban ethos comes closest to representing the older sense of the city as a place of adventure, into which one traveled from the countryside to seek one's fortune (e.g., the film *Page Miss Glory* from 1935). In fact, the city bends to Minogue's will and bounces to her beat, in the final scene flashing the lights of its office towers to her Euro-dance rhythms and choreography. The video shows Minogue as truly in charge of the urban environment.

In the contrast between Minogue's mastery and the Geto Boys' tragic victimization, then, one can quite clearly see how the urban ethos posits not just one mapping but a highly differentiated set of mappings of the city. As the urban ethos at all times projects such a variety of experiences for different subjects and such a spectrum between personal agency and geographic determination, it will always prove telling to examine it internally and to see how such a broad range of representations is distributed among artists, songs, and so forth. The examples explored so far do quite clearly suggest that the variety of experiences within an urban ethos is distributed in a far from random way. Musical genres clearly operate prominently, here, as the character of representations often seems to correlate with some combination of genre with the star-text of the artist. The differences between the kinds of city represented in "Geto Fantasy" and "Can't Get You Out of My Head" bespeak a generic gap between rap and pop/disco, as well as a gap between the public identities of the Geto Boys (a hardcore rap group from the Fifth Ward of Houston) and disco diva Kylie Minogue. Indeed, American notions of genre in popular music have often born a distinct relation to different mappings of the city, often tied to notions of origin and authenticity. The rise of rap and the widely circulated images of a ruinous-looking South Bronx in the late 1970s acquired close public associations,[22] whereas disco always contained notions of urban freedom and experimentation (to be discussed in Chapter 3), and British invasion pop in the early 1960s never lost its association with street toughs and urban rebellion. The relationship of changed perceptions of "The Urban" to popular music, however, probably finds its most comprehensive figuration not in any individual genre but rather in a popular-music *genre system*, "genre system" here meaning simply the constellation of all possible musical genres, taken as a system of relational signification. Thus, for example, the genre known as "drum and bass" is identified, and effects its social functions, not as a self-defined group of sounds and practices, but rather in relation to jungle, techno, industrial, trance, and so on (and, of course, more distantly, in relation to power ballads, hardcore, and rockabilly). In a previous book I described the applicability of such a concept specifically to rap music, referring to a "field of production and consumption in which relations among genres are defined, maintained, and often transformed. Those relations, in turn, enable the constructions of identity which are more properly the objects of much work in cultural studies" (*Rap Music*, 91).

By extension, if popular-music genre bears such an intimate relation to publicly disseminated views of cities, the possibility arises that the urban ethos, too, offers an analogous mapping, but in this case of the possibilities for urban experience. The parceling out within the urban ethos, then, will be less a distribution of representation alone than a more generalized parceling of social possibility, just as the genre system partitions potential kinds of engagements with music, investments in music, and social activity around and about music. In any case, given the close relation of city image to the rise and fall of music genre, a properly musicological/music theoretical approach to genre, which offers formal classification, could well illuminate more than simply isolated or abstracted aesthetic experience. Of course, such projects inevitably become quite messy, because, as Susan Crafts and the other authors of *My Music* point out, the consumption of music (not to mention its production) often straddles genres.[23]

At the level of audience reception, such codes surely do not work by simple psychological identification, as one can see in the oft-trumpeted white suburban teenagers' infatuation with rap music. Rather, it would make more sense to argue that audiences may articulate the urban ethos with larger aspects of their ideological outlook, including their notion of the role that music plays in their lives and society. Indeed, there must always be a reciprocal effect between production and reception of city representations, in which the associations of urban mappings with some particular genre mutate in response to changing public perceptions of the city overall. Hence, for instance, the fact that although American rap music has always been associated with the "inner city"—read: black ghetto—the kind of inner city represented, and the relation between that location and the agency of those found there, has, in fact, changed remarkably since rap was first marketed commercially.

The mutual encoding of music genre and urban geography also works through musical poetics, though never purely or in an unmediated way. Although the examples offered so far have, at times, implicated lyrics and video imagery, the connection through genre argues strongly that the urban ethos also implicates the *sound* of music; and although the sound may rely at one point on visual cues for its semiotic value, it also thereafter may work with relative autonomy. The muted jazz-like trumpet soloing at the end of "Downtown" offered a particularly straightforward example; beyond that, the sounds of musical tracks and rhythmic delivery for "Geto Fantasy" are cued through the hardcore-rap lament tradition to a certain tragic notion of the ghetto, whereas the melodic contours and instrumental textures of Petula Clark's "Downtown" cue a conception of that district as an ecstatic solution to life's challenges and dreariness. And the retro style of Costello and Bacharach's "Such Unlikely Lovers" attributes to the surroundings an equally antiquated sense of romantic adventure.

The distance among these four representations can be measured musicologically in sound, visually in media culture, semantically in lyrics, and historically in the shifting characters of the cities they describe. All of these parameters ultimately may be separated conceptually, but they work together, so that the most adequate approach would try to think them simultaneously.

New Possibilities, Lost Possibilities

Just as the urban ethos always offers a range of possible experiences and cities, so does it never offer *every* conceivable character of cities or every possible experience; in other words, it has its limits, and the limits change over time. In fact, tracing those limits will normally offer the most diagnostic value, especially when the representational apparatus is considered in light of changes in the cities of the developed world. Two instances that have already been considered in this chapter are 50 Cent's "In My Hood" and the Geto Boys' "Geto Fantasy," with their visions of the impacted ghetto, which was simply not available to the urban ethos of the mid-1980s, or any time before. But Kylie Minogue's "Can't Get You Out of My Head" offers a less obvious but perhaps more telling glimpse of something relatively novel, at least something not widely seen before, say, the mid- to late 1990s, namely what one might call the *abstract city of fantasy*. The computer-generated city in the video appears simultaneously bright and abstract, impeccably clean and without any particular localizing feature. Both as a backdrop to the dancers and as a environment through which Minogue drives, the city embodies the abstract geometry and placelessness of a dreamscape. Unlike the fake city backgrounds of, say, old Hollywood musicals, Minogue's background presents itself as pointedly generic, cleared of even the possibility of any orienting landmarks in a fashion that suggests the city as a location of the sublime, in the sense that it is simultaneously stimulating, inaccessible, and overwhelming. Like the impacted ghetto of hardcore rap music, Minogue's abstract city of fantasy also finds its concrete embodiment in recent developments within the cities of the industrialized world, namely (as discussed in the Introduction) the transformation of downtowns into centers for the production of information and business services, along with the provision of spectacular entertainment. That dual transformation simultaneously hides the laboring infrastructure within almost indistinguishable office buildings—very much unlike the older concentrations of factories—and also foregrounds the spectacle of the city, its face of design, desire, and consumption. The abstraction of urban areas into glistening, interchangeable forms in "Can't Get You Out of My Head," then, becomes not simply a representation but also a filtered view of a lived reality for those who navigate cities and experience, on a daily basis, their public faces. Although undeniably some of the chilly urbanity of the Minogue video may be attributed to the computer generation and thus determined technologically, computer-generated cities need not be abstract or free of place markers. On the contrary, with any technology, even including the painted urban backdrops of earlier Hollywood film, place and specificity were, and still are, used when intended and appropriate to the aesthetic circumstance.

In both the impacted ghetto and the abstract city, then, one can find examples of arguably the most illuminating aspect of the urban ethos, namely the pushing of representation into previously unknown areas—or conversely, the abandoning of previous possibilities. Changes in the very outer boundaries of the urban ethos suggest the inseparability of representation and the spatial contours of cities themselves, because they point to *conditions of possibility* for expressive culture in changing regimes of capital accumulation (conditions that may, of course, operate mutually). Attention to such shifts proves especially valuable because a great many, probably most, kinds of representation remain constant across many urban ethoi. Thus nowadays, as back in the mid-1980s, one may find the city of romantic squalor and alienation, the frenetic city, and even the urban playground for young adults. Yet even within such continuities, some projections of downtown life require new modalities as the urban ethos changes—as was seen in the cases of "Such Unlikely Lovers" and "We Trying to Stay Alive."

Gender and the City

Modalities of presentation within the urban ethos need not involve simply musical poetics; though modalities usually do encompass musical poetics, they may often embrace other representational and social categories. One particularly prominent recent instance worth examining is the common foregrounding of gender in our current urban ethos and the imbrication of certain conceptions of femininity to concepts of the city. The internationally successful American television program *Sex and the City* (1998–2004) may be taken as a first symptom, particularly in its presentation of a privileged group of late-youth white women who share their personal agonies and victories in one of the most sanitized urban environments ever seen on television. A vast majority of the time, the series omits even the lighthearted foibles of city life and its dangers and inconveniences; the protagonists' private lives are rarely disturbed by yelling neighbors, strewn garbage, or traffic jams, let alone the deadly menace one sees in television series like *The Corner* (2000) or the old-fashioned haunted quality of the various *Law and Order* series (e.g., *Law and Order*, 1990-present). Here one may most valuably recall the urban ethos as a set of representations of who can do what in the city and with what degree of autonomy from the effects of space; *Sex and the City* offers the vision of certain privileged white women who can go just about anywhere and act with blissful freedom in an urban environment. The obstacles that they encounter in their lives, far from being intrinsic to urban structure (as in "Geto Fantasy"), result from personal shortcomings, bad decisions, or complicated personal relationships. The city, conversely, enables rather than blocks the women's ambitions, providing the beautiful housing, the chic restaurants and bars, and, of course, the men and women occasionally adopted as lovers or sex partners. The show's encouragement that the viewer empathize with the experiences of such privileged urban subjects, and its evident success, given the widespread popularity of the series in North America and Europe, might in itself be taken as a troubling historical sign. But such a representation need not be considered as necessarily socially regressive or exclusive in every sense; after all, not too long before its production, even privileged women had been limited in their mobility and enjoyment within cities (and, of course, in reality still are). Such a double edge will always accompany the continuing admission of previously excluded groups to higher social levels. Attention might more usefully be directed to the program's consistent cathexis of Manhattan, one which must have somehow resonated in both the United States and Europe, given that television series' popular success, and probably not solely among women of the same social class as that of the protagonists. High production values indubitably contribute to the series' appeal; but *Sex and the* City more distinctively implies something more salient to the present discussion, namely, its need for a purified urban space for staging a certain conception of femininity.

This last notion finds support in some roughly contemporary music videos in which a white female's distance from spatial restriction, and her psychological reflection on that space, become constitutive of her gender and agency. The 1998 video "Thank U" by Alanis Morissette (1998) offers illustration, as does Sarah McLachlan's 1997 video "Adia."[24] With such music videos, in which young, white alienated females move freely and reflectively through a softened urban environment, one can perhaps begin to see representations of the city as highly gendered. Such particular alienations of female personas differ fundamentally from the male-gendered urban alienation of, say, *film noir* or feature films like *Midnight Cowboy* (1969) or *Trash* (1970).[25] In the latter classic masculist alienations, the protagonist truly inhabits the metropolis and acts as an agent, occasionally a victim, who either learns how to survive, through cunning or evasion, or is crushed by urban cruelty. Life and death are at stake, and city structure itself poses a threat, the tough streets and marginal, if not menacing, characters imprinting the necessity for cunning and struggle. But the female protagonists of recent music videos like these exist only liminally in their surroundings, and the urban structure per se offers no particular threat. Both McLachlan and Morissette move abstracted through the city without seeming regard for its dangers or limitations: Morissette advances detached from her surroundings, naked and vulnerable, while McLachlan wanders or stands pensively, separated from her environment both by temporality and by the fleeting status of other people, all of whom are apt to disappear suddenly and without a trace. Such characters could not possibly threaten her, as they are projected visually to exist in another realm entirely. Instead, Sarah McLachlan appears most preoccupied, first, by her difference from those around her (which is figured in both their different speeds and their aptness simply to vanish), and second, by her periodic attempts to touch them—attempts that succeed only with a small child in front of a shop picture window. Standing and singing amidst the imposing exterior architecture of the opening and closing scenes, and amid various crowded scenes of (presumably) strangers, she nevertheless can view people and places only with a distanced and soulful detachment. Although her gestures and her abstraction from the temporality and ontology of the city clearly mark her as in some sense distanced and vulnerable, still, McLachlan by no means lacks power in this video; on the contrary, unlike most masculized icons of urban existence, protagonists battling the city for supremacy, sometimes winning and sometimes losing, McLachlan exercises mastery directly through her states of subjectivity. One can safely assume that viewers and listeners are not to take literally the shifting temporality of the anonymous crowds and their eventual disappearance from every scene. Instead, the singing protagonist projects her own subjectivity onto the urban environment—such a projection being, of course, the only tangible link between the lyrics, about failed love and postulated innocence, and the visual settings of the video. In that sense, the gendered aspect of the city in "Adia" and "Thank U" combines extremes of vulnerability and power, both of them figured in the effects of feminized subjectivity. The vulnerability of such representations might seem obvious enough, given the persona of the singer-songwriter and the mode of musical delivery, not to mention the bodily gestures and lyrics of the two videos. The protagonists' power may at first seem less obvious, but one may at least claim the evidence of authorial voice in the case of Morissette's "Thank U." While promoting the album, Alanis Morissette explained to Carson Daly her decision to wander about naked in the city for her "Thank U" video in the following terms:

> I was in my shower one morning—we had just mastered the record—and I was trying to think, or "feel" rather, what this video could be—and I was naked in my shower, and I just felt very … I was feeling very raw, and very real, and very myself, and I felt like "Thank U" is about that.

> It's sort of the heartspace that that song was written from, and also the rest of the record, really. So I just thought it was appropriate to be naked in it and to be "powerful" and "vulnerable" at the same time.[26]

Naturally, only the most naive media theory would cite an excerpt from an interview as unmediated evidence of cultural signification, but certainly it offers at the very least a consistency of public presentation—the interview and video imagery complement each other to form a recognizable discourse of "the feminine" inside our contemporary urban ethos. In fact, the city's disappearance as an agent (including its loss of menace) gives way to the women's power, whereas the conventional signs of vulnerability (e.g., McLachlan's open-armed gentle embrace toward the camera) may not only offer the balancing qualities necessary for the viewer's and listener's identification but also sneak into the scenario more traditional notions of femininity.

The more empathetic properties cannot ultimately be separated from both McLachlan's and Morissette's star-texts, or from the air of sincerity that must surround their public image as singer-songwriters. Such a linkage reinforces the earlier assertion about the intimate correspondences of urban representation and musical genre. But more crucially, the television series *Sex and the City* and these videos all demonstrate that beyond star persona, the current urban ethos calls for a certain kind of imagined city environment in order to construct a certain notion of femininity, one that proves most hospitable to staging a notion of feminine subjectivity and agency.

If gender inflects the urban ethos—that is, if it goes to determining the kinds of cities that one might show, and the ways (perhaps including genre) in which one might show it—then it is at least conceivable that other social categories might as well. The examples already discussed from Chaka Khan and the Geto Boys leave no doubt that regimes of urban representation differentiate by "race." In fact, the whole shock to public perceptions of cities occasioned by the rise, in the 1970s and 1980s, of the impacted ghetto continues to find resonance in images of American urban life, even in the first decade of the twenty-first century, in which the widespread fascination with "the ghetto" has arguably faded. One should also not be surprised to find gay cities, cities of youth, and other life stages and, of course,[27] representational differentiation by social class. Such divisions underline that the urban ethos tells the stories not just of changing cities, but also of where and how different kinds of people may move, with what degree of autonomy from space, and what kinds of experiences may be available to them. As all of these factors change as cities themselves change and play host to new kinds of capital accumulation, such differences are always registered as profoundly *historical* facts. They will originate in real, material social relations and the changing spatial strategies by which cities adjust to accumulate capital. But they will then be imagined in representational strategies and sometimes even used to refashion cities themselves.

Now that the urban ethos has been defined and illustrated, several caveats merit mention. As should be quite evident by now, the considerations surrounding the urban ethos in this chapter confine their scope to the Anglophone media products that circulate freely in North America and the British Isles. Although the boundaries between these musical (and other) practices and those of other regions and languages are by no means impenetrable, the frequency and energy with which music, film, television, print media, and the Internet circulate within those regions and institutions boundaries argue that they may well form a reasonable set of (at least provisional) boundaries. The claims made here for the significance of the urban ethos surely are ambitious enough without extension to the rest of the world, and yet considering global aspects of it would surely prove at least as intriguing as theorizing the urban ethos in the Anglophone Atlantic, as would comparative studies. Second, in the course of writing this book, I have often spoken to people, academic and otherwise, about this aspect of the music/urban-geography project, and I have frequently encountered the response, "Oh, you're talking about perceptions of cities—that must have changed enormously since September 11"—referring to the terror attacks on New York City and Washington, D.C., on September 11, 2001. The surprising fact is that those attacks appear to have influenced the urban ethos very little. The initial response, particularly in US television, was, of course, predictably sharp, but in the course of the years since then, the urban ethos appears remarkably similar to its state prior to the events. There have appeared, of course, some media products like the television series *Rescue Me* (2004 to the present) that refer directly to the attacks; but, far more relevant to present considerations, the overall character of city representations now differs little from those before the attacks. Such resilience may reflect less any simple act of repression than that the true sources of practices like representing cities lie in experiences of everyday encounters, rather than exceptional (albeit important) events. That such quotidian experiences, on the part of those who create and shape media culture, might occupy a sort of hidden center stage for producing images of urban life suggests the possibility of creating a linkage among theories of representation, musical sound, and the relations of production. Theorizing the urban ethos represents an initial approach at creating just such linkages, with the view to building truly contemporary theories of music and historical materialism.

2

Space, Place, and Popular Music in Curaçao and Elsewhere

In Chapter 1, I posited the urban ethos as a determinative and interpretive tool for a symptomatic reading of expressive culture. There, the urban ethos offered a historical window on publicly circulated and shared ideas about how cities are and how people live in them and move through them. As a regime of poetic procedures, the urban ethos clearly forms an aspect of *representation*, in the broad sense that the word has developed in (postmodern) cultural studies. At the same time, however, I carefully underlined at key points that the urban ethos cannot develop autonomously, but rather it forms something of a continuum with the real unfolding (i.e., nonrepresentational—which is not to say that representation is not itself real) of urban space related to changes in capital accumulation (the latter having been outlined in the Introduction). Therefore, although in the first chapter of this book I detailed some crucial workings of place hitherto unstudied, I also pointed toward a more comprehensive, totalizing view in which shifts related to capital production played a central role. That nod toward totalization figured especially in the boundary possibilities, i.e., in those aspects of city life that moved in and out of sight, even as perhaps the vast majority of urban representations persisted through changes in the day-to-day metropolis. In the present chapter I offer a preliminary rationale for that more comprehensive view—though in reality, all the remaining chapters of this book can be taken to illustrate equally well the inseparability of changing city spatial structures and the poetics of expressive culture. But this chapter specifically and explicitly contrasts the approaches to music and urban geography through place and through space, arguing for a shift of emphasis from the former (which is currently rather popular) to the latter.

The participation of music as a focal point in urban cultural industries has not escaped the attention of urban geographers.[1] The centrality of cultural industries to certain forms of postindustrial economic regeneration has formed a nexus of research among some of them. Such scenarios, based on classic cases like those of Manchester or New York, persuade in their breadth and detail.[2] Transforming swaths of the metropolis into centers of leisure, tourism, and cultural consumption offers, among other things, the opportunity to keep or draw into the center those who earnings afford them significant disposable income. Insuring that the income be spent locally may be crucial to many cash-strapped cities that, in earlier stages of capital accumulation, could have relied on manufacturing and related industries. Often vast sums of public money are devoted to such development, in the name of the common good of regenerating the city, although many have argued (e.g., Hannigan, *Fantasy City*, 129–150) that the benefits hardly trickle down to those already disadvantaged by urban restructuring. Overall, in fact, the effects of culture-based regeneration are highly differential, even aesthetically. Although large sections of the inner city may indeed be transformed into exciting or luminescent spaces and adventurous, eclectic experiences, access to and enjoyment of such areas remains highly class-bound (not to mention weighted toward young, childless adults), especially in tandem with the privatization of space entailed in many such development schemes. Nevertheless (or perhaps not even contradictorily), culture-based regeneration, as it is often called, appears to have accumulated such broad appeal that even cities with arguably few cultural links to other centers (e.g., Edmonton or, more successfully, Bilbao) float the idea or try it, under the most implausible circumstances. The famous tragic-comic example of Flint, Michigan, as described by Michael Moore in his classic 1989 documentary *Roger and Me*, illustrates the dangers of relying on culture and tourism to stimulate the economic growth of cities devastated by structural changes in world production. In fact, the very notion of culture-based regeneration assumes, in the first place, either a sufficient local capital accumulation to support continuous expensive leisure pursuits, or the ability to attract moneyed consumers on a large scale from far-flung locations.

Whatever the dangers or pitfalls of stimulating metropolitan growth with music halls, art museums, and lovingly renovated Victorian factories, it is difficult to locate a major city in the developed world that has not, to some extent, been touched by the phenomenon, sometimes on a massive scale (e.g., New York City), sometimes much more modestly (e.g., New Haven, Connecticut). Given the extent to which such economic/cultural activity emphasizes local touches—the renovation of historic buildings, the contributions of local musicians and artists, the marketing of regional foods and crafts—cultural regeneration may well project itself as a phenomenon of *place*. Developing, maintaining, and projecting a local uniqueness has embedded itself in the goals of many urban planners, enhancing the value of a city as a destination for locals and tourists alike.[3] Such dynamics could be taken to argue strongly that a theorist foreground *place* as part of any consideration of music and urban geography. Surely, after all, the character of any city and its outlying region constitutes a central dynamic of the culturally driven economies offered up enthusiastically by some urban planners. And indeed, any consideration of the new structures of urban economies that does not take account of the position that place occupies in the competitive dynamics of tourism, shopping, and entertainment misses an important factor. But the point to be underlined is that the aspects of place that drive such factors are not simply formed from natural aspects of the existing city, nor are they invented discursively from whole cloth. Rather, they are a mixture of natural geographic features, historical structure (itself largely formed from earlier economic/cultural configurations), and economic and cultural dispositions of the present. To treat place as first and foremost discursive, therefore, is to risk obscuring the complex levels that inform the place identity of any city.[4] In particular, by seeing place as discursive, one might obscure the extent to which the current preoccupation with place (scholarly and otherwise) itself mirrors contemporary aspects of production.

The remainder of this chapter will be devoted to demonstrating the political economy often obscured in discussions of place, and specifically to showing how music's role in shaping the discourse of place may hinge on urban transformations that are inseparable from larger patterns in global development. Furthermore, in this chapter I will also shift focus away from the cities of the developed world to an urban location whose fate and character differentiate it from most others discussed in this book. Indeed, the vast majority of recent theories about so-called post-Fordist cities, "global" cities, and so forth concentrate (sometimes by their very nature, such as Sassen's global city theories) on developed cities as their objects (or sometimes on transitional cities, such as Shanghai).[5] But many of the processes described in developed or transitional cities may be observed in the developing world as well, albeit often in different combinations and proportions. Indeed, a close look at music and urban culture and production in a developing country may offer a measure of the scope of changes discussed in this book so far. It may also indicate important differences, worthy of more thorough investigation than a generalized and introductory study like the present one is equipped to offer. Perhaps most important, a close look at a city in the developing world, and its dynamics of music and urban geography, will suggest the global reach of urban restructuring, the fragmented but still totalizing force of world capital, and its spectral force in the musical culture of a far-flung island in the Dutch Caribbean.

The present chapter will therefore pursue two different directions, the first one concerning popular music theory, and the second one a small island in the western Caribbean. The two directions lead to the same place, but they do so at different scales—and the point of bringing them together is to show that, ultimately, they tell the same story. It will prove most effective to *start* the story at the theoretical level in order to lay bare and arrange the stakes. The particularity of Curaçao can then be allowed to raise issues peculiar to that place, as well as some issues that are more broadly applicable. For urban change does not simply occur in the developed world, and its uniqueness in every *particular* location suggests the value of sometimes grounding its description in a single place. Although its city Willemstad hardly comes naturally to the fore in discussions of urban change, its very eccentricity with respect to standard discussions of the "new" metropolis will eventually prove to be a strength, as it suggests both the scope and the flexibility of any consideration of music and urban change. So that while the first discussion in this chapter approaches the issues of space and place more or less as theoretical objects and examines their configuration in recent scholarship on music and culture, the second will see the unique strewing of those objects across the streets, buildings, and cultural practices of Curaçao.

The theoretical story begins with what must almost certainly be a healthy development in popular music studies, namely the framing of social issues as somehow fundamentally geographic. That trend has been increasing with essay collections and important monographs that foreground spatial aspects of musical production, circulation, and reception.[6] Although diverse in their approach and method, such studies somehow work popular music through space and the way it is lived by particular groups or people. All of this is not to mention the seeming proliferation of geographically focused sessions at the conferences of the major music-scholarly societies and special conferences with regional or national foci. Even though some of the latter surely continue a long-standing tradition of regional studies and therefore might not represent any significant theoretical shift, the publications just mentioned surely do. Such a focus on geography in music studies will illuminate some powerful determinants of social life: not all social relations are fundamentally spatial but just about all of them are somehow *spatialized*, whether in regional distributions of populations, heavily policed urban barriers, or transaction-rich hi-tech districts on the edge of, or just outside of, many major cities.[7] The examination of music through that rubric, therefore, offers the possibility to see music as both part of the spatialization of social relations and also as a consequence of that spatialization. As an example of the former, one could cite the use of music to repel undesired populations (as classical music has been used in Toronto's Kennedy Subway Station) or to reclaim urban space, whereas the distribution of performance sites and recording retailers across urban districts could offer an instance of the latter.[8] The tendency to see music as an *agent* of spatiality has thus arisen on a number of fronts in recent years. Although such a trend indubitably reflects an important reality, the tendency to attribute political/social agency to cultural production remains widespread (in some quarters, seeming obligatory) enough to attract legitimate suspicion. One useful countermeasure may be to think about music not as an agent, pure and simple, in the sense of an originating cause, but rather to figure it as an integral part of a larger complex of social forces—not a point of social origin (or more optimistically, as in much cultural studies, a point of social "intervention"), so much as a unique location in a front of worldwide change. Music as a location in the social body may claim uniqueness in at least two respects: one, that of geographic specificity (or place), has received exhaustive attention from popular music scholars, geographers, and other concerned scholars, as discussed above. The other uniqueness, that of the mechanisms by which music partakes in wider aspects of social change, remains a good deal more obscure in recent discussions of music and geography.

The reason for the latter gap in the scholarly literature presents itself readily enough: the near dogma concerning the autonomy of expressive culture—sometimes qualified as "relative" but ultimately treated as absolute—militates against treating music (among other art forms) as an object of anything more than superficial or contingent determination. By such a view, determining forces offer little more than a background against which music exercises its compelling agency. Under such a regime of cultural analysis, music may become a force of liberation against a background of determination, all the more powerful because of its presumably nonrepresentational properties and their ineffable abilities to move large populations emotionally (a property, ironically, often presenting itself, in contemporary analysis, in forms largely untouched since nineteen-century romanticism). The resulting operating procedures project an agonistic cultural struggle between two terms that it will be useful to designate as *space* versus *place*. In such dichotomies, roughly speaking, "space" represents coercive forces of social constraint, for instance, the social inequalities of so-called globalization, or the homogenizing structures of the shopping mall and service-industry employment. In the context of scholarship that is critical of capitalism and cultural domination, therefore, space acquires a generally negative force. Against the negative value of space, "place" then assumes a liberatory force in this dichotomy, representing the ways in which people and their expressive cultures revalidate localities, create symbolic attachments, and reaffirm the importance of their specific and unique corners of the world. Place, in other words, becomes, in this most common rubric of analyses, the model of liberatory resistance to space. Arif Dirlik exemplifies this conception when he asserts that "[t]he struggle for place in the concrete is a struggle against power and the hegemony of abstractions."[9] Whereas Dirlik is particularly explicit about his theoretical framework, most scholars of cultural geography validate the cultural processes of place more implicitly, by allowing its social formation and definitions to become the central drama in a humane narration of everyday activity. To take one example specific to music studies: in their examination of a cultural scene known as Northern Soul (essentially a social network centered on dance and musical appreciation of soul records from the 1960s and 1970s), Joanne Hollows and Katie Milestone evince an awareness of the shaping force of regional domination. In this case, the southeast of England asserts its centrality, marginalizing culturally (and otherwise) the eponymous north of England.[10] The bulk of the essay focuses, appropriately, on the contours and practices of Northern Soul, emphasizing the practices of exchange, pilgrimage, and the production of meaning that constitute the scene. Hollows and Milestone compile an impressive and potentially quite significant argument concerning how appreciation and reception create surprising geographical affinities, and how the scene that they discuss "highlights the complexity of the relations between space, power, and musical cultures" (p. 97).[11] It does indeed, but the limitations of the view stem from the fundamental disconnection between structural situation (i.e., regional domination) and the affective investments of the actors which constitute, to some extent, a response to that situation. The situation remains suspended, as a premise for the activity described and apparently resisted by it, but in fact, holding no dynamic relation to any particular cultural situation described in the essay. The social activity and creation of sentiment—in short, the making of place—thus emerges as a thing in itself, a clearly significant human activity but with no more than an initial connection to its broader situation (plus its eventual transformation of it). Hollows and Milestone's procedures are assuredly different from Dirlik's: whereas the latter deploys the ideological regime of liberatory expressive culture against oppressive forces being discussed here, Hollows and Milestone offer the "weaker" version of such a picture, in which the local investments of place are simply presented as music geography per se. Musical "place" thus becomes a locus of freedom, individual self-making, and the layering of sentiment over a landscape of economic production, domination, and other forces that serve merely as a background (albeit a crucial one to understanding the significance of the actions described). Hollows and Milestone's approach arguably forms far more the norm than the exception. The contributors to *Music, Space, and Place*, for instance, underline how performers and audiences of popular music deploy it strategically, to reclaim their own identities and that of their surroundings. In extreme cases, nostalgia for such acts of resistance appears to form the only discernible content of a given discussion.[12] Whether one examines the starker (and more common) opposition of determination versus expressive culture's freedom exemplified in Dirlik's essay, or the softer and perhaps more informal version presented by Hollows and Milestone, music ends up occupying roughly the same role in social formation, namely as a loosely constructed set of individual (or locally collective) acts, forming the uniqueness of a person, localized group, or indeed, a place.

It is worth noting here how the social forces line up: place represents the human-scaled world of the concrete, struggling against the presumably oppressive abstraction of space.[13] Some closely homologous dichotomies also creep into music studies. Some analysts celebrate the "local" over and against the "global," decrying how so-called globalization erases the uniqueness of local life.[14] Or in yet another related theoretical gesture, a normally denigrated location receives its validation from this or that musical practice, resisting the spatial order that normally favors some more dominant locale. Thus, for example, some studies reassure us that hip-hop assists in shoring up ghetto residents' sentiments for their neighborhoods,[15] whereas Joanne Hollows and Katie Milestone, as already discussed, celebrate consumers of Northern Soul in their cathexis of northern England, opposing the cultural and political domination of the southeast.

It would surely be exaggerated to deny the cultural salience of these theoretical celebrations of place and locality. Among other things, such studies remind us that whatever the force of a social totality, it cannot determine every detail of cultural production, nor, for that matter, of any part of the production/consumption loop, including the ways in which individuals construct their own sentimental attachments to place. The agonistic tinge of many such examinations also serves to remind readers that expressive culture may serve as a battleground in which something is at stake (though the battle is rarely as evenly pitched as is often implied). Nor would it help to erase the dichotomy of space versus place or even to deny categorically the positive force ascribed to the representation of place. Indeed, it is true that world capital increasingly homogenizes at some scales, and it is equally true that many expressive cultures resist that homogenization symbolically. No doubt, that resistance *does* serve important and desirable psychological functions for real human beings, on a daily basis.

But there remain compelling reasons to suspend that vision of a fundamentally *resistant* geography of place, and to consider the possibility that analyses of popular music that treat the expressive construction of place as liberatory generally do so by *misconceiving the relation of space to place in the contemporary world.* In particular, far from being separate and opposed realms in which we can cheer one side against the other, space and place increasingly merge in the contemporary world, becoming two different faces of a single, overarching hegemonic process. In other words, to oversimplify for a moment, the global is, in fact, the same as the local; space becomes place.[16] To cheer one term over and against the other, therefore, misconstrues the geographic reality of the contemporary world. The merging of space and place will now be outlined in a generalized fashion, before the argument is instantiated through the particular example of Curaçao and one of its unique and indigenous musical genres, *tumba.*

The Merging of Space and Place

The merging of space and place has arguably been a fundamental aspect of capitalism since its inception. After all, Marx and, more recently, countless generations of location theorists have insistently reminded us how the development of capital structures the growth of particular localities. But even so, the intermingling of space and place arguably accelerated, in the advanced capitalist world, sometime in the early to mid-1970s. Although to some extent periodizing a tendency that is, in the first place, endemic to capitalism might arouse legitimate suspicion, it is important to specify that time, because right about then some specific and crucial processes, already begun, achieved some generalized visibility. The most important of them is *design-intensive production*, in our society in general and in the cultural industries in particular.

Design-intensive production, already outlined in the introduction to this book, bears clear relationships to the new kinds of capital accumulation practiced in cities in the last few decades.[17] Not surprisingly, then, that kind of production, though it has always existed, accelerated with the rise of post-Fordist strategies of accumulation. As deindustrialization ravaged many cities in the developed world, certain heavy manufacturing industries moved either away from cities into rural areas or overseas to developing economies. In first-world cities, design-intensive production became one vehicle for industrial renewal, manifesting itself anywhere from software and information industries to the music and film industries, to the production of designer coffeepots, so-called "ethnic" foods, and both mass and niche-market tourism. All of these products and services derive much, sometimes most, of their market value from the development and packaging of symbols, information, or aesthetic properties, rather than physical materials. That is not to say that their material content becomes irrelevant to their value: clearly, for instance, a designer coffeepot must be resistant to high temperatures, solid, nontoxic, and so forth. But even given the material requirements of certain objects, a substantial, sometimes overwhelming, aspect of their market value, if they are design intensive, will be their informational, symbolic, or aesthetic distinctions from other functionally similar products. And the same goes for services. Many tourist agencies, for instance, may transport one to New Zealand, but only certain eco-tourist businesses will do so in a way aimed to a certain niche consumer, whereas in the burgeoning information industries, all actors might produce blackened paper or electronic data, but the informational content forms the real market value.

Most significantly for the present discussion, *place* itself provides one of the fundamental symbolic values for many of these commodities and services. And while the role of place may be blindingly obvious in the case of tourism, location also emerges visibly in the constitution of ethnic foods as well, in "Scandinavian"-design furniture, in popular and so-called world music—in short, across both the performing arts and an enormous range of design-intensive consumer commodities. When one combines such developments with the turn in urban economies to tourism, as discussed above, place seems to have saturated the urban environment and the experience of cities for visitors and residents alike; whether one is visiting a city that has remade itself (or parts of itself) as a tourist destination or whether one is simply shopping for ethnic food or world music, routes through post-Fordist cities are often laden with the signposts of place—not only the place through which one literally moves, but also other places that enhance the value of goods and services. Some geographers and musicologists treat the prominence of place as a matter of simple human nature; numerous studies, for instance, either assume that defining place occupies an intrinsically central aspect of people's relation to music, or else follows the fates of various characters' relation to place as if to suggest a timeless, transhistorical geographic process.[18]

But as the previous narrative suggests, the prominence of place in contemporary life is by no means transhistorical or intrinsic to human nature; whereas some attachment to particular locations may be argued to reside in human nature, historical and social phenomena clearly (at a minimum) enhance such a tendency. These phenomena participate in a particular configuration of capitalism, in which place acquires something of a branding value. In other words, place has acquired a value-added function that is quite specific to our present socioeconomic life. That is not to say that, previous to this, place played a minor role in human life or that place acts only as a value-added property for goods and services. Rather, it is to suggest that the omnipresence of place in our cultural life, as well as (importantly) the scholarly interest in place that has so permeated music studies, has undergone its vast recent expansion for a reason; it is not a matter of coincidence but, rather, an aspect of the changing developmental circumstances of the capitalist world. Explanations that fail to historicize the prominence of place in our contemporary musical life thus run the risk of mystifying, rather than illuminating, a phenomenon that presents itself as thoroughly contingent.

Studies that treat place as a timeless, essential geographic force also miss how its recent prominence reflects something of a merging of place with space. It is precisely larger changes in the accumulation and distribution of capital—that is to say, space—that have allowed place the enhanced role that it now plays in cultural production. This is true not only in the relatively oft-cited (and perhaps banal) sense that products and services from around the world now circulate more freely than ever before, especially in large cities of the world, thus offering a greater marketplace of geographic origins.[19] It is also true in the perhaps profounder sense, namely place's role in offering relative surplus value for cultural products, consistently with the greater role that symbols and information play in the values of products and services generally (Castells, *End*; Lash and Urry, *Economies*; Sassen, *Global City*). The emergence of information and symbols as leading forces in economic and cultural production itself partakes of the greater spatial order of post-Fordist capitalist production. It structures (and is structured by) the networks of electronic communication that connect international banks to each other, just as such networks facilitate the spread of homemade remixes of popular music on the Internet. For this reason, it may make sense—as heretical as it might seem—to conceive of the emergence of place in recent years (including scholarly interest in the subject) as a subheading of the greater shift in the spatial order of capitalist production. Once one has effected such a conceptual shift, the merging of place and space becomes clearer, as it also becomes clear that the merger does not occur on equal terms: it is the shift in the spatial logic of capital that serves as the precondition for the enhanced significance of place. New urban logics of space also, of course, encompass many areas of social life that have nothing to do (directly) with place, such as (to take one of many possible examples) the concentration of information and service industries in so-called global cities (Sassen, *Global City*). But the specific context in which the importance of place emerges provides a crucial link between many of the discussions in this book, on the one hand, and the more placed-oriented studies that have been popular in recent years among musicologists, music theorists, ethnomusicologists, and popular-music scholars.

For strategic reasons it will now be useful to recall what was supposed to be the initial distinction between space and place, the one that structured the purported liberatory force of place. "Space" was supposed to refer to the objective, large-scale and relatively impersonal forces that shape our geographic environment, whereas "place" was supposed to refer to the more intimate, affective localization. But what reality remains in such a distinction, when suddenly the global forces of spatial reorganization demand that cultural products and practices be saturated with the symbolic content of place? In particular, how does one celebrate the affective power of place in popular music, when the spatial forces of global reorganization demand, in many cases, that music be tagged with a presumably "resistant" locality?[20] If the geographic structure of space operates largely, sometimes even principally, through the symbolic force of place, then the notion of locality as somehow "resistant" would seem to risk gullibility or even absurdity. (At the very least, such a notion would be outdated.) This is one reason to retain a certain skepticism when music scholars celebrate the construction of place or the overturning of dominant localities by dominated localities. To celebrate along with such theories may be to entertain the same insidious ideology which has captured the imagination of hordes of consumers of "world" music, "local" bands and electronic dance styles, and so forth.[21] But this is only one reason to question the purported liberatory force of place; to argue a subtler but more pervasive reason, it will be instructive now to turn to Curaçao.

Place, *Tumba*, and Curaçao

Associated in many North Americans' minds with the eponymous sweet liqueur, Curaçao is one of three major islands comprising the Netherlands Antilles, the others being Aruba and Bonaire.[22] Too barren to support major agricultural industry, Curaçao instead served, during the many years of slavery in the New World, as a first outpost and central trading point for slaves newly transported from Africa;[23] its main industries, in the present day, include oil refining, ship repair, and tourism. With a relatively well-developed economy by regional standards, Curaçao also boasts a high (again, by regional standards) per-capita GDP estimated (in 1998) at $11,800. However, it also suffers, as is common in the Caribbean, from a high unemployment rate (14.9%, estimated in 1998) and intransigent pockets of extreme poverty. Willemstad, a city with a population of about 144,000,[24] is Curaçao's capital and also the capital of the Netherlands Antilles.

Although the Netherlands Antilles nominally gained its domestic independence in 1954, it remains part of the Kingdom of the Netherlands and retains, like many former colonies, a complex dependence relation with its colonizer, involving foreign relations, public-sector transfer payments, immigration, and commercial contacts. Like most Caribbean islands, Curaçao is poor by developed world standards, though because of the transfer payments from Holland and a relatively lucrative oil refinery, it remains better off than the worst in the region. Oil refining and transshipment, in fact, have been a mainstay of Curaçao's economy since 1915, and that, in turn, develops another complex dependency relation, this time with Venezuela. The latter's crude oil feeds the Curaçaoan industries of oil refining and transshipment, and Venezuela operates the oil refinery (located in an inlet from the ocean within Willemstad itself), which is the island's largest employer.[25]

Unlike its neighbor and countrymate Aruba, Curaçao did not successfully develop its tourism industry during the 1960s and 1970s, the initial boom period for Caribbean tourism, especially from the United States.[26] As a result, Curaçao still scrambles for tourist dollars in competition with Aruba. Both Willemstad itself and the outlying areas of the island offer some tourist amenities. The outlying areas house facilities for nature-related tourism (especially snorkeling and fishing) and some of the larger (especially all-inclusive) resorts are there. Willemstad itself, on the other hand, offers the stretch of brightly colored waterfront buildings that line the shoreline of Punda, the oldest part of the downtown. Partially on account of them, Willemstad was declared a UNESCO World Heritage Site in 1997, and reproductions of that stretch of buildings constitute an emblematic representation of Willemstad in tourist guides, restaurant menus, and downtown hotel advertisements, among other things. Also in Punda can be found the Western Hemisphere's oldest synagogue, Mikve Israël Synagogue, built in 1730 to service the then-growing community of Jews fleeing persecution in Portugal (and now paired with a Jewish Cultural Museum). Other buildings registered as contributing to the city's UNESCO status include the waterfront fort and the bright yellow eighteenth-century Penha department store. To some extent, all these architectural features anchor the urban tourism that helps sustain Willemstad's economic life. A floating bridge connects Punda to Otrabanda across the St. Anna Bay; Otrabanda's rambling and in some places decrepit streets also offer attractions to tourists, and most of the downtown hotels are located there. A casino (with hotel) abuts the waterfront of Otrabanda, and restaurants agglomerate around the waterfronts both of Punda and of Otrabanda. Also agglomerated near the waterfront of Punda are a good number of duty-free shops, which attract shoppers mainly from the cruise ships that dock either in St. Anna Bay or, in the case of the newer supersized liner, at the recently built oceanside passenger-ship dock specifically designed for the largest cruise ships. By contrast, the north (inland) part of St. Anna Bay is dominated by the ship-repair, oil refining, and oil transshipment facilities.

The aforementioned oceanside dock, which welcomes the largest crowds of ship-bound tourists, usually hosts small numbers of local musicians during the day, along with stalls selling tapes and CDs of "authentic" Curaçao music. In fact, Curaçao claims several indigenous musical traditions, all of them ultimately related to its mixed heritage of African slavery and European colonization. By far the best-known indigenous musical genre, at least to locals but probably also to tourists, is the *tumba*. Related to other Caribbean popular-music genres like the Venezuelan *rhumba* and the *salsas* and *socas* that circulate throughout the region, the *tumba* nevertheless borrows from indigenous genres like the *tambu* and has achieved a status close to an official national musical form.[27] The annual February *Tumba* Festival, central to Curaçao's annual *Karnival* celebrations, dominates the island's media culture. Audiences at the venue instantiate startlingly well the ideology of music's unifying force, bringing together socioeconomic classes and Afro-Curaçaoan with European Dutch, in uninhibited, ear-splitting celebration. The festival dominates the local television station *TeleCuraçao*, local media coverage, and as far as I could tell, discussion all over the island. Within several weeks of the festival, which is also a contest, a special CD is released of the top-ranked performances, taped live. The CD sells briskly in all of the island's record stores. The festival is held early in the *Karnival* season, and the winning song becomes a quasi-official anthem for its duration. The island's dominant institutions, and locals I have interviewed, all prize *tumba* for being particularly and uniquely Curaçaoan; combining the slave tradition of *tambu* music with the nearly ubiquitous Caribbean *salsa*, it also most importantly flaunts the local Creole language Papiamentu. In all these senses, *tumba* acts as an emblem of Curaçaoan nationhood. Although the character of *tumba* lyrics varies, a good many, if not the majority, are self-consciously uplifting and patriotic, praising Curaçao and urging listeners toward pride and achievement.

The emotional popular adoration for *tumba*, and its integral status to local experiences and cathexes of Curaçao, together suggest the very soul of the idea of place. It constitutes the "local" in its most everyday and authentic sense on just about every conceivable scale, from the annual gatherings of Curaçaoans, watching the festival on television at local bars, to the proud work of the musicians and the operation of official institutions. *Tumba* palpably participates in constituting listeners' (and musicians') concepts of what it means to be Curaçaoan, their sense of the uniqueness of the island and their culture—in short, place. Practitioners of cultural studies would urge us to consider *tumba* as profoundly constitutive of Curaçaoan nationhood, nearly unmatched as it is in its social saturation throughout the population. In this sense, virtually no expressive culture marks "place" as firmly for Curaçao as *tumba* itself. It will be helpful at this point, therefore, to take a look at a recent winner of the *tumba* festival, "Much'i Otrabanda" from 2001 (sung by Izaline Calister with the instrumental group GIO Fuertisimo), and to try to draw some lessons from it about space and place. In perusing the lyrics, reproduced below with my own English translation, readers will want to know that Awasa is the harborside neighborhood within Otrabanda that hosts the main parade of *Karnival.* More will be said presently about Otrabanda and Awasa.

Much'i Otrabanda (2x)	Children of Otrabanda (2x)
Sa sa na Áwasa (2x)	Dance at Awasa (2x)
Rekonosementu di un pueblo na un pueblo	Recognition from one people of a people
Anto Otrabanda t'e símbolo di rekonosementu	So Otrabanda is the symbol of recognition
Otrabanda t'e símbolo di renasementu	Otrabanda is the symbol of rebirth
Dje pida baranka ku yama Kòrsou	Of the piece of rock called Curaçao

Otrabanda ta kargá ku historia Ku ta yena kada un di nos ku orguyo I e fanatísmo di un much'i Otrabanda Ta demostrá ferviente idealismo	Otrabanda is replete with history Which fills each of us with pride And the enthusiasm of a child of Otrabanda Shows a passionate idealism
Oh	Oh
Anto karnaval, ta much'i Otrabanda Su lombrishi ta derá, den pleno Otrabanda I tur karnavalista, ta much'i Otrabanda T'esei t'e kurasón di nos karnaval	So Karnaval is the child of Otrabanda Its navel is buried in the midst of Otrabanda And all karnavalists are children of Otrabanda Therefore, they are the heart of our Karnaval
Quinta, Shon Toms, Panama ku Domi Mundu Nobo, Charo, Baraltwijk ku Rif Colon i Marchena	[These are all proper names, of neighborhoods within Otrabanda.]
Até, atá, até, até, atá (2x)	Over there, look, over there, over there, look (2x)
[Pregón:]	[Refrain:]
Figuranan masha popular ta (Much'i Otrabanda) Aurilio Hato i Rina Penso Percey Pinedo i Orlando Cuales tambe tá Ay ami mes masha ten mi tin ta purba Tur hende sa, or'e tumb'aki zona Hai ku nos dushi karnaval ta...	Very popular figures are (Children of Otrabanda) Aurilio Hato and Rina Penso Percey Pinedo and Orlando Cuales also are Me myself, I have so much to show Everyone knows, when this tumba sounds That it is our dear Karnaval
Anto Áwasa ta sentr'i Otrabanda Einan ta kulminashon, di tur kos bon Anto ún pa ún nos ta bai Ún pa ún nos ta bai	So Awasa is the center of Otrabanda They are the culmination of all good things So one by one we go One by one we go
Sa, sa, sa... sa sa na Áwasa Sa, sa, sa, sa sa na Áwasa Sa sa na Áwasa (Sasa na Áwasa) Sa sa na Áwasa	Dance, dance in Awasa Dance, dance in Awasa Dance in Awasa (Dance in Awasa) Dance in Awasa

Mi ta kana ta toka ta toka ta tumba	I walk, play, play, tumba
Mi ta kana ta toka ta toka ta tumba	I walk, play, play, tumba
Huntu den legria (pasa barbería Jopi)	Together in joy (passing Jopi's Barbershop)
Karnaval den pas i harmonía (bula baila kanta i gosa hopi)	Karnaval in peace and harmony (Jump up, dance, sing and have a great time)
Bula bai, baila bai nos ta pasando den Roodeweg	Jump up, dance, we are passing through Roodeweg
Sa sa na Áwasa	Dance in Awasa
Sa sa na Áwasa	Dance in Awasa
Anto nos ta bai (Ún pa ún)	We are going (one by one)
Nos ta move	We are moving
Rib'un rust	On a tear
Yen di energia	Full of energy
Anto nos ta bai	So we are going
Nos ta move	We are moving
Rib'un rust	On a tear
Yen di energia	Full of energy
Sa sa na Áwasa (Sa sa na Áwasa)	Dance in Awasa (Dance in Awasa)
Sa sa na Áwasa	Dance in Awasa
Mi ta kana ta toka ta toka ta tumba	I walk, play, play, tumba
Mi ta kana ta toka ta toka ta tumba	I walk, play, play, tumba
Hai ku nos man na laira, nos ta kana t'e mainta	Our hand to the sky, we walk until dawn
Nos ta kana henter dia, sin doló di pia	We walk the whole day, without foot pain
Sasa na Áwasa	Dance in Awasa
Sasa na Áwasa	Dance in Awasa
(Mambo)	(Mambo)
David de Voet	[These are again neighborhoods of
Kamama likdor	Otrabanda.]
Dó puitu	
Di Otrabanda	

The musical poetics of this song open geographically in multiple directions, shaping rhetorically the force of the lyrics. The most obvious of those directions comes quite simply from the semantic parameter of the lyrics. Amid the blustery rhetoric of praise—not unusual for *tumba*, by any means—and the equally generic encouragement to celebrate, the song enjoins listeners to cathect Otrabanda as a place. For example, in the very first verse, Otrabanda is not only the "símbolo di rekonosementu" ("symbol of recognition") but also the "símbolo di renasementu" ("symbol of rebirth")—an optimistic assessment, perhaps, but not unusually so for the normally upbeat, boosterish lyrics of *tumba*. The song highlights the centrality of Awasa to the parade, in many ways the culmination of the annual *Karnival*, thus conflating that neighborhood with the general ethos of patriotism that clearly serves much of the ideological function of the festival. It is worth pointing out that among *tumba* songs that I know, a fixation like this on one urban region and neighborhood is quite novel, as the majority of the songs touting locality celebrate the whole island.

The sequence of geographic scope within the song also suggests a particular path, clear and consistent enough for impact on a first listening. The opening verse locates Otrabanda on the rocky island, with the following verse-and-a-half extolling its virtues, centrality in *Karnival*, and "popular figures." Halfway through the second verse, however, the scale narrows to Awasa, introduced as the "center of Otrabanda," followed by the rhetoric deeming it the "culmination of all good things." Immediately, the scale narrows down yet another level, to that of the dancing, celebrating individuals: "Anto ún pa ún nos ta bai" ("So one by one, we go"). The song's formal structure underlines these scale shifts and ties the last two together—Awasa and the individual—with the arrival of the refrain: "Sa, sa, sa … sa sa na Áwasa" ("Dance, dance in Awasa"). The connection of these last two scales—the neighborhood of Awasa and the individual—in the personage of the dancing "karnavalista" remains the final geographic context, and the rest of the song repeats and elaborates the connection of the celebrant to Awasa. The entirety of the song, therefore, narrows the listener's focus from the island down to the neighborhood Awasa, then cementing the individual's pleasure to that final, most localized scale.

Characteristic aspects of *tumba* and this song also convey a sense of locality; Figure 2.1 shows how. "Much'i Otrabanda" shares the basic formal design of many *tumbas*, with an initial introduction and verse/refrain alternation leading into an extended jam. That two-part structure handily corresponds to the semantic parameters of the lyrics: the verses perform the geographic telescoping from Curaçao to Awasa, whereas the jam enjoins listeners to dance and celebrate. The song is a bit messier than all that, however, because a truncated third verse is actually repeated late in the song in the midst of what is otherwise labeled a jam—that is what Figure 2.1 labels "verse 3 fragment." But coming as it does four measures into 128 measures of jam, it cannot strongly project the character of a section. Instead, it works as an interjection, an interruption of the two-part process. Most important, it is this truncated third verse that finally narrows the focus of place to Awasa itself, while shifting the character of the music from verse/refrain alternation to the jam. The relevant moment sets the following material:

A (verse) material, telescoping to Awasa:	
Anto Áwasa ta sentr'i Otrabanda	So Awasa is the center of Otrabanda
Einan ta kulminashon, di tur kos bon	They are the culmination of all good things
Transitional upbeat material, link of Awasa to celebrating individual:	
Anto ún pa ún nos ta bai	So one by one we go
Ún pa ún nos ta bai	One by one we go
Sa, sa, sa… sa sa na Áwasa	Dance, dance in Awasa
Sa, sa, sa, sa sa na Áwasa	Dance, dance in Awasa
B (jam) material, enjoinment of individual to celebrate:	
Sa sa na Áwasa (Sasa na Áwasa)	Dance in Awasa (Dance in Awasa)
Sa sa na Áwasa	Dance in Awasa

The lyrics here situate Awasa as the place of arrival, not only with the introductory gesture "anto"—meaning "therefore"—but also by designating the neighborhood as the "kulminashon di tur cos bon" ("the culmination of all good things"). When the following transitional structural upbeat then interrupts the verse, it therefore reinforces a

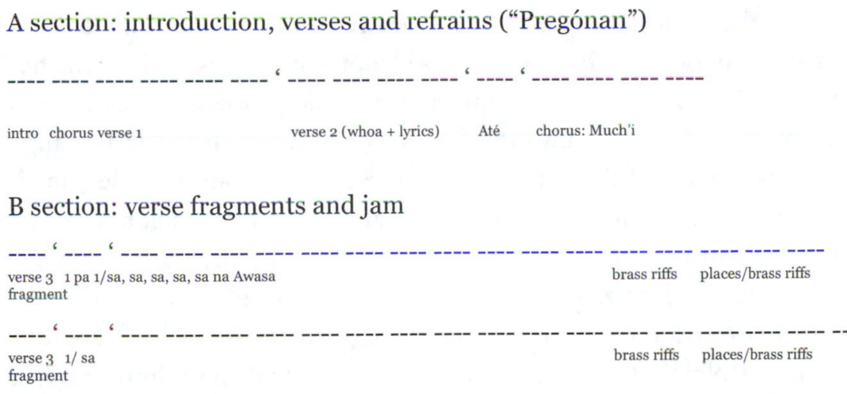

Figure 2.1 Two-part form in "Much'i Otrabanda."

clear geographic logic: once Áwasa has been established as the locus of dancing and celebration, the singer can instruct the listeners to celebrate and dance: "anto ún pa ún nos ta bai / ún pa ún nos ta bai / sa, sa, sa / sa, sa na Awasa." The jam takes over at just that moment by repeating and recontextualizing the line "Dance in Awasa," the dance rhythms focusing, stabilizing, and intensifying as the singer directs the listeners—the celebrants of *Karnival*—to party all night. The repetition of that truncated third verse, therefore, serves to focus the link of Awasa to celebration, whereas the opening line of the jam underlines the link of the dancing individual to that neighborhood. So this structural transition establishes not Curaçao, Willemstad, or even Otrabanda, but specifically Awasa as a locale for the investment of pride, pleasure, and emotional and physical release. The process sutures the listener, the dancer, as a celebrant not only *in* Awasa, but also *of* Awasa.

It has always seemed to me that two-part musical structures such as this, not uncommon among forms adopting the Cuban *son*, effect a complex teleology with respect to that final jam. In a sense, the jam serves as a musical goal and thus a release of tension in the traditional sense that, in Western classical music theory, music scholars attribute to cadences. On the other hand, that goal constitutes anything but a resting point, even in the highly tenuous sense that cadences do in classical music; instead, it marks the high point of energetic engagement, the moment when the dance enters its most frenzied abandon. In that sense, the material preceding the jam serves both as transition and as introduction, while the jam itself both stabilizes and intensifies the musical material. Harmonic and melodic processes contribute to all of this, as in the jam of "Much'i Otrabanda," the melodic range narrows to forceful interjections while the harmony whittles down to an insistent dominant/tonic alternation. Such a resolutely bipartite structure has more in common with songs like Lynyrd Skynyrd's "Freebird" or Led Zeppelin's "Stairway to Heaven" than it does with the verse/refrain structure that forms part of the generic expectations of much North American popular music.[28] And most important, it divides the semantics of the lyrics into an analogous two-part structure: the verses and chorus serve to narrow the geographic focus to a concentration on Awasa, while the jam then enjoins the listener to invest that locale with the full energy of the celebration of *Karnival*. The content of "Much'i Otrabanda" 's jam cannot be surprising, given the tendency of *tumba*, like *Karnival* music generally, to foreground the act of celebration. But the most important effect of the song's two-part structure is its seamless elision of the localities of Otrabanda and Awasa with the joy of carnival and national pride.

According to the most widespread theoretical tendencies in popular music studies, therefore, "Much'i Otrabanda" should present a thoroughly resistant locality, as Curaçaoan listeners cathect the neighborhood against the homogenizing and denigrating forces of globalization. In the more forceful versions of such an approach, such a cathexis should also go to influencing mainstream, or majority, perceptions of Curaçao (though if that is indeed happening, I have yet to notice it). And in fact, such a perspective would surely accommodate the most literal possible reading of the lyrics. The conscious purpose of such relentless praise of Otrabanda, of Awasa, and of Curaçao could hardly be anything other than local pride, and it is not by any means farfetched to expect listeners to be aware of the slow (or sometimes quick) process by which forces, both local and global, are eroding living conditions on the island for the majority—and thus to be conscious of the song's thrust as some form of symbolic resistance.

But the argument being advanced here, of course, insists on the growing inseparability of place and space, such that they cannot be separated, with one side cheered against the other. Yes, of course, songs like this could, at least temporarily, help listeners (and perhaps performers) feel better about their environment; but then to celebrate that symbolic "resistance" fetishizes the artistic gesture and thus obscure its ultimate compliance with the same political/economic forces that structure the gesture in the first place. To demonstrate how that occurs in this case, now that "Much'i Otrabanda"'s forming of locality should be clear enough, the logical next step will be to specify what it is about Willemstad that actually renders that locality compliant with global forces of capital.

Willemstad Becomes Place …

David Harvey (*Condition*, 66–98), John Hannigan (*Fantasy City*), and other geographers have described and theorized first-world cities, as they busily remake their devastated inner districts and now-moribund industrial areas into tourist and entertainment centers, shopping malls, and other sites of upscale consumption. In transformation to an object of tourism, a city produces *itself* as a design, produces *itself* as a symbol. Its effectiveness in doing so then powers the tourism and entertainment sectors that have partially replaced industrial production. As such strategies have become popular in cities throughout the developed world (from Leeds to Bilbao), Harvey, Hannigan, and quite a few others have carefully delineated the winners and losers of such development, and perhaps not surprisingly, the two camps closely resemble the winners and losers of quite a few other "postindustrial" growth schemes, with larger investors and corporations reaping most of the benefits while the labor force increasingly tends toward low-paid, part-time service-sector work.

Such studies of urban geography and new urban development tend, understandably, to focus on the developed world, in which most of the processes manifest themselves most plainly, and in which, not coincidentally, most of the intellectuals who describe them live and work. And while critically important to an understanding of the world as a system (including the developing world), that body of literature offers only a passing glimpse of the forces at work elsewhere in the world, in places, that is to say, like Curaçao. Conversely, while quite a bit of literature exists concerning new urban geographies in the developing world, the scholarly literature remains rather barren concerning events in Curaçao.[29] There, many of the processes described by geographers of the developed world apply, as well—for instance, privatization of formerly public services, the shrinking of the welfare state, and, especially relevant to the present context, the conversion of city centers into loci for tourism. But some of the other developments described in cities like London or Tokyo may not apply to the same extent, if at all, in a location like Willemstad: as an example, neither the infrastructure nor the demand would likely exist to convert it into a center for financial control, advanced business services, or media production. Cities like Willemstad, instead, have fewer options, limited by history and geography, and channeled by natural environment and regional traditions and capitalization. At the same time, as will be seen, some of the styles and strategies of the developed urban center may also be replicated in Willemstad, albeit on a much smaller scale.

So when the Dutch government, at the behest of the International Monetary Fund, began cutting its transfer payments to Curaçao—payments that, among other things, supported much of the island's welfare payments and public expenditures for infrastructure—the government of the Netherlands Antilles faced little choice but to pursue the few avenues that were open to it. The default measure in much of the Caribbean is, of course, tourism, and dutifully, the government has pursued that option, among other things with the measures described above to enhance its viability as a tourist destination.[30] These measures have been partially successful, with increases in the tourist sector outpacing many other sectors of the island's economy. Most important for the current argument, though, the transformation of cities into touristic spaces also merges space (i.e., the systematic nature of tourism's economic necessity) with place. So despite its placement in the developing world, Willemstad, in fact, replicates many features of both the design-intensive city and the merging of space and place in tourism and urban consumption.

The large-scale embrace of tourism comes after many years of struggle to establish more economic independence, with some at least temporary success. While Curaçao has long shared the extreme poverty characteristics of most Caribbean cities, two factors have historically served as relative stabilizers. The first has been the all-important oil refinery, which dominates the first inland dip of the city's central St. Anna Bay. In fact, until the early 1960s, the refinery was largely responsible for a stable working class on the island, an unusually high literacy rate, and even a flourishing body of indigenous literature. The mid-1960s, however, saw the island suffer an economic body-blow in the form of automation and worker dismissal in the refinery, and the 1980s and 1990s introduced a more insidious and intransigent dynamic, the infamous "globalization of labor" that threatened the refinery's very presence on the well-unionized island. The Venezuelan government, center of the oil business that farms out its refining to Curaçao, periodically threatens to move the operation elsewhere unless the local union continues to sacrifice job benefits and security. So that one rare economically and socially salutary factor on the island has now, for a couple of decades, been eroding steadily. The other major historical stabilizer for Curaçao has also been eroding, namely the continuing colonial dynamic with the Netherlands, and especially the transfer payments with which the Dutch have long supported their ex-colony's public expenses, including the rather expensive social safety net. That system itself has now come under threat from a familiar source, the International Monetary Fund, which there, as elsewhere in the world, actively pressures the Netherlands Antilles government to slash its public sector, especially its social programs. Even in the so-called industrialized world, such measures have been infamously destructive to lower social classes; one may imagine its effect on an island like Curaçao, with its chronically high unemployment rate. The labor threat to its refinery and decimation of its public sector have together precipitated an unprecedented social crisis in Curaçao, exacerbating already widespread poverty, increasing crime, and leading to historic levels of emigration, especially to the Netherlands.

The government of the island has not reacted passively to these circumstances, however, and their response rejoins the theme of space and place, as the principal countermeasure in Curaçao has, indeed, been tourism. In mid-1990s the island began developing comprehensive plans to revitalize the economy with tourist dollars. The first measure was the construction of the so-called Megapier within the city of Willemstad, designed to host the new gigantic cruise ships run principally from Miami and Puerto Rico. These ships normally run tours of parts of the Caribbean and dock in Willemstad for a few hours or the full day, leaving money mainly in the form of docking fees, taxi fares, food and beverage consumption, and duty-free and souvenir shopping. As one might expect, the local music industry responded to the Megapier, with musicians showing up to perform live for handouts, small souvenir stands selling CDs and cassettes of local music, and other musicians staking out the arriving tourists in the more picturesque downtown.[31]

The central and best-known part of downtown Willemstad is divided by the harbor into two districts, one of them, of course, Punda, the United Nations World Heritage site. Most of the buildings lined up against the harbor were built in the seventeenth century by the Dutch colonists to imitate the architecture of Amsterdam, then painted with day-glo colors, folklore has it, to mitigate the blinding reflections of the tropical sun. Indeed, that small stretch of Punda enjoys reproduction on tourist brochures, websites, CD jewel cases, and posters worldwide, circulating as assuredly the best-known image and emblem of the island. The preservation and fetishized representation of this morsel of the urban environment has long served as a staple of Curaçao's public image; but the current and more structurally crucial push to remake the island as a tourist haven has focused energy, symbolic weight, and finances on the district facing Punda from across the harbor, none other than Otrabanda itself. Literally meaning "the other side," Otrabanda has been historically a major center of culture and commerce in Willemstad's downtown. Despite being less widely circulated abroad than Punda as an image of place, Otrabanda remains, in fact, a more lively cultural and tourism center, hosting many of the major downtown hotels, casinos, restaurants, bars, and retails stores. In the center of Otrabanda's harborside lies what, during my first visit in 1998, was little more than a gutted plaza: Brionplein ("Brion plaza," named for Pedro Luis Brion, a local hero and native Curaçaoan, who, under Simon Bolivar, fought for independence in Venezuela and Colombia). In the colonial (i.e., pre-1954) days of the twentieth century, the elegant Hotel Americano anchored the district, an upscale business that marked Otrabanda as a center of colonial commerce. Riots in 1969, however, which led to governmental reforms' placing political control in the hands of the Afro-European majority, also destroyed much of Brion square, and as in many developing world cities, the area, despite its obvious centrality and waterfront location, was not rebuilt until the beginning of the twenty-first century. But in the recent push to tourism, it has now been renovated as a tourist complex, anchored by a Howard Johnson hotel.[32] The harborside of Otrabanda will also host a new, highly stylized apartment complex (under construction at the time of this writing) with some office space, the Annabay View apartments, while on Awasa itself an older hotel has been upgraded and renamed Hotel Kura Hulanda, now paired with a heritage museum bearing the same name, thanks to the financing of resident Dutch multimillionaire Jakob Gelt Dekker. Other, smaller-scale capital investments mirror this already small-scale remaking of waterfront Otrabanda. Houses long abandoned, or left in disrepair, close to the harborside are being touched up, mainly with mixed private and public funding. And to the south, oceanside, the old Dutch fort is undergoing gentrification into historically themed restaurants and shops, echoing a process common in developed cities.

While such developments could be (and, of course, have been) argued as improvements over the former stagnant and decrepit state of Otrabanda, the new locality hosts a distinct version of urban life, designed specifically for cultural tourism and entertainment—in other words, the kind of city life described by John Hannigan and other geographers of flexible accumulation (*Fantasy City*). But Willemstad's version of such activity embodies features specific to the developing world and to Willemstad itself. It is both far smaller in scale than analogous transformations in cities like London (or Barcelona, for that matter), and it is far more concentrated on tourism as an economic growth engine. In Willemstad's case, as a matter of fact, the facilities for cultural tourism and entertainment far outweigh any provision for producer services, targeting visitors to the island rather than the local population, the island's economy structurally being able to host only limited producer services in the first place. Thus, the city's mix of so-called postindustrial facilities is decidedly shaped by its developing economy, as is the modest scale on which it all takes place—though from a local standpoint, the changes are dramatic indeed.

But modest or not, the touristic and service-oriented revamping of Otrabanda remains a high priority for the governments of Curaçao and the Netherlands Antilles with, of course, the blessing of the International Monetary Fund, which on my second trip there (in 1999) was visiting and actively encouraging the government further to trim its public expenditures. And with the island converting its economy to rely more heavily on tourism, despite evidence that the economic benefits do not spread very far through host countries, the *significance of place* reemerges with a vengeance.[26] Now, Otrabanda as a particular place with a cultural history and unique geographic properties acquires a value-added function, with crucial impact on the socioeconomic restructuring of the island. Stories of the arrivals of cruise megaships and planned touristic innovations often dominate the local Papiamentu newspaper *La Prensa*, next to lurid stories of violent crime among the island's indigent population mainly untouched by tourism's benefits. In a region crowded by tropical islands, beaches, and resorts—and on an island bereft of major stretches of sandy beaches (despite some world-class snorkeling sites)—the cultural and historical aspects of Otrabanda's locality have been leveraged as a competitive edge and (more important) produced in precisely that context.

… and Place *Is* Space

The examples of *tumba* and Willemstad demonstrate the theoretical bedrock of this chapter: the pleasures of place have now become unified with the structuring force of global space in contemporary cities. Place does work, of course, as it is often treated by many cultural geographers and ethnomusicologists—a matter of attachment, symbolism, memory, and constant cultural recreation. But it is also one of the crucial cornerstones of the economic remaking of cities, conditioned by the movement and reproduction of global capital. In the present example, the crushing force of global liberalization, taking the direct form of the International Monetary Fund and many oblique forms like labor mobility, forces Curaçao toward revamping its sense of locality. Its foregrounding of place then reaches articulation in architecture, in tourism infrastructure, in city form, and of course, in "Much'i Otrabanda." The multiple points of articulation around a single geographic process indicate the imprecision, if not the flaw, of considering space and place as somehow opposed, and especially of thinking of place as somehow a folk resistance to the impersonality of space. On the contrary, the foregrounding of place and locality forms, to a great extent, the cutting edge of our current global economic regime. In the meantime, scholars in popular music and cultural studies, perhaps curiously, continue to celebrate locality as if it were somehow resistant to cultural or economic domination. Such approaches, relying on modernist conceptions of spatial development and early postmodern critiques like those of Jane Jacobs, may have been more salient in the 1960s and 1970s, but by the early to mid-1980s, when the Thatcher government in England was remaking Manchester for its cultural industries and the uniqueness of place, geographic realities and transformations in capitalist production called for more nuanced contemporary analyses in which global capital and local sentiment are more closely intertwined.[33] The present analysis of "Much'i Otrabanda" aims at outlining a conceptual basis for such an analysis. One more point about that song will serve to illustrate how the merging of space and place in our world may inform theories of music and culture.

In the midst of the remarkable coordination of geographic and musical processes already detailed in the song, a small part nevertheless retained a functional detachability. The repeated refrain "sa, sa, sa / sa, sa na Awasa," in the wake of Izaline Calister's victory, acquired the status of a musical slogan for the entire season of *Karnival* 2001. This is, of course, the same line whose repetition served as the great sectional transition for the song. Reproduced word for word on souvenir T-shirts, it was repeated relentlessly, often excerpted, on Curaçao television, on radio, in cafés, and blaring from loudspeakers in trucks that roamed the streets of Willemstad. Such deployment of an excerpt from a winning *Karnival* song constitutes more the rule than the exception in Curaçao. And yet even the fetishized treatment of the song's structure retained its place-building function, as hundreds of spectators jammed the streets of Awasa, later in that *Karnival* season, to cheer the "Gran Marcha" ("Grand Parade"), wearing the T-shirts and singing along with the refrain as floats passed by, echoing the song off the stone buildings of the narrow streets. Such scenes may be said to embody the moment of truth in celebrations of locality that celebrate everyday pleasures and the building of communities, especially among subaltern subjects. Even if such moments represent little in the way of social change, or more cynically, encourage the population to cathect the powers that suppress them, the joy of the moment nevertheless remains palpable. Even in its life as musical snippet, then, "Much'i Otrabanda" enacts Arif Dirlik's (and many others') definition of place, the great struggle for the investment of emotion, sentiment, and memory in a highly particular location. (One could walk across Awasa in about 10 to 15 minutes, and it is certainly culturally and physically unique.) Indeed, Awasa embodies in many respects Dirlik's great heroic struggle against the hegemony of abstraction, the Curaçaoan people's courageous resistance to the global financial pressures of the International Monetary Fund. To those interested in cheering and promoting "place" and "the local," "Much'i Otrabanda" exemplifies affirmative culture on the part of some of the more disadvantaged people in the American hemisphere.

However, by now, the pitfalls of such a happy scenario are all too evident. The localization, psychic investment, and distinct identity of Otrabanda all work in tandem with transnational capital, Curaçao's compliant solution to the fiscal crisis it faces from the mobility of labor and capital, and from the International Monetary Fund, with its program of liberalization. That is not to say that Curaçaoans who produce and consume such music do so knowingly, or happily, nor that their situation allows many better choices. Indeed, if one were interested in judging morally (which I am not), little could be said against "Much'i Otrabanda" and its celebrants. But as the recent history of Willemstad illustrates, "place" and "locality" act, for Otrabanda as well as for Willemstad and Curaçao more generally, as value-added processes in the building for tourism, one of the few economic options left to the island in the face of its devastated public sector and fiscal crises.

Far from resisting some putative trend toward worldwide standardization and abstraction, the projection of Otrabanda and Awasa as enhanced localities rejoins a much larger dynamic of multinational capital, acting as a force of local differentiation. The scenario that emerges in this case has already been noted by sociologists and urban geographers; but in disciplines such as popular music studies, with their closer affinities to cultural studies, such a recognition still seems slow in coming (and similarly in music studies overall). Instead, music that rehabilitates otherwise denigrated spaces remains *ipso facto* cause for celebration. The lesson to be inferred from examining Willemstad is that these portrayals of place and locality as somehow politically progressive, or socially salutary, rely on a mistaken, or perhaps simply outdated, idea of economic geographic development as a uniform force of standardization (most famously perpetuated, of course, in the scenarios of Adorno and Horkheimer).[34] Nor would one strengthen such a position by drawing a distinction between corporate players and genuinely popular cathexis of place; such an intellectually fragile distinction elides the systematic force that embraces all players, large and small, in the same economy of place. Here, the official institutions and personal sentiment work in tandem, rather than in any cycle of authenticity and cooptation.

A more fruitful way to conceive of place in "Much'i Otrabanda" would suggest that capital development and popular sentiment may often coincide (and why should they not, as they both often follow such winding and twisted courses?). Willemstad, in fact, manifests with remarkable consistency exactly what economic geographers have argued with respect to more developed cities: "place" and "locality" are as integral to capital's mobility, and the resulting attendant social devastation, as the forces of economic abstraction and the more calculated calibration of economic exchange. In fact, paradoxically, the specific features of localities often lie at the center of economic abstraction itself, as place, like information and design, acquires an economic value that must be taken into account; in that sense, abstraction may now take place not in the form of ever more formally similar architecture or spatial layouts (as in the infamous case of the International Style), so much as in the overarching and totalizing forces that differentiate and distribute place.

In fact, the designs of the newer buildings in Otrabanda themselves thoroughly embody aspects of locality: both the Annabay View luxury apartment complex on the west end of Otrabanda and the total rebuilding of Brionplein embody place sensitivity and enhance the visual consistency of locality. The developers, the Kimatrai group, have explicitly patterned the Brionplein structures after existing local styles, such that the new Howard Johnson hotel resembles none anywhere else in the world but rather projects the image of an unusually well-kept Curaçao structure. And the waterfront Annabay View apartments will update visually the Art Nouveau styles of formerly elegant landmarks in Willemstad, just about all now fallen into ruin. None of this should surprise anyone who noted and retained, almost two decades before my research in Curaçao, Sharon Zukin's warning that urban design had started brandishing place as a strategy of capital accumulation, for the consumption of those mainly urban educated cultural workers that Bourdieu called the "new cultural intermediaries."[35] Somewhat ironic in the context of Curaçao, however, is how thin and precarious such elements of the "new middle class" are locally, mainly appearing briefly off luxury cruisers or jaunting out the doors of the harbor-front hotels.

Still, none of this story will be unfamiliar to those acquainted with cities in the developed world, many of whose economic revitalization has relied on the influx of knowledge and information workers. A brief glance north to a mid-sized city like Austin, Texas, would provide a suitable contrast: the revitalization, in Austin's case, has deployed, among other things, the combination of culture industries (especially popular music), and the one–two punch of a major university and high-tech industries. The music industry in Austin (and its famous South By Southwest festival) remains in many respects every bit as place-dependent as the tourist industry of Curaçao, whereas the high-tech sector depends more crucially not on place but on another aspect of late-capitalist urban development, the combination of vertical disintegration and transaction-rich agglomerations. But in fact, both the music *and* high-tech industries that characterize Austin's place-related profile depend on the character of the city as a locality, the attraction of educated, culturally sophisticated workers to the urban area in all its unique specificity. In the meantime, areas like its Warehouse District exemplify revitalization through entertainment. In that city, as in the otherwise distantly related city of Willemstad, the entire rubric of "place" ends up being pivotal to strategies of capital accumulation, rather than being somehow culturally oppositional. Place, in Austin as in Willemstad, *is* space, rather than being a liberatory force opposed to space and its regimes of social and economic domination.

This chapter has elaborated a theoretical framework, and a set of illustrative concretes, that together suggest a good deal of skepticism toward the tenacious attachment to "place" so prevalent in music studies. Whatever the force of my arguments, it might be objected that despite the compliance of "place" with globalizing social conditions, it nevertheless represents the sentiments of common human subjects, or in favored cases, subaltern subjects—even if I am correct that those sentiments work harmoniously with the force of capital. The objection could even be parlayed into an issue of morality, that it is somehow unfair to contest the significance of people's emotional investments, relying on totalizing arguments about social change and culture. That "place" represents the intimate experience of real human beings stands, of course, as perfectly true, and no better argument could be advanced to prove that our theoretical attachments to place and locality are instances of sheer ideology. After all, what could more convincingly brand a sentiment as ideology than the deeply felt embrace of social and economic domination as personal values by the dominating and the dominated alike? Such is, in fact, the very definition of ideology—both by the early Marx's definition, namely the worldview of the dominant class, and by the much-circulated Frankfurt School definition, namely false consciousness, coercion embraced as a matter of personal choice and self-expression. The emotional uplift indubitably felt by the audience in Curaçao as they listened to "Much'i Otrabanda" may well be—in fact, certainly is—important from a humanistic standpoint, as the experience of real people, but that fact renders its ideological stakes and the need for serious analysis more, rather than less, pressing. One need not dismiss the emotional investments of human subjects simply in order to contest the scope and character of their overall significance.

Perhaps there is one final way to conceptualize place and space, rather than as domination and resistance—that is, to think of them dialectically, in the very strict sense of dialectics that is rarely used anymore. Sometimes in music studies the word *dialectics* seems confined to the notion that one bounces back and forth between two poles, maybe in a developing way. But I mean "dialectical" to denote a stricter sense of the word, namely that, from some later, posterior perspective, two apparently opposite terms turn out to constitute each other, after all, in ways impossible to grasp at that earlier stage. So while in popular music studies now a majority of scholars might think of local music and the love of one's place as somehow a healthy, politically progressive viewpoint, one might, from a newer perspective, appreciate it as both resistance *and* compliance—not only in Curaçao and Austin, and not only in the song "Much'i Otrabanda," but also in music scenes the world over, in beautiful small musics and industries, and in the emotional investments of people in their neighborhoods and cities. The love of place, of one's neighborhood, city, or nation, liberates us, pleases us, enriches our lives—and may, in many instances, further subordinate our fate to the production of multinational capital. That apparent paradox, which is not really a paradox at all, can be considered the last laugh of Karl Marx, close to two decades after the fall of the Eastern Bloc regimes that had claimed his name. One of his legacies to us, after all, was the project of mapping capitalism and its reliance on properties that often appear to standard morality as opposites. Nothing has bequeathed us more powerful tools than that mapping project for sensing the spatial contours that surround us, of social, and musical, development.

3

Mourning the Impossible Libidinal City in *Boogie Nights*

If the complex of sentiments and beliefs that constitute "place," and its merging with space, could help map the course of music under twenty-first century capitalism, as argued in Chapter 2, then music could perhaps in other ways act symptomatically, revealing to us a unique angle on the cultural workings of our totality. So far in this book, the discussion of those processes has focused exclusively on music—arguably appropriate, given the title of this book. But treating music in isolation from other media risks fetishizing it, attributing to it powers that it may hold only in combination with other media, from advertisements to radio and films. Perhaps rather randomly, the present chapter groups music with film, proposing the idea that it serve as exemplary of any number of pairings (or larger groupings) of "music with," and that the results be taken as reflecting larger theoretical contentions, rather than as privileging disco as a genre or *Boogie Nights* as a film (as important as both may be). At the same time, it is crucial to recognize that grouping music with predominantly visual genres like film risks the rather facile use of visual cues to interpret music, all the more common because we have so much better-developed tools for assigning semantic values to visual media. In the present case, attempts have been made throughout to allow music not to be interpreted through visual cues, but rather in conjunction with them, and in all its own specificity.

Although disco may still be present in our musical culture—generally under the rubric of "house music"—its popular representations cannot be (and never could have been) disentangled from the historical concept of the 1970s, and specifically the mid- to late 1970s (e.g., the character Disco Stu from *The Simpsons*); and though the latter qualification stems from the history of disco itself, it also corresponds roughly, intriguingly enough, to Fredric Jameson's periodization of the 1960s (which, by his account, extends to roughly 1972–1974).[1] Since roughly the mid-1990s, the association of disco with a generalized image of the 1970s has significantly complicated any discussion of the genre, as images of the 1970s have saturated the fields of fashion, television, film, and advertising. From *The Brady Bunch Movie* to *Boogie Nights* and *54*, from the revival of bell-bottoms to *That '70s Show* and numerous satirical television commercials, the whole topic of disco cannot be engaged without bringing along an entire constellation of historical discourse. Still, it will be argued here that disco occupies a special place that cannot be confined to the recent preoccupation with that earlier decade and, furthermore, that as music, it constitutes a special site for ideas about history and, especially, about urban life and its possibilities. Although the present discussion necessarily sidelines more specific histories and deployments of disco (especially those of African Americans and gay men, the latter significantly invoked by Richard Dyer), I would maintain that the more generalized context to be described here bears on those histories, as well, albeit in a highly inflected manner.[2]

In the most general context, recent deployments of disco (especially in *Boogie Nights*) will turn out to figure metonymically senses of changing possibilities for urban life, changes that can be traced in economic restructuring and built space itself. Issues of the qualities of urban life—what kinds of places cities are, who lives in them and where, and how—are ultimately at stake here, historicized and transcoded as kinds of musical experience. In other words, representations from the 1990s of disco, and the 1970s, figure as a small but unusually telling instance of the urban ethos of the 1990s (for which see Chapter 1).

Any attempt to historicize the present of disco should begin with the recollection that the public afterlife of disco has always been active and has in no way been dependent on the more recent fascination with the 1970s. The popular cultural phenomenon of the modern dance club, with the special bass-heavy sound system and resident DJ, as well as genres such as house and techno (with their constantly multiplying subgenres), have assured that disco retains a legacy in musical style and urban space alike. That the name "disco" has been eradicated both as a musical genre and as a type of club (at least in English-speaking countries) thus will constitute in itself a telling symptom. Clearly, the avoidance involved has to do not with musical style but rather with some other aspect associated with the label "disco." But in some ways more significantly, disco has remained a force in our society as a site of negative cathexis, as a symbol somehow for the greatest aesthetic nadir, the butt of humor with the strongest possible distancing force. One might recall a *Time* magazine commercial featuring visuals of a purportedly classic disco scene and a middle-aged white man dressed to look young and dancing awkwardly, captioned "What were we thinking of?" In such moments, the particularly brutal repression of which disco has been the object comes into clearer focus.

The contours of such repression seem remarkably consistent across the numerous representations: the music as part of a larger, repellent cultural phenomenon, as often signaled by clothing as by music; the participant's obliviousness to the indignity of the dancing, the music, and the clothing—in short, the entire spectacle of sheer bad taste. The almost obligatory reference to disco in print media as a music utterly without merit (matched frequently only by similar hit-and-run slams at rap music) has become a cultural commonplace. More generally, disco may easily be invoked as a point of simple reference, representing musical culture at its most shameful nadir, a spot in the history of the music industry in which commercial forces and aesthetic decay were most visibly joined—the apotheosis of mass-culture theory come to life and now sealed forever as such in public memory. Loving African-American musical traditions, as well, would seem, by some accounts, to involve disliking disco, as figures like Nelson George remind us;[3] despite the obvious black participation in disco's origins and early dissemination, disco here is figured as smothering the legacy of R&B, growing, perhaps, from a seed of Philly soul but then developing into its caricature, mocking it rather than building on its legacy of African-American achievement. Disco sucks, indeed, such representations would seem to reassure us; the references and images of the seemingly vapid and silly people who enjoyed the music serve to reinforce the Othering process by which we may eliminate from view the pleasures that were obviously at one point experienced and desired. The situation has long been different, of course, in some gay communities; but that such a differing memory and representation should be marked as gay goes all the more to reinforce a broader denigration of disco as a genre, enabling large sections of the population to intertwine the reputation of disco with broader structures of homophobia.[4]

Or so it was until fairly recently. The condition just described has been greatly complicated by the recent fascination with the 1970s, which began in the 1990s, as the former period's music has been reinvested with a certain libidinal attraction. Such a development is, in retrospect, remarkable, when one recalls that what was at one time called "New Wave" music, as well as punk, were long heralded as welcome reactions to purported earlier musical excesses and commercial deformations, precisely in the late 1970s. Disco has, to some extent, benefited from the cultural libidinal reinvestment. Revival shows and recordings by artists such as Gloria Gaynor (long treasured in gay communities) and the Bee Gees, among many others, attract little of the ridicule formerly heaped on them, although, significantly, the music is now revived shorn of the dancing, the clothing, the fashion, the modes of social interaction—in short, of the context that thickened disco initially into a socially significant phenomenon. But it is precisely the *modality* of the recent reinvestment in disco that requires close attention, for within it one may read images of more far-reaching cultural processes. That does not necessarily mean that the original context, so often repressed in recent celebrations of disco, need be restored, but it does indicate that the means of revival, as well as the appearance of disco itself, require examination and interpretation. That interpretation, in turn, will end up raising questions of urban change and show them to be at the core of our ambiguous revivals of disco and of the 1970s in general.

The film *Boogie Nights* (1997) may be an instructive, if atypical, place to begin. It is instructive because of its commercial success and the centrality of the time setting to its theme, but it is perhaps atypical in that therein, disco *does* stand revived with the ensemble of its contexts, or at least certain selected portions thereof—the lurid, lingering shots of hair styles, clothing, and décor often dominate the composition of various shots. But precisely those added elements (or rather, elements often not explicitly present) of disco may help one to read symptomatically, to recognize ensembles of attitudes sometimes hidden in more limited representations. *Boogie Nights* has, in fact, attracted more popular and academic attention than many films, but that attention has often focused on director Paul Thomas Anderson and his attitudes toward pornography, or his innovative visual style. Although both those issues will figure in the following discussion, the concern in this chapter will be more about what the music of the film tells us. Furthermore, the agency of Anderson will be of little concern here, compared to the result of the finished product, the film itself, and in particular, the way in which it produces the 1970s (and by contrast, the 1980s) for the viewer. *Boogie Nights*, in fact, is particularly instructive precisely because of the unusual degree to which the presentation approaches some kind of framelessness—that is to say, the unusual degree to which something like a genuine historical hermeneutic is attempted, in which a certain currency and seriousness is suggested for a music somehow appropriate to its time. Thus, Robert C. Sickels actually observes that *Boogie Nights* celebrates, above all, "what Anderson sees as the halcyon days of the 1970s."[5] But the film will elicit even more interest here for the ways in which that attempt at framelessness fails, and the specific ways in which *Boogie Nights* ends up being thoroughly contemporary to the late 1990s. In fact, it is the movie's more general problematizing of the 1970s that ultimately negates the possibility of a fully sympathetic hermeneutic. That problematizing works through the means of what I will call the "distancing frame," in which disco music is invoked and provided as a source of pleasure, but always in carefully contextualized—and contained—ways.

The first appearance of the distancing frame is, in fact, fully musical, and it consists of the stakes set on the distinction between diegetic and nondiegetic music, which in the opening scene only gradually develops out of an initial confusion. As the camera pans from the film title (displayed on a movie marquee) to Jack Horner's car, approaching Hot Traxx (the discotheque featured in the film), the Emotions' "Best of My Love" plays as seemingly nondiegetic music;[6] but on his entrance to the discotheque, with no apparent change in the sound, the music seems to become diegetic, with on-screen characters introduced dancing to its rhythms. Similarly, in the next discotheque sequence, not only is the Chakachas' "Jungle Fever" introduced over the end of a preceding scene (a common enough maneuver), but more important, its volume is not adjusted for the displacement of Roller Girl to the kitchen, where she goes to seduce Eddy Adams, and it continues even into the following outdoor scene;[7] thus, music initially presented in such a way as to suggest that it is diegetic turns out to be nondiegetic. Of course, films' playing with the diegetic/nondiegetic distinction, slyly turning one into the other, is most common; that in itself does not distinguish *Boogie Nights* from many other (especially recent) films. But what should be underlined about these two pivotal early moments is the significance of the discotheque itself as the locus that conveys such an ambiguity, caught as it is in a dual dynamic fully typical of recent representations of that period. For the discotheque cannot be separated, in the film, from the lurid and vaguely repulsive world of pornography and immodest (often carnal) self-indulgence, designed to shock (and, of course, attract); instead, the discotheque shares the sexual excess and egotistical self-absorption, and it provides their musical apotheosis.

The liminal status of the music continues into the opening party scenes at Jack Horner's house, perhaps best exemplified when Eric Burdon and War's "Spill the Wine" actually becomes foregrounded, saturating the soundtrack, as a swimmer enters Jack's pool and the camera follows her under water.[8] After such a classic indication of the transition from diegetic to nondiegetic music, more confusion mounts, as the soundtrack then distorts the song, imitating the effects that being under water enact on hearing—and thus suggesting a diegetic point of view once again, that of the swimmer. Such a playful approach to scoring, with its comic undertones, belies the stakes of the confusions concerning diegetic versus nondiegetic music in the film. If nondiegetic music tells us how to feel about a scene and viewers are more distanced from diegetic music, then musical tricks like this (and the others already mentioned) help to form an ambiguous or suspended judgment concerning how to feel about the world that the viewer sees. Caught between empathy and distance, the viewer of the film is drawn into the ambiguous attraction and revulsion more generally invoked by the visual and narrative aspects of *Boogie Nights*. Kelly Ritter, thus, must be seen as wrong in believing that music functions in the film to create viewer empathy;[9] on the contrary, the visual and verbal narrative works far more consistently to create empathy, at most points, than does the music. The latter, on the contrary, encourages ambiguity.

Other games played with soundtrack songs from the party scene contribute to the combination of playfulness and suspended judgment that characterize the film's portrayal of the 1970s. The songs, for one thing, often act as sly commentary on the action onscreen: Andrew Gold's "Lonely Boy" accompanies Amber Waves' son's unsuccessful attempt to call her at the party, and Elvin Bishop's "Fooled Around and Fell in Love" frames Little Bill's humiliating discovery of his wife's having public intercourse with yet another lover—foreshadowing his eventually killing her, and himself, in a desperate, jealous rage.[10] Something closer to a conventional, straightforward framing follows when Scotty first spots, then centers in tunnel vision, Eddy Adams, to the accompaniment (still suspended between diegetic and nondiegetic status) of Hot Chocolate's "You Sexy Thing";[11] Scotty's later humiliation at his drunken advance toward Eddy receives here its sly foreshadowing.

To some extent even more telling are the moments when music seems to be introduced as diegetic but never seems fully to achieve that status. One encounters this phenomenon not only in the disco scenes discussed earlier, but also after the first filming in Jack's house, when the viewer sees a needle drop onto vinyl and then hears surface noise segue into KC and the Sunshine Band's "Boogie Shoes."[12] Even then, the music projects itself only as ambiguously diegetic, filling the soundtrack more like nondiegetic music and then continuing over scenes in shops and then the discotheque. By far, in any case, the song's most emphatic function is to set nondiagetically the immediately following scenes of clothes and shoe shopping, leading to that return to the discotheque. Once the characters have returned to the discotheque, the music appears diegetic once more, as characters (and extras) seem to be dancing to the same rhythm, and Buck and Reed suffer (comic) mishearings over the music. Thus, the music even becomes an agent in the film. So now, music shows a suppleness, a pliability in being capable of moving from diegetic, to nondiegetic, back to diegetic status, a playfulness perhaps analogous to the in-jokes of Jack Horner's earlier party. Those in-jokes with the audience did not constitute the same phenomenon as the suspension of boundaries between diegetic and nondiegetic music just described, but they were clearly closely related. Both procedures suggest a coy refusal to use soundtrack music either purely to create empathy or purely to impose distance for the viewer.[13]

After the viewer has seen "Boogie Shoes" lead through the orgy of consumption back into the disco, the trick of shifting the music between diegetic and nondiegetic status repeats almost immediately, this time with The Commodores' "Machine Gun," at which point a certain reversal comes into focus: instead of the established film practice of leading diegetic music into nondiegetic scenes and thus saturating the movie with the sentiments of a certain character, "Boogie Nights" uses the sentiments of the film (or the coy suspension between sentiment and withholding emotional investment) to lead the viewer always back to the discotheque.[14] This reversed technique, in fact, is one way in which it is made clear to the viewer that the same ambiguous investment that s/he is encouraged to make in clothing, home design, and shoes must ultimately also apply to the discotheque and disco music as well. Given the centrality of the discotheque in the universe of *Boogie Nights*, such a suspension of emotional judgment then extends over the entirety of the garish and, for sure, also attractive world of disco, drugs, the pornography industry, and the late 1970s overall.

Once that suspension has been established, none of the "period" music of *Boogie Nights* can act analogously to the ubiquitous power rock song played so often over movies' closing credits (particularly in comedy genres) nor is it quite the equivalent to mood- (or place-, or personality-, or time-, or ethnicity-) setting, nondiegetic soundtrack music that often accompanies a visual setting of place and/or time. Instead, a generalized note of irony hangs over the musical settings, something of a wink and a nod consistent with the tendency of everything in the film toward excess: the eye-popping colors, lingering shots, and ubiquitous promiscuity form the backdrop for something short of genuine fulfillment, whose possibility seems denied. After all, Amber Waves' tragic family situation and, especially, Dirk Diggler's (i.e., Eddy Adams') descent into drug abuse, musical (worse than) mediocrity, and prostitution provide the hangover to the dizzying champagne of sex, drugs, and disco. In contrast to the fast-paced, garish visuals of the establishing shots, those scenes of emotional turmoil and transformation are shot sympathetically and feature purely nondiegetic, emotionally wrenching music. Thus, the movie does, after all, offer unambiguously nondiegetic music and endorse viewpoints and emotional responses—but only to the characters' descent into pain in scenes, importantly, prominently set in the 1980s.

What is more, the music for the post-1970s scenes is remarkably anachronistic: the Beach Boys' "God Only Knows," which sets Dirk's return as the prodigal son to Jack Horner, was first released in 1966.[15] In its conspicuous, and highly unusual, origins well outside the period being represented, and in its nondiegetic usage over a moment of climactic emotion and transformation, the song removes itself from the borderline nondiegetic/diegetic world of the disco and Jack Horner's house. As nonperiod music, "God Only Knows" appears to rise above the historical contingency attached to the majority of the soundtrack's music, and thus the song seems to escape the overwhelming web of determination that saturates the majority of the film. Dirk's supplication to rejoin Jack Horner's "family" now falls outside of the strict contingency, the historically marked world of Lycra stretch pants and the Emotions' "Best of My Love." As unambiguously nondiegetic music, too, "God Only Knows" brands Dirk's return to his surrogate 'family' as the emotional core of the film. Here, for once, is a moment that the soundtrack marks as truly emotionally compelling, a scene in which the audience is not encouraged to smirk knowingly. But of course, that same scene projects events distanced in time from the 1970s fetishized in most of the film; so that the emotional weight attached to it, if anything, throws into relief the relative weightlessness of the previous scenes.

One of the truly remarkable features, in fact, about the song's presentation in the film is precisely the degree to which it is *staged*, that is to say, presented as if it could not possibly form anything like a "natural" background of time and place (i.e., could not be "establishing" music). In this sense, it serves a very different function from, say, the time-setting use of the Four Aces' "Mr. Sandman" when Marty arrives in the 1950s during *Back to the Future* (1985).[16] In the latter case, not only is the music nondiegetic, but it also performs its work precisely by being so distanced from the aesthetic sensibility of the filmgoing audience. Hence, it constitutes a more effective choice for establishing the time than would have, say, a song of Chuck Berry, descendents of which remain part of the (then, i.e., in 1985) present-day musical landscape. "Mr. Sandman" works its time-setting function partially by not being a likely object of aesthetic pleasure and emotional cathexis to a 1985 audience, exemplifying what one might call a *spatio-temporal establishing* function. However, such a seamless and powerful use of a song for setting time and place may be unimaginable in *Boogie Nights*, in any case, given how the film, up to this point, has simultaneously foregrounded "period" music and drawn attention (in such an ambiguous way) to its character. The crucial requirement that music seem 'naturally' suitable to a scene, to set time or place, with no sense of irony or distancing, could hardly be imagined by this point in the film. The distancing frame has already been too strongly established.

But further than this, and more specifically to the imaging of disco, I would like to suggest one strongly projected aspect of the film as particularly revealing how disco as a genre is constructed for the audience to interpret, based on the thick cultural environment that surrounds it and a rather blunt periodization that the film performs. Namely, the setting of the film as a rise-and-fall story, together with the equally important scenes of reconciliation and bonding at the end, involves strategies of musical deployment that communicate a great deal about disco, as *Boogie Nights* constructs it. Briefly put, one may divide the plot of the film roughly as follows. Much of the film concerns itself with the rise of Dirk Diggler's (i.e., Eddy Adams') career, from a menial employee at the disco to a Best-Cock-winning porno actor. Much admired by his peers and well compensated, Diggler escapes a troubled home life and achieves his dreams by capitalizing on his natural gift and a supportive (if itself quite troubled) surrogate family. The summit of his success features an upbeat montage of clothing and shoe purchases, industry awards, a custom-decorated apartment, and disco dancing (the scenes earlier discussed as accompanied by "Boogie Shoes" on the soundtrack). Following not long after the celebratory display, however—and pointedly set just after the 1980s begin—arrives the fateful combination of drugs and a younger rival, spawning paranoia, a flare-up with the director Jack Horner (and the father of the surrogate family), and Dirk's ultimate downfall. The next stage of the film describes a painful self-funded stab at a rock career, combined with continued drug abuse and culminating in broke desperation, hustling, violence, and finally a failed and costly attempt to rob a drug dealer. The last stage of the film brings about a reconciliation with Jack Horner and the surrogate family and a revival of Dirk's film career, albeit represented in a more low-key manner than the initial flourishes. Such a description clearly leaves out quite a few details and subplots, but it will suffice for the following discussion.

What is crucial here is the musical treatment of the segments, and their relation both to the plot, most generally, and to chronological representation and the characters, more specifically. These factors change remarkably cleanly with the story as presented here. In the first section of film—that is to say, that which portrays Diggler's discovery and his rise to fame—the music is nearly constant and consistently 'period,' at least within certain parameters. The last qualification simply indicates that there is some 'give' in the selections with respect to the specific years indicated in onscreen titles[17]; nevertheless, allowing for some 'give' to within a few years, which is a reasonable provision anyway considering many people's listening habits, the music is at least pointedly cued to "period" and prominently featured. And let us not forget that the years of the film's setting are not only displayed prominently on screen; they are also objects of frequent reference (as, for example, in the extended scene of the party welcoming in the year 1980). The alternation among 1970's pop (e.g., Andrew Gold's "Lonely Boy"), funk (e.g., Eric Burdon and War's "Spill the Wine"), and, of course, disco (e.g., the Silver Convention's "Fly Robin Fly") often provides the only sound accompanying scenes without dialogue, or with only sparse dialogue and foregrounded music.[18] Within the span of genres, disco plays a special role. It is, of course, a disco that forms, along with Horner's house, the locus of social interaction and bonding. Disco music forms the soundtrack to that interaction by people usually not dancing but, rather, seated at a table on the side of the club. In quite a few scenes in this section of the film (e.g., party scenes), of course, it is not clear whether the music one hears is diegetic or not, because of the sly and coy treatment described above. The pervasive scenes of socialization and the playful approach to music instead impart the ambiguous investments in disco. But such is not always the case, and the exceptions themselves are most telling. To elaborate on both the ambiguity in diegetic and nondiegetic functions, and on the telling exceptions, a link needs to be established from the music to the film's visual object world.

One striking visual feature of *Boogie Nights* is the degree to which it foregrounds material style and consumption in conjunction with the ambiguously (non)diegetic music. Fashion and the stylized consumption of commodities bring material culture in close proximity to music—not in any essential way (i.e., not to suggest that music is somehow intrinsically close to stylized commodity consumption), but because of the proximity of music to stylized commodification in media culture.[19] In effect, the insistent ostentatiousness of the object world throughout the film serves as something of a counterpart to the infamous excesses of disco. And the growing interdependence of music and various aspects of both visual culture and more general aspects of "style" and design has been widely remarked by scholars as diverse as Hal Foster and Scott Lash and John Urry, among many others.[20] What is more, the tremendous horizontal integration of culture industries over the past two decades has furnished a political-economic environment to foster that interdependence; it is not sheer imagination on the part of the filmmakers. Of course, the proximity of music to design aspects of other commodities is not essential, either, but nakedly historical. In that sense, *Boogie Nights* may be somewhat anachronistic, projecting onto the late 1970s a degree of integration between music and the world of designed articles that had not yet been achieved. What is perhaps remarkable about the film, then, is the force with which it not only projects that dynamic into the 1970s, but also makes it seem like the most natural possible process. Perhaps the apotheosis of *Boogie Nights*' blending of music into consumption and style is the scene, discussed earlier, that immediately follows Dirk Diggler's first receiving his film awards to the enthusiastic reactions of industry colleagues. At that point, the soundtrack introduces KC and the Sunshine Band's "Boogie Shoes" as a (non)diegetic accompaniment to a montage of scenes.[21] The character of those scenes is crucial to the point being made here, for they all engage aspects of material culture constructing a certain representation of the 1970s.

That representation specifically engages notions of exuberance and sensuous consumption. Lurid clothing and shoes impossible to imagine nowadays except in the category of "camp" instead are eyed and purchased by the characters with the enthusiasm of conspicuous social climbers. For much of the montage, Diggler proudly shows his new and lavishly decorated quarters to Amber, as the camera slowly and lovingly pans décor, music equipment, furniture, and (on entering a walk-in closet) clothing. The ambiguously diegetic accompaniment of "Boogie Shoes" underlines a notion of joyous indulgence and investment in this sparkling, eye-poppingly colorful object world. Diggler observes his portrait being painted, while a stereo system customized by Buck insures that music finds its visual stake in the object world. If somehow the viewer manages to miss the exuberant indulgence and aggressive garishness with its relation to the music that dominates the soundtrack, then later scenes underline the point by contrast, with starkly different combinations of interior-scapes and music: the scene at the house of Rahad Jackson (the drug dealer) is a dark, demented, and menacing interior with early 1980s-style power ballads (to which Jackson manifests comically inappropriate pleasure), and a grim and seedy recording studio registers the pathetic stab that post-pornography Eddy and Reed make at recording careers with corny and formulaic arena rock music. The synthesis of sound and object world underlines the effect already accomplished by the soundtrack.

All in all, then, the musical soundtrack in *Boogie Nights*—a structure so imposing that virtually every commentator has remarked on it (e.g., "Spectacle")—conveys with cues, sometimes subtle, sometimes overt, sometimes outright playful, a nevertheless clear but ambiguous structure of emotion for the viewer. Disco music, in particular, and the stylized object world in which it existed, come across as simultaneously desirable, ludicrous, and impossible. Or at least, music and its design environment unfold before the viewer with an ambiguous mixture of beckoning and repulsion, and at the same time, the film—specifically, the music—always places its world just out of range of accessibility. The viewer ultimately cannot enter, or empathize with, the eye-popping world of disco and the late 1970s; symptomatically of that, the lavish, brightly colored object world no longer assaults the viewer in the second half (i.e., 1980's part) of the film, when empathy for the characters becomes necessary for the film to work its emotional effects properly. As a phenomenon of the movie *Boogie Nights*, this 1970's era of attraction, repulsion, and impossibility is in itself worth noting, but greater interest and relevance lies in the notion of this film as symptomatic of a more widespread attitude toward that time in the mid- to late 1990s. That attitude finds manifestations not just in 1997's *Boogie Nights*, but also in the Fox television series *That '70s Show* (first airing in August 1998), the video for Wyclef Jean's "We Tryin' to Stay Alive"—an entire, strikingly wide range of representations of the late 1970s (often just referred to as "the 1970s") that conveys a remarkable uniformity of attitude.[22] For the simultaneous attraction and repulsion, the impossible "pastness" of the era, the ironic framing that turns events and (equally important) the object world into simultaneous coveted experience and absurd comedy—these features of *Boogie Nights* are far from unusual, and in fact remain standard, in recent representations of "the 1970s"; *Boogie Nights* simply does us the favor of projecting the viewpoint elaborately, and on a grand scale.[23] What calls for explanation, therefore, is not so much the particular approach or attitude projected by the music in *Boogie Nights*, as it is a view of "the 1970s" that seems evenly distributed across an entire media environment of the mid- and late 1990s. The scale of such an explanation, in turns, suggests that one seek a mode of inquiry that transcends the status of the fad or the trend. Instead, a need for a true historical framework presents itself, a way of thinking through why the later time finds a need to see the earlier time and its music through such a lens. One clearly confronts an unusual case, here, in which the subjects of an earlier point in history are consistently distanced from listeners/viewers. For recent representations of that earlier period, an assumption of transcendent human nature about which Foucault so famously complained, together with its corollary of empathy, seems not to exist.[24] Why such a conspicuous hole in one of the basic rules of film, in which viewers are normally encouraged to empathize with one or more of the characters? What about the late 1970s and disco simultaneously tempts and repulses those who think about it a mere twenty years later, and why do later subjects find in that era's music and culture such an aura of impossibility, such hopelessness in accessing its mindset? What is so impossible, and so attractive, about those earlier years?

Having outlined the questions to be addressed, and having generalized away from *Boogie Nights* to that era and its music, one can begin to advance and privilege (as is inevitable) factors that seem to separate and differentiate them. And since we are now talking about representation, it would make sense to invoke the urban ethos defined and described back in Chapter 1. In that chapter I suggested that one of the great untold stories of musical genres is the extent to which they seem to reflect publicly shared images of urban possibility, i.e., notions of what kinds of places cities are, who can live in them, and where and how they would live in them. To state things otherwise: the view of disco and the late 1970s formed in the mid- to late 1990s was a particular, and particularly suggestive, case of the urban ethos. And to be sure, public discourses of city life changed substantially between the heyday of disco (say, the late 1970s) and the initial revivals of interest in that genre. A comparison could be made across a number of North American media, ranging from film (e.g., the genre of "hood" films of the early 1990s) to television (e.g., the genre of crime "reality" series stretching from the mid-1980s to the present) to the news media (e.g., the near-obsessive reports of crime waves and the fear of inner-city residents). What such media accounts or representations repeatedly offer is a new vision of the (American) city, in which publicly shared pleasure seems no longer possible; in which citizens instead either avoid the city altogether or pursue pleasure privately, often heavily guarded or in considerable danger; in which sexual freedom and indulgence have been obliterated, either by AIDS, by social distrust, or both; in which the optimism and freedom associated with "the 1970s" quickly (and increasingly) are framed as naive, short-sighted, or irresponsible; and in which the associated fashions (musical and otherwise) are painted with the analogous brush of bad taste or loss of (presumably aesthetic) perspective.[25] From a space of possibility and promise (among other things, of course), the city, since roughly the time of disco's demise, becomes, at least imaginatively, the kind of place where sociality such as that found in the discotheque is no longer possible (or at least, not imaginable). And while criminality and danger have nearly always formed important components of public representations of the city, what seems new in the last twenty years or so is the sheer bifurcation of "the urban" into, on the one hand, a place of sinister threat and, on the other hand, a place of protected escapism—neither notion (and they are, of course, complementary) being hospitable to the freewheeling social environment of the disco. Thus, for instance, by the time the disco "revival" begins, one has encountered in American film a plethora of what one might call "dangerous city" films such as *Falling Down* (1993), *Sugar Hill* (1994), and *Clockers* (1995) (significantly, all racialized in varying ways), as well as what one might call "fantasy/denial" films such as *The Sixth Sense* (1999) (with its remarkably sanitized Philadelphia) and *Singles* (1992) (with its absurdly bohemian Seattle). But the city as locus of adventure, mobility, and libidinal investment had nearly vanished from popular film (and remains rare now). The genre, for instance, of "poor country girl/boy goes to metropolis to make good," comic or tragic (like *My Sister Eileen* of 1942 and 1955), can only be traced in older features, virtually freezing such pictures either into black and white or into geographically far-flung places for American audiences (e.g., in the Jamaica of *The Harder They Come* [1972]). It is instructive to recall that such representations of urban life had once been prominent in American cinema (even when used to moralize against urban values, such as in *Mr. Deeds Goes to Town* [1936]), surviving today mainly only as spoof and urban theory alike—not to mention popular music itself, in which the allure of urban life has been one of the foundational contexts from almost the beginning of rock. Naturally, if, as Fredric Jameson argues, the distinction of the urban and rural, which used to structure so much geographic representation, has broken down to any great extent, then we might not wonder that without its more tranquil and socially isolated counterpart, the city can no longer contain categories of novelty, energy, and exploration in quite the same way—an old lesson from semiotics.[26] But such a development could only partially explain the far more comprehensive and varied changes in urban representation over the time period being discussed here.

And in such a climate, the seemingly reckless self-indulgence and aesthetic abandon of the late 1970s would have to seem foreign, indeed, including the spirit of sociability that it assumes, so that portraying it would have to involve some kind of distancing frame such as those described above. Jameson's most salient observation to this point is that the film genre system provides a map of possibilities, and it is just that aspect that reconnects with the changing geography of (especially) American cities.[27] (One might think of Gene Kelly's famous performance of the title song from *Singing in the Rain* [1952] and try to imagine a similar scene being staged today, in order to get a sense of changes of possibility.) For if media representations have registered the loss of the possibility of certain urban experiences, then it would not be surprising to find such a sense of loss registered in the genre system of popular music. And if, as Jameson suggests, one of the most telling aspects of a genre system is precisely the sorts of things it excludes, then *Boogie Nights*' inability to play its representations of the late 1970s "straight" (as it tellingly does after 1980) can be taken as emblematic of just such an exclusion. In recognizing this, one begins to see one of the boundaries of our contemporary ethos.

The argument, then, is that disco has slipped past the bounds of the urban ethos precisely because it, along with the sets of social and spatial relations that it implies, represents a now-defunct perception and use of urban life. It has become impossible, and its impossibility is marked by *Boogie Nights*' distancing frame. Disco can, of course, be reproduced, represented, and even appreciated, but not in the kind of (relatively) unself-conscious and committed manner that had been possible in the music's heyday. The gap between the two historical possibilities of engagement was traced, of course, precisely in *Boogie Nights*'s profoundly hedged appreciation of the music and its object world, but one can find it across a broad range of responses to disco and its world.

Thus, when that *Time* magazine commercial from the late 1990s shows a (stereo)typically late 1970's dance floor of mainly white, out-of-shape, and garishly dressed disco dancers with the caption "What were we thinking?"—and the headline of a review of a disco exhibit at the New York Public Library for the Performing Arts asks precisely the same question—one viable answer is "We were thinking that the American city was a very different place from how it now seems to us."[28] Such a conviction allowed disco a place in the American popular musical genre system that no music could now hold—including house music, for example, which may bear historical and musicological affiliations with disco. What disco crucially held in the time of its commercial dominance was the image of an urban public space of collective pleasure and libidinal exploration. Of course, in order not to endorse the latter uncritically, one should keep in mind that the community it presents in most recent representations is almost always circumscribed: middle-class, white or sufficiently assimilated to 'mainstream' culture, adult, and straight. And imagining such a demographic as disco's exclusive audience involves considerable historical erasure. But that erasure in itself points to a useful hermeneutical suggestion, namely that disco, especially in its more denigrating representations, must be tied to bourgeois propriety or impropriety, and to unmarked subjects, as if to reflect not so much a particular set of acts or attitudes, as the spiritual illness, or at least intoxication, of an entire *Zeitgeist*.

If, as suggested in this chapter, the estrangement from disco may be traced, through the mediation of the urban ethos, to changes in (especially) North American cities since its peak of popularity, then the question might arise of why it is that disco seems to have been subject to that estrangement more than other genres. Why, in other words, are not movies like *Boogie Nights* being made that focus, instead, on mainstream pop? One foremost reason has already received some discussion here, namely that it is the kinds of urban *sociality* specifically associated with disco that are felt to be lost. As a symptom of that, one may look to those kinds of social interaction that appear in the film, such as the free-wheeling sexuality—not only pornography and its loss of "greatness" in the personage of Jack Horner, but also the promiscuity, and the dancing and gathering at the disco itself. Disco quite clearly occupies a certain cultural niche where the music remains inseparable from ideas of dancing, of a dance floor crowded with adults of a remarkably wide age span (and hence, perhaps, the current representation of discoers as a bit too old for what they are doing), and of a safe area for libidinal investment within the city.[29] Of course, in disco's heyday, there existed alternate locations for disco social interaction—though tellingly, not many rural ones—as when the disco-laden theme music for the television series *The Love Boat* (1977–1986) promised "Love, exciting and new ... " and encouraged the viewer to "Set a course for adventure, your heart on a new romance..." This final lyric communicates equally tellingly, since romance and adventure, excitement, and exploration were never far from the semiosis surrounding disco at the height of its popularity, and although *The Love Boat* transferred the setting from the city to the high seas, the normalized setting of disco pleasure remained the great American metropolis of *Saturday Night Fever* (1977). It may even, indeed, be argued emphatically that the events surrounding *Saturday Night Fever* demonstrate just to what degree disco's social force was inseparable from notions of urban life. As the opening shots of the film establish Brooklyn in the greater context of New York, the camera pans from aerial views of Manhattan, across the bridge to Brooklyn; that, together with the famous, and oft-troped, images of Tony Manero walking the city sidewalks, establish the setting for the opening credits. The decidedly urban (Italian-American) working-class community of the film's setting forms a crucial setting for the marketing of disco and its greatest commercial dominance.[30] That the setting also involves an erasure of disco's black and gay contexts demonstrates all the more powerfully how a certain *kind* of urban space is inseparable from ideas of those who inhabit it and the music that they consume.

The extent to which the existence of such safe, publicly accessible urban areas forms a foundation for public memories and representations of disco underlines that sometimes the layers of mediation between the imaginative mechanisms of an urban ethos and the larger world of social relations may not be excessively thick. After all, the urban ethos deals with possibilities, rather than any individual representation, and limits on possibility tend to involve matters of overwhelming force, social developments whose scope transcends any particular discursive tradition. The changes, then, in both objective urban space (increasingly dramatic class polarization, skyrocketing crime rates, gang activity of excluded youth, etc.) and in public perceptions of cities (moral panics about gangs, increasing villanizing of young black males, etc.) combined to foreclose the imagined possibility of the urban setting disco implied—at least that setting imagined in the most popular memories, the space of pleasure, bodily freedom, and libidinal exploration for working- and middle-class (mainly white) heterosexuals. The urban space for pleasure, freedom, and exploration also proved foundational, again at least in popular memory, to the broader object world and design styles of that period, rendering them emblems of all that was presumably tasteless, garish, and inexplicably popular in the mid- to late 1970s: "What were we thinking," indeed! Although such a postmortem reputation is consistent with some then-contemporary critiques of disco (e.g., as repetitive, standardized, and soulless music), its elevation to a cultural truism suggests changes of a more sweeping nature. It is worth remembering that, at various points in their histories, similar things were said about jazz, rock 'n' roll, and rap with equal vehemence. Only the critique of disco has endured in such a widespread and thoroughly naturalized manner. In that sense, it has taken on the role of a coded history of urban life from the late 1970s to the present, in which the real object of resentment and derision is the investment of city space with such libidinal hope and optimism, the feeling that the (principally) American city was a safe place for straight white working- and middle-class people to play out dramas of libidinal investment and desire.

Indeed, the urban ethos soon after disco's demise contained no space for a social equivalent to the music and its attendant social practices. Punk and its crossover cousin, New Wave (even when, as in the music of Blondie, it incorporated components of disco), not only spelled the oft-recounted reaction to disco and arena rock, they also announced different perceptions of city life, in which squalor and class-based rage could no longer be denied or contained. If such a notion of cities found early musical figuration in England, the resonance in North American cities, where class and racial warfare was beginning to accelerate and "deindustrialization" had begun to enter the popular vocabulary, was profound and shook the popular music genre system, and the overall urban ethos, to their core. Musicologically, it is not true that disco simply died; its afterlife, its musical poetics, continued in house music and various techno genres, not to mention some more mainstream incarnations like the music of Madonna. But the latter genres scattered within an urban ethos in which no broadly based notion of urban freedom was implied. It is telling that Madonna's music, although often sonically often very close to disco, nevertheless encompasses quite a few musical genres and finds its unity more

Table 3.1 The Bifurcation of Class in the United States, Beginning in 1970s

	REAL FAMILY INCOME GROWTH BY QUINTILE	
	1950–1978 (%)	1979–1993 (%)
Bottom 20%	+138	–17
Second 20%	+98	–8
Middle 20%	+106	–3
Fourth 20%	+111	+5
Top 20%	+99	+2032

centrally in her star-text. Meanwhile, the dance offsprings of disco settled into the status of "scenes," appropriate to the increasing physical fragmentation and race/class segregation of the 1980's American city, in which the libidinal freedom of some came increasingly at the expense of—and increasingly required protection from—the increasing misery of others. Although the spatial segregation itself is best traced in studies such as those of William Julius Wilson and Mark Hughes, perhaps most striking as an overview of American society is the bifurcation of income traced by the United States Census Bureau and beginning (quite significantly, in the present context) in the late 1970s.[31] Table 3.1 provides such an overview.[32]

As classes divided dramatically during the 1980s, the notion of widely shared urban experiences, always something of a fiction in any case, became increasingly untenable. From then on, the sites in which disco's exploration and freedom had thrived in some sense were less publicly shared and celebrated, could never again contribute theme music for top-twenty television programs, and could never again constitute a broadly based public dream (however disdained critically) about adventure and exploration in the city. Or, rather, any revival of such a dream would have to distance itself from it, celebrate it carefully, and at a pronounced remove—precisely as *Boogie Nights*, of course, does.

Such a history of disco, the city, and the urban ethos may also help us to understand the surprisingly powerful revival of interest in the 1970s that is observable at the end of the 1990s and the current revival of interest in disco in particular. A return to *Boogie Nights*, with the present discussion of the urban ethos in mind, can allow the modality of disco in that film to resonate with changes in urban geography and current views of that period's culture, as well as the late 1990's revival of interest in the mid- to late 1970s. In particular, we can again focus on the deeply bifurcated attitudes of envy and disdain coded musically and visually. In the film, audiences see the camera's slow and loving caress of the painfully colorful clothing, along with its amicable panning of dancing couples at the discotheque as they hear the near-constant accompaniment (on that crucial cusp of diegesis and nondiegesis) of 1970's pop hits. The sense of temporal separation and estrangement establishes itself well beyond the relatively scant eighteen years that separate the film's release from the last moments of libidinal investment (i.e., 1979) in the film. In the 1970's part of the film, the object world becomes unusually marked visually—with the unrelenting bright colors and the foregrounding of historical markers like Buck's clothing, hair fashions, and stereo equipment—while the music enacts the distancing force discussed at the beginning of this chapter. And, tellingly, such lurid visual environments constantly beckon in scenes of social interaction. Of course, the viewer sees scenes at the discotheque but also parties at Jack Horner's house, something like a housewarming party at Dirk's house, awards ceremonies, and film shoots. In fact, the first 1970's section of the film distinguishes itself for its predominance of socializing crowd scenes, presented, of course, in a relentless rhythm of celebration;[33] and by contrast, the later, 1980's section of the film presents no such large groups, only solitary individuals (e.g., Dirk waiting for clients as he prostitutes himself) and small, dysfunctional groups (e.g., Dirk's drug-addicted group of friends). So the modes of social interaction in the film—the possibilities for how, how many, and what kinds of people may gather for mutual pleasure, libidinal investment, and celebration—end up falling quite strictly into two categories: the freely indulgent crowds versus the trapped and unhappy individuals or small groups. And such a contrast is by no means accidental; the association of disco's pleasures in the contemporary urban ethos with the possibilities of public urban openness and large-group celebration structure precisely this dichotomy in *Boogie Nights*.

So not only with music and the colorful object world, but also with the mode of social interaction, *Boogie Nights* marks the difference between the perceived public realms of the 1970s and the time that followed (and with the customary oversimplification, of course, as things literally change on January 1, 1980).[34] That mode of interaction, in turn, supports the image of disco, not only in the film, but also in the (often denigrating) representations of disco in our society more generally. Those mocking images of garishly dressed, overly aged men and women dancing in those television advertisements came, after all, into precisely such an urban environment whose loss the film encourages us to mourn. The film, in that sense, narrates an irretrievable loss that, nevertheless, partially disowns, even parodies, the mourned object. The object, of course, is not so much disco itself as a constellation of cultural practices and attitudes for which disco (and related music in the film) may be a metonym—as well as the urban spaces that once could host them. To some extent, the pornography industry itself in *Boogie Nights* points to a similar historical loss, but in a quite different way. The industry does not point toward sex as a lost object; on the contrary, the little on-camera sex is campy and humorous, decidedly and deliberately unsexy, whereas the few non-pornographic sexual situations involve humiliating gay desire, child pornography, and flagrant infidelity culminating in a murder/suicide. The lost object of the pornography industry, instead, is Jack Horner's love of the movies as art, presumably defeated by the industry's rapid transition to video.[35] Here, unlike the case of the mode of social interaction supporting disco, the viewer may watch the confrontation between Horner and Floyd Gondolli, in which Gondolli admonishes him that video and amateurs would be the future of pornography, in full knowledge that Gondolli's vision of the future will turn out correct. The film also provides the further service of showing the sad consequences, as Horner lives, frustrated, through that transition. It is probably going too far to suggest that the audience's watching of Horner's films in the porno theatres after ejaculation because of their artistic merit (Horner's stated intention early in *Boogie Nights*) constitutes another mode of social interaction lamented in the film. But the story of pornography does reinforce, on its own terms, the film's depiction of disco and its lost urban possibilities: Horner's artistic fate rejoins the classic, vaguely Adornan (but also popular) story about the loss of artistic ambition and achievement in the face of the march forward of mass production. It thus dramatizes, by metonym, the irresistible and tragic force of history itself. And the transition to video, with Horner's onscreen degraded film career, provides the visual counterpart to the musical transition from disco to arena rock. The tangible force of history's regress unfolds, dramatizing a more generalized decay of the spatial environment. That environment never finds itself foregrounded in the film but rather dramatized via its cultural life; in the meantime, the more direct dramatization of urban change, from *Falling Down* (1993) to *Menace II Society* (1993), usually omitted anything more than the more localized consequences or lurid physical threats. Such fractionalized portrayals of the total urban environment convey perfectly why totalizing concepts such as the urban ethos—as unfashionable or untimely as totalizing may be—may turn out, ironically, precisely the most useful concepts for the fractured and presumably incommensurate world of post-Fordism.

The loss of earlier urban possibilities could even be traced through more abstract aspects of *Boogie Nights*'s music, including much of the nondisco music, such as its seeming cheerfulness (in the 1970's part of the film, of course). That apparently carefree and optimistic worldview, inviting the same mixture of attraction, fascination, contempt, and ridicule, should be familiar to those who have observed the more general revival (and revision) of 1970's culture in the 1990s, from the Brady Bunch movies (*The Brady Bunch Movie* [1995] and *A Very Brady Sequel* [1996]) through the Abba Teens. However, disco may be singled out as having a rather special status, even among these outstanding tongue-in-cheek revivals of schlock: long before the generalized cultural interest in the 1970s, disco was remembered, in a narrow sense, as a singularly poor (and inexplicably popular) music, and in a broader sense, as emblematic of the (presumably) inexplicable poor taste of 1970's popular culture.

Still, even the nondisco music in *Boogie Nights* carries the same indexical qualities, and here it is worth remarking how much of the popular music on the 1970s shares disco's stigma. A linking term among all that music can best be glimpsed in the theatre, especially those with good sound systems, because it involves properly sonic qualities independent of pitch and rhythm (though if one listens properly, even in those parameters shockingly little difference can be noted between much music from that era and much from our own). The upbeat performance style and vocal delivery of even lugubrious songs like Andrew Gold's "Lonely Boy" and Electric Light Orchestra's "Livin' Thing" (played over the movie's closing credits) suggest a near-tireless cheerfulness, which offers the same simultaneous allure and revulsion as disco or classic pornography. And at the same time, the production qualities of the music itself—what can only be termed the *slickness*, and what would, from the retrospect of 1980's punk and new wave, be seen as "overproduction"—beckon the listener to be enveloped in an embracing wall of sound. That sound character, in turn, can only be, like disco itself, the object of a highly mediated reception, be it irony, camp, or guilty appreciation. Cheerfulness and optimism most obviously serve as dividers of the film along the usual (1970s versus 1980s) line, but in many of the other cultural productions listed here, they serve more explicitly as indices of reactions to urban change. In *The Brady Bunch Movie* (1995), for instance, whose one running joke involves the tirelessly cheerful family's inappropriateness to the 1990's world in which they find themselves, that very contrast finds its greatest articulation in the outdoor shots, which show family members stepping outside the creepily calm suburban-style house into a rundown, threatening urban environment, with police or ambulance sirens blaring in the background. The characters continuing boundless cheer and seemingly impervious passage through the menacing city, provide a particularly broad illustration that cheerfulness or optimism themselves may index time-appropriate (or inappropriate) demeanors.

Boogie Nights most powerfully teaches the cultural analyst the experience of glimpsing impossibility, the modalities of presentation that may arise in expressive culture when one urban ethos views a cultural practice no longer perceived as possible in the present. Once (and still) a comical index of an era of poor taste, disco now to some extent finds itself longed for, not as great music but rather as a lost experience of the American city. Or, more accurately, the desire for disco indicates a much larger complex of social and spatial experiences, which it can only signal indexically: the urban discotheque where adults of varied ages and background mingled and indulged sexual fantasies and desires, the safe city in which adventure and libidinal experiment were possible. Of course, to call these "historical experiences" rings a bit generous, as they involve a good deal of selective memory. The question of just *who* ever had access to such experiences of disco must be posed; determinations involving race, class, and gender intervene (such as the notorious straightening and whitening of *Saturday Night Fever*), though it can quickly be added that racial segregation in most American cities greatly increased during the 1980s and that many discotheques were indeed available to a wide range of people by today's standards.

But the important question at hand is not 1970's disco *als es eigentlich gewesen*, but rather what function it seems to serve more recently, as an object of desire. To that end, and with the mediation of the urban ethos, it can now be advanced that the ambiguity of disco's deployment in *Boogie Nights* signals precisely an imagined historicity about American urban life and the possibility for libidinal exploration in urban space. Insofar as the viewer is encouraged to indulge the sonic and visual pleasures of the film, the value of a remembered 1970's urban life is signaled and invoked. Insofar as those pleasures are parodied and otherwise distanced from the viewer, the irretrievable loss of such pleasurable possibilities intervenes. The impossibility of disco as an object of desire figures poetically the perceived irreversibility of the historical prism through which it can only be viewed. Nobody appears to believe that American cities will return to their earlier configuration or that such a cheerful optimism and libidinal freedom could be recovered. At the same time, such presumed impossibility allows the music to be retrieved despite its intransigent popular bad reputation: disco can be embraced precisely because the embrace remains partial, discarding the presumably impossibly naive optimism that characterized disco's view of urban life. As it can only be invoked via an ironic distancing, the aesthetic and emotional engagement remains always mediated, always hidden behind something of a wink and a nod. In that sense, *Boogie Nights* rejoins other cultural productions of the 1970's "revival" in the 1990s (and beyond)—which is not, of course, a revival at all—in which the earlier period is consistently invoked through an ironic prism and in conspicuously metamorphosed forms. One might invoke the Abba stage musical *Mamma Mia* (premiering in London in 1999 and enormously successful), Snoop Dogg's video for "Snoop Dogg (What's My Name?, Part 2)," or even the Fox sitcom *That '70s Show* (premiering in 1998).[36]

It would be overstating the case to assert that the revival and redeployment of interest in disco, in *Boogie Nights* and elsewhere, finds its simple and unique determination in urban-geographic change and notions of the city's social possibility. Other determinations, ranging from generational aging, through AIDS, to the broader tendency of popular culture to recycle historical periods as objects of consumption, could well be cited and developed in tandem with the present argument. They may be regarded as supplements to geographical explanations. At the same time, contemplating cultural products like *Boogie Nights* through the mediation of the urban ethos and geographic change best conveys the irony and ambiguity of recent representations of the (late) 1970s. The emphasis here on those spatial explanations also further develops the much larger idea that histories of popular musical genres may sometimes secretly be histories of cities and, equally important, popular perceptions of their dangers and possibilities.

One cautionary note can be sounded, as the previous discussion addresses recent interest in the 1970s in a purposefully generalized fashion and thus may seem to impute a more unitary nature to that interest than, in fact, exists. It could be argued, for example, that some forms of African-American popular (and commercial) culture inflect that decade (and others) in particular ways: the pimp figure in hip-hop culture never entirely lacks traces from Blaxploitation film or Iceberg Slim's writings; Spike Lee's *Crooklyn* (1994) relies on a specifically African-American experience of the (almost) eponymous neighborhood; and the Digable Planets' 1960's (visual and musical) styles, even the Roots' ?uestlove's Afro, are not comprehensible without some basis in specifically African-American history and memory. These caveats remind us that specific histories inhabit and inflect generalities, not nullifying them but opening to their own indefinitely expansive byways. Thus, some attempts to return disco to its largely black and gay origins (such as the Experience Music Project's 2004 traveling exhibition *Disco: A Decade of Saturday Nights*) end up underlining all the more emphatically the recent interest in subaltern histories and how this music (like any music) can never enter the same historical river twice.

4

Marxist Music Analysis after Adorno

How Adorno Stands in for "Marxism" in Popular Music Studies

No book-length study claiming a Marxist approach could proceed without tackling that most perplexing and inevitable presence, Theodor Adorno. His shadow looms over the present project of Marxism and urban geography from two related perspectives, that of musicology and that of popular music studies (though, of course, "high" genres figure in this study as well, especially in Chapter 5).

Until the end of the 1980s mainly shunned as overly speculative and reliant on old-fashioned idealist philosophy, Adorno has undergone what must have been one of the most stunning rehabilitations in musicology. From the spates of translations, through the innumerable conference sessions, books, essays, articles, and university courses, he has now established himself, improbably, as one of the central figures of contemporary musicology. At times, his connection to work that invokes his name might seem tenuous, as in the early days of American cultural musicology when Adorno seemed to serve as little more than a *tenant lieu* for the notion of socially engaged music studies, sometimes bafflingly mischaracterized. In such cases, any notion of an Adorno *als er eigentlich gewesen* seems to disappear, and he stands reborn as a sort of way of legitimating, with the Germanophilia common to musicology, little more than cultural studies (in a way that would, of course, have scandalized him). At other times, a more serious effort at reconstructing and understanding Adorno as a historical figure implies a continuing (or perhaps renewed) relevance to a rather old project of connecting musical form and social structure, often combined with a distanced (or hermeneutic) approach to his more idealist tendencies.[1] In yet other cases (most commonly, in popular music studies), Adorno seems to appear as little more than a stick figure against which to construct more disciplinarily acceptable theoretical frameworks. In other words, we now inhabit a musicological world with quite a few different "Adornos," not always commensurate (perhaps appropriately, to a posthumous and postmodern existence).

But present he is, and to complicate matters, his position at the center of what has come, for better or worse, to be called "Western Marxism" has seemingly intractably associated any Marxian approach within musicology to his name. Such associations linger, despite the fact that quite a few commentators have pointed out how distant Adorno's theoretical premises lie from most strands of Marxism and the difficulties of connecting Adorno's convictions with Marx's ideas.[2] Although the recent fascination with Adorno's musicology, in both North America and the United Kingdom, often sidelines (most curiously) Marxism as an explicit consideration (with some notable exceptions such as Max Paddison),[3] perhaps unfortunately, such a neglect of that Marxist context has not yet succeeded in displacing Adorno as an almost knee-jerk invocation to any mention of Marxist thought in analyzing music. Judgments about Adorno thus sometimes serve to substitute for any independent understanding of the traditions of Marxist thought, and such judgments, when coupled with the cultural studies or postmodern allergy to their collective parent tradition, has long tended to forestall any serious consideration of revisiting Marxist ways of thinking about art and society. Musicology, of course, was one of the later disciplines even to embrace postmodern thought and cultural studies, and their literary-theoretical relatives, and surely these bodies of work have exercised tremendous rhetorical effect, with their tendency to index Marxism implicitly with dismissive cues like "totalizing" (decontextualized and emptied of content to the point where it means little more than "overgeneralizing").

In such circumstances, one might be forgiven for advancing Theodor Adorno as one of the single greatest obstacles to developing a Marxist analysis of music. Nowhere does Adorno's looming presence prove so vexing as in popular music studies; there, even the most strenuous validations of the music seem, at some point, out of necessity, to look back to Adorno's shadow and exorcise the weight of his critiques. His well-known, perhaps notorious, rubrics of mass production, standardization, false differentiation, and the regression of listening seem to lie inextricably as a foundational trauma in the discipline; and even those, almost certainly the majority, in popular music studies who contest his descriptions nevertheless find it necessary to confront them. By the influence of now somewhat routine cultural studies, promoting a music genre or subculture as political resistance and a disruption of discursive consensus entails explaining how that genre or subculture disrupts Adorno's projected deadening conformity of the music industry. Claiming the progressiveness of a community's reception of some mainstream music involves arguing the productive effects of reception against Adorno's seeming one-way circuit from producer to consumer. And the presumably crucial emergence of subaltern voices in contemporary popular music must disown Adorno's vision of the homogenizing effects of the industry. The spectral presence of Adorno can be traced even in work with an apparently vast disciplinary distance from Frankfurt critical theory, such as the post-Marxist cultural studies of George Lipsitz or the populist audience-focused research of John Fiske, both of whom seem regularly to need to counterpose their more optimistic scenarios to an already assumed condemnation of media industries.[4] Adorno's presence in popular music studies seems most often to resemble that of a pinball bumper, against which scholars all at some point fling themselves in order to bounce somewhere else with renewed energy and theoretical momentum but always with the horrifying threat that gravity will bring them back down in the same direction. Anybody wanting a measure of his seemingly invincible presence need only peruse Keith Negus' *Popular Music in Theory: An Introduction* and watch sections on Adorno open the first two chapters, with responses to his work dominating the contributions that follow.[5] There, as Negus explicitly traces a trajectory away from Adorno concerning first audiences and then the music industry, Adorno seems to loom ever larger, as the reader watches opinions flee his central contentions, like so many planets fleeing a great, originary cosmic explosion. The extent to which the "Adorno" rejected in such studies resembles the historical man and his true views can always be questioned; certainly, many of them deal with inaccurate or oversimplified versions of his thought. But recognizing that simply displaces the spectre from an historical person to a more recent collective construction.

As tempting as it may be, it would ultimately be simplistic and counter productive simply to shout "Get over it!," as if the weight of historical constructions of popular music could simply be offloaded and researchers could enjoy a newfound freedom by sheer dint of will. If Adorno is the popular music scholar's scene of primal trauma, then repression would offer little relief: at least one can say that the talking cure lived out in journals and books itself proffers more than its share of productive discussion, even if, as will be seen in this chapter, its very framework remains deeply flawed. Furthermore, just about nobody, most likely, would want to contend that (at least the conjured) Adorno was completely wrong. Why would one resist an Adornan vision of the seemingly endless worldwide proliferation of young-boy pop/R&B groups, or of this month's new, deeply sincere, and touchingly pained singer-songwriter? Or who could have expected that the Backstreet Boys would in retrospect almost seem hip, next to the endless stream of even less interesting knock-offs? Clearly, Adorno was not wrong about everything.

But arguably today the most damaging effect of Adorno's shadow stems precisely from the widespread conflation of his name with the entire broad and diverse field of Marxism, at least by many practitioners of music theory, musicology, and popular music studies. The development of that sad state of affairs constitutes too long a story to retell here, involving the dominating presence of so-called Western Marxism in traditions of critical humanities scholarship. While Western Marxism deviates sharply in many respects from other Marxist traditions, it nevertheless remains the only tradition related to Marx that many humanities scholars encounter in any depth or detail (i.e., in any state beyond allusive reference or caricature). Just next door, disciplinarily speaking, in the social sciences, Marxism manages to exist in other forms and names in the work of scholars like David Harvey, Neil Smith, and Ellen Meiksins Wood; and even a discipline (in some ways) as close to musicology as literary studies hosts such differing (and towering) figures as Terry Eagleton and Fredric Jameson. But the historical gravitation in music scholarship draws musicologists and music theorists to traditions of Marxism preoccupied by the problematic of mass production, a powerful but sometimes limiting problematic that often fails to convey the full cultural (including economic) scope of capitalism. What is more, the problematic of mass production and its intersection with the commodity fetish arguably become ever blunter tools precisely as our own societies come increasingly under the sway of those same commodities, while it diversifies from mass production (as outlined in the Introduction to this book).

But Adorno's legacy (or, as some would have it, his distortion) in popular music studies has really tended to stream in two directions, namely the twin notions of cultural imperialism and standardization of product lines. And, notably, his classic stances within those problematics have come, in many studies, to be equated with Marxism itself: Dominic Strinati and Peter Manuel, for example, leave cultural imperialism and formal standardization as the remnants of Marxist theory in their own narratives of popular culture, which their own corrective positions then undertake to modify or reject.[6] "Marxism," in such a disciplinary context, takes the form of an outdated structure against which the more 'contemporary' theorist must struggle in order to build something more modern, something more appropriate to the new world in which she finds herself. Given such placeholders for the rich and diverse traditions that have characterized (and in some disciplines, continue to characterize) Marxist thought, a scholar wanting to centralize Marxism in the study of popular music faces formidable obstacles. Whereas the previous chapters (particularly Chapter 2) have already foregrounded strengths for a Marxist approach as a corrective to the (by now) traditional cultural studies framework, the first task of the present chapter will be to historicize Adorno with respect to the present moment; in that section of the chapter I will argue that both (the rare) proponents and opponents of Adorno's vision of the music industry tend to wrap their debates around conditions that have been at least partially surpassed historically. The second task of this chapter will be to suggest a means of Marxist music theory more adequate to our times, positing that if capitalism changes in history, then a Marxist music theory needs to change with it, being, to quote Lenin, as "radical as reality itself"[7];

the changes in cities wrought by reorganizations of urban production will be seen to implant themselves in patterns of sound far more directly than in the examples cited in Chapter 1.

Flexible Accumulation (or Why Adorno Should *Not* Stand in for "Marxism" in Popular Music Studies)

In the industrial era of capitalism, when economies of scale were transforming the landscape and the very pace and character of life, including art, Adorno's vision proved extremely perceptive, even prescient for a few decades to come. If nothing else, Mike Davis' extraordinary description of the Los Angeles that surrounded Adorno should suggest that the nightmare of enlightenment had its real embodiment and a profound moment of social truth.[8] Contrary to the image of an unrehabilitated idealist sometimes imposed on him, Adorno was living the reality that he was describing. But it is possible to recognize, from a present perspective, that the character of social life to which Adorno responded was itself historical and did not carry nearly the longevity that he imagined. What Adorno took for an inexorable process turned out to be historically specific, to have not just a birth but also a developmental process, one that followed directions he could not have predicted. What intervened, and what Adorno could not have theorized in his lifetime, is, of course, the advent of flexible accumulation or so-called post-Fordism, which received some outlining in the Introduction to this book as a major determination of the changing spatial and social characters of contemporary cities. At this point, a more detailed examination of flexible accumulation will offer a specific rejoinder to his vision without the moralizing critiques that invoke cultural snobbery (as if calling somebody a bad person somehow constituted a cogent refutation of her or his contentions).

Flexible accumulation does not represent a step away from capitalism—far from it—or even a fundamental shift in its basic social mechanisms. Rather, it describes a mutation in capitalist accumulation that has sufficiently inflected cultural processes as to call for new ways of theorizing music and its social effects. The difference that constitutes flexible accumulation occurs at the level of *regime of accumulation*, that is, specific strategies of accumulating capital. Its characteristics have been debated, both in their detail and in their scope, but for the purposes of discussing Adorno and Marxism, a simplified schematic description should suffice.[9] The most salient aspects for the present discussion include the following, listed in more or less random order and condensing some related items from the list given in the introduction:

1. A switch in many industries from mass production to the production of a variety of products in small and frequently changing batches
2. Design intensity in production, while automation and programmability allow for quick and flexible design change
3. A shift, especially in the most economically developed countries, away from manufacturing and toward the provision of services to producers (such as payroll and back-office operation)
4. Increased consumption by individuals of personal services in addition to goods, from restaurant delivery and Internet access provision to specialized mail services and "spiritual" counseling
5. Vertical disintegration of large firms, as companies subcontract to independent operators what had previously been done in-house, creating a whole sector of business service and information companies ranging from Federal Express to temp firms
6. A flattening of corporate decision making and the removal of managerial layers, as job descriptions increasingly merge and expand
7. At another place in the work force, large numbers of laborers being *forced* into flexibility, with a far larger percentages of new jobs being part-time, temporary, and without previously normal levels of benefits
8. Feedback loops from consumers becoming more quickly and thoroughly integrated to design (as when one designs one's own CD or, indeed, computer online)
9. Mergers and buyouts, forming huge multinational conglomerates
10. Vertical disintegration and outsourcing, spawning specialized regional economies
11. Surviving manufacturing movement out of inner cities, either overseas or to suburbs, exurbs, or rural areas

Scholars also differ greatly on when flexible accumulation began to exercise significant influence on cultural and economic life, with some seeing signs just after or even before World War II, and others not seeing it as significantly developed until some time during or just after the 1970s; most commonly, though, its beginning is traced to the 1970s, as a response to the global recession that characterized the beginning of that decade.[10] Many of its characteristics, especially numbers 3, 7, and 11, received mention in the Introduction to this book as particular determinants of urban change. As must have become clear in the intervening chapters, all of the aspects of flexible accumulation just mentioned inflect significantly the kinds of lives lived in contemporary cities of the developed world.

What is more, the culture industries, especially the popular music industry, have long occupied privileged sites of explanation for theories of flexible accumulation, even to the extent that Scott Lash and John Urry take popular music as the exemplary instance of what they (perhaps somewhat optimistically) call "postorganized capitalism."[11] And yet, despite the extensive discussions of flexible accumulation in the social sciences, musicologists, music theorists, and cultural studies scholars seemed to have overlooked its rather striking relevance to debates concerning Adorno.[12] Given his theories' quite evident reliance on the mechanisms of older, more thoroughly Fordist mechanisms of production, one could only imagine that any stance toward Adorno (or, for that matter, Marxism in popular music studies) must at least address more recent theories of capitalist organization. And even though debates have raged about both the extent and the nature of the economic and geographic transformations involved, very few scholars doubt that changes in technology, communications, and computerized design have altered production and consumption. Even theoretically modest (and yet empirically rich) studies like Alfred Chandler's *Scale and Scope* mark significant departures from older industrial organization at some point around or after the middle of the twentieth century.[13] Certainly, when one narrows one's focus to the music industry itself, considerable aspects of post-Fordism have been notable for quite some time by now.[14] Although Adorno assumed that mass production proceeded roughly the same within the music industry as in other sectors of the economy, it nevertheless will be helpful to turn to those aspects specifically of the music industry that have indeed shifted during the period normally associated with flexible accumulation. Those changes affect the rubrics both of standardization and of cultural imperialism, which, it will be recalled, remain the principle rubrics under which discussions in popular music studies tend to retain traces (often negative) of Adorno's thought:

Standardization. The changes wrought by developing music technology on the structure and character of the music industry have been much remarked.[15] Some of the discussions of this massive topic have gushed with an exaggerated enthusiasm for imagined liberatory possibilities (particularly in connection with the Internet); such accounts and predictions can be taken to demonstrate the fallacy of technological determinism, as capitalism enacts the triumph of the social system both by shaping the development of technology and also by reacting, sometimes stumbling, but, in the end, triumphant.[16] Few things demonstrate such a dynamic better than the proliferation of inexpensive digital technology in the past couple of decades. The costs of professional-quality production, in the wake of ever cheaper digital technology and programming, have enabled profitable independent music production on a smaller scale than Adorno could ever have envisioned. Of course, such independence exists only in the most attenuated state, as "indies" perform an integral role in a system that also embraces and supports the "majors."[17] But more germane to this discussion, the other, complementary face of flexible accumulation, inseparable in a broader context, soon appears, namely the rampant acquisition of otherwise independent companies by ever larger entertainment conglomerates, not to mention the latter's merging into ever larger entities like Vivendi Universal or Sony BMG. The trend of entertainment giants to absorb smaller record labels and maintain their valuable brand name mirrors, to some extent, the already existing tendency among major record companies to separate off musical production by genre, forming units that function quasi-autonomously (Negus, *Genres*, 31–62). Such units and wholly owned former independents often stress innovation and diversity with no less enthusiasm (and, dare one say, sincerity) than the genuine indies, and yet they are the very substance of large-scale music-commodity production. In the meantime, inputs from aspiring artists, amateur musicians who straddle the technological line between consumption and production, and even established artists draw on a greater variety of sounds accessible through near-instantaneous communications infrastructures, with the ability to manipulate and restructure sounds unprecedented in history; such inputs enter a production structure both centrally owned and functionally dispersed. The resulting musical commodities are then broadcast, promoted, and advertised in a media structure of unprecedented concentration, especially in the United States, where liberalization of ownership laws has facilitated the worldwide trend to concentrate media ownership. The net result is an industry with more centralized ownership and greater product diversification *at the same time*. Independent record companies are relatively inexpensive to start and can be run on shoestring budgets impossible in the era of large-scale standardized production; the flip side is that the profitable independent labels, or their rosters, are almost always absorbed by larger companies, or enter distribution and licensing deals that transfer significant profits to the majors*.[18] Such trends result in a configuration Adorno could never have imagined: a concentration of wealth with a deconcentration of control, an industry of a small number of majors inseparable from a veritable Lego construction of minors. With flexible and highly localized decision-making structures ultimately answerable financially to a small number of dominant players, the music industry begins to manifest some of the well-known attributes of flexible accumulation more generally.[19] An unprecedented proliferation of musical genres destined to niche markets can now be served profitably on a small scale; at all levels, the industry can respond ever more rapidly to changes in consumer demand. Geographically localized and ethnically specific trends and music can generate commercial activity whose scale, in previous years, would not have attained economic viability. Now, unlike twenty years ago, one can locate dozens, if not hundreds, of constantly mutating dance genres in specialized urban shops, just down the street from a Tower Records mass-marketing Patty Griffin's singer–songwriter sincerities, next to an import shop or Internet café offering access to Swahili rap or dub poetry. Yet in a situation presenting such a dazzling circulation of music large

* Lee, "Re-Examining," pp. 28–29; Hesmondhalgh, "Flexibility," pp. 478–481.

and small, four major record companies (as of the time of this writing) produce the recordings that represent more than 85 percent of the world's phonogram sales.

In such a situation one may recognize an inadequacy of an Adornan conception, as the unprecedented concentration of the music-recording industry does *not* necessarily promote an increasing homogenization of the product (form or content) and does *not* necessarily entail ever more standardized, falsely differentiated musical forms of deadening similarity. Listening does not have to regress in order to capture the variety of popular music being produced today; on the contrary, the proliferation of music can probably be tagged as sublime in the most literal sense, producing both a pleasure at the adventures of music and a fear of being cognitively overwhelmed by the endless developments. The world of musical objects thus produces its own replication of Fredric Jameson's famous sublime of multinational capital, perhaps in itself an illustration that Adorno was correct in his overall hypothesis of music's absorption into the dynamics of commodity production, even if mistaken about the particulars.[20] But, of course, it is precisely those particulars that structure the scholarly literature examined here. Given such a concrete repudiation of the Adornan nightmare, some scholars may be tempted to project an uncritical picture of market capitalism in the music industry. As with any celebration of capitalism, they would be partially correct: being by far the most dynamic and agile force of economic organization in human history, capital should surprise nobody in enabling such a bewildering array of musical delights. But, of course, Adorno himself would presumably have been surprised (at least from his vantage point—an unfair perspective, perhaps); the dialectic of enlightenment has indeed taken a dialectical turn for which Adorno could not have prepared us.

Cultural Imperialism. Adorno concerned himself more with capital per se than with the fate of nations and local culture; the hidden force of creeping imperialism structures much of the discussion in "The Culture Industry: Enlightenment as Mass Deception," as Adorno's and Horkheimer's stunning opening panning of a nightmarish city openly spatializes the dynamic they are about to unfold.[21] Of course, subsequent discussions of the popular music industry more openly traffic in visions of a creeping or galloping (usually American) cultural imperialism, with an earlier fashion of disparagement eventually giving way, in the wake of trends in cultural studies, to studies that present themselves as more nuanced visions of "globalization."[22] And, of course, the latter school of thought has sunk its roots not only in academic intellectual trends but also in discussions of the technological and institutional changes since the heyday of the "cultural imperialism hypothesis"; the music industry's ability to respond to feedback from audiences, and the increased production for small specialty markets, do an end run around the problematics of cultural imperialism, as traditionally conceived, and at least greatly complicate the well-worn questions of producer control versus audience inflection. Both substantial independent record companies and localized branches or affiliates of international conglomerates now design artist rosters and repertory of staggering variety and attunement to local markets, though, of course, the blockbuster title designed for "international" markets still takes precedence economically. Conversely, music from far-flung locations like Cape Verde and South Korea can be packaged and niche-marketed globally, forming the boom in so-called "world music" that has constituted one of the most widely remarked transformations in the music industry over the last decade. If such large-scale marketing of the marked local constitutes cultural imperialism—and good, cogent arguments could easily be advanced that it is precisely that—it nevertheless forms a cultural and commercial configuration far from the kind envisioned in the problematic we have inherited from Adorno, or, for that matter, from Lenin. The latter, writing in 1916 and not surrounded, as Adorno was, by both the mechanisms and the products of the mass music industry, nevertheless proposed arguments profoundly influential in their theorization.[23] So-called "active audience" theories that developed in response to such visions can, to some extent, claim vindication in commercial reality: the affordability of quick, small-batch production in the music industry has rendered audience agency visible in ways that belie Adorno's nightmare of mass passivity and uniform transformations of consciousness. The feedback loops and quick, small-batch production just mentioned exemplify, of course, flexible accumulation as an economic process, and yet their palpable relevance to old debates about active and passive audiences seems to escape the literature about popular music.

But the most crucial point that needs to be made about all these affronts to Adorno's vision (or that attributed to him) is that they are *fully a formation of capitalism*. Nothing about flexible accumulation resists capitalism (except insofar as capitalism embodies its own contradictions) or departs from its basic procedures, such as the extraction of relative surplus value—and of course, the same "globalization" that enables the wide circulation of localized musical styles and traditions itself participates intimately in the boosting of relative surplus value, as corporations seek low wages and far-flung markets around the world. The infinite variety of world music, including those produced and consumed by subaltern subjects, has always existed as a silent objection to the nightmare of mass consumption, but it is only the flexible-accumulation wrinkle that has allowed much of that music wide-scale commercial representation. And although audiences have always inflected music and integrated it to their lives in locally unique ways, it is only with the profusion of, for example, niche-marketed dance labels and other small-batch producers that those inflections have undergone properly developed production and marketing. The coming-into-representation of audiences, including subaltern subjects, can be taken as a partial realization of a Foucauldian dream and perhaps a challenge to Gayatri Spivak, and can easily be an occasion for celebration;[24] to state the negation, and to argue the preferability that such small-scale music remain hidden, would seem downright perverse. But the flip side of the equation is equally important, because the same mobility of capital that enables such developments also allows the increasingly concentrated owners of that capital to outmaneuver the classes that struggle against it—including, it should quickly be added, many of the subjects whose representation one would have been tempted to celebrate. In other words, the material/social infrastructure of the situation, and the class relationships that it develops and deepens, seem to contradict the implicit direction of the discursive liberation. The subaltern earns its right to speak, or at least its niche in the marketplace, alongside the weakening of regulatory power in collapsing nation-states, neo-liberal regimes with their devastated public sectors, and, as part of the regime of flexible accumulation, labor structures that harden the lines between the haves and the increasingly trapped have-nots. One need only recall Table 3.1 in order to understand the material fates of many of those subaltern (and other) subjects in the United States since 1979.

Although one would not want to underestimate the importance of "small" music's attaining commercial viability, the seeming divergence of representational liberation from class relations (defined the old-fashioned way) must at least give pause to those championing the cultural-studies-related notion of the transformative power of "resistant" representations; Adorno's notion that capitalism, to thrive, must (among other things) homogenize and standardize artistic products seems to have outlived its viability. After all, in the popular music industry, the gradual disappearance of many even large record companies such as Atlantic, and the whittling down of the number of "majors" suggests Adorno's very nightmare, along with the implied concentrations of wealth and power. But that concentration in many ways proves remarkably adaptable, through flexibility and instant communication of information, to diversity and change in markets. Thus, for instance, the remaining independent labels distribute and market their products in most cases precisely through the increasingly centralized networks of the majors. The Internet itself provides a handy illustration of the separation of centralized control from mass-produced and standardized product, its virtually unlimited input possibilities and staggeringly diverse content running through lines principally owned by one conglomerate (Cisco Systems).

The relation of increasingly centralized economic organization to diversified cultural result is *not* upside down; one might be tempted to think that it is, simply through having naturalized Adorno's equation of centralized ownership with standardization and mass production. But no essential and unchanging relation exists between ownership concentration, on the one hand, and method of production and qualities of products, on the other hand: *the relationship is always and everywhere historical.* To continue arguing using Adorno's assumptions, or against his assumptions, without checking to see whether those very assumptions even pertain any more may be one of the great looming flaws haunting recent scholarly discussions of popular music. In regimes of flexible accumulation and just-in-time production, enormous inequalities in power (including but not limited to wealth) may not just be consistent with, but even may *depend* on, the stylistic, ethnic, and geographic mobility and diversity that pervade the current cultural sphere.[26] And one can observe that dependence every day in the marketing strategies of businesses ranging from fashion through computers to circuit assemblies, in which far-flung and "exotic" products whirl by like so many twirling parasols and hybrid cultural transgressions dance playfully. In such an environment, nobody should wonder that the distinguished consumer should be omnivorous—and that such boundary-transgressing tastes, far from being somehow revolutionary, in fact constitute the essence of bourgeois preference.[27] Norms and dominant identities continue to exist, of course, but consuming their combination and transgression also falls well within dominant (or, if one prefers, "hegemonic") cultural patterns of consumption, rendering celebrations of hybridity and norm violation, now common in popular music studies, music theory, and musicology, moot.[28]

How Cultural Studies Approaches Take the Same View of Capital as Adorno

The detachment of centralized ownership from uniform mass-manufactured product must crucially be distinguished from some prominent objections to Adorno's vision that have arisen most especially in communications, literary, and cultural theory. Those fields arguably form the closest thing to a mainstream in popular music studies, and by and large their practitioners argue forcefully against Adorno's theories (or theories that they attribute to him), from John Fiske to Iain Chambers to Lisa Lewis.[29] But by and large, even those who decry Adorno's pessimistic vision base their own optimism on the *same conception of capital itself.* In their work, the assertion of local or subaltern voices and cultural practices becomes a rebuke to totalizing, the contamination of dominant discourse by symbolic resistance is celebrated and encouraged, and the polyvalence and mutability of the world of discourse is underlined as a challenge to domination. Whatever moment of truth lurks behind such celebrations, the fact is that the studies that produce them, working in and against the shadow of Adorno, adopt precisely his premises about the nature of capitalism and culture, differing only by projecting the cultural sphere as more multiple, resistant, and filled with subaltern voices and practices than Adorno allowed. Indeed, such arguments are correct, on all counts (except possibly the resistance), but they fail to grasp that the cultural processes that they celebrate do not oppose the effects of capitalism, but rather form *integral parts of it*. What prevents theorists from seeing the present-day musical kaleidoscope as a phenomenon of capital stems from a conception of capitalist hegemony culled from theorists like Gramsci (via Dick Hebdige and other Birmingham theorists), whose frame of civil society draws on the national boundaries, dominant identities, and cultural homogeneities that flexible accumulation has been gradually displacing.[30] Cultural practice, then, like our current music industry (and the other culture industries from which it has grown inseparable), which profit from challenging or complicating national boundaries, dominant identities, and cultural homogeneities, acquires value precisely for having challenged hegemony—and not coincidentally, for having disrupted the deadening sameness embodied in Adorno's nightmare. But hegemony, like the Adornan mass-production vision, attaches the workings of capital closely to conformity and narrowed, large-scale product lines (albeit less directly, via the mechanisms of representation). One should not wonder, then, that practitioners of cultural studies, in exposing cultural challenges to hegemony, should attach themselves to the same model of capitalism as that of Adorno—and in so doing, distance themselves from relevance to recent social life.

Popular music studies thus end up populated by, on the one hand, Adorno, with very few adherents and viewpoints on culture based on earlier formations of capital and, on the other hand, a plethora of studies that validate the cultural processes of popular music, but do so on the basis of the *same* conception of capital's relation to uniformity and discursive domination. If scholarly consensus measures the strength of intellectual positions, then the mainstream positions in cultural theory and communications studies may claim truth-value; very few popular music scholars accept completely Adorno's account of the culture industry, and it is usually a safe bet, theoretically, to champion the musics of subaltern subjects and their cultural effects. In fact, the literature in popular music studies trumpeting the symbolic upsetting of consensus surely has constituted one of its growth industries since studies began appearing to celebrate the powers of artists and audiences to inflect discourse.[31] Thus, at least by consensus, the hegemony-fighting power of production and consumption (and presumably distribution as well?) has triumphed. But the history of capitalism, one should hasten to submit, has, in the meantime, walked right past the terrain of struggle into a stage in which discursive domination and capitalist organization bear a strikingly different relation to each other, something that Gramsci would not recognize. Under the view proposed here, capitalism is no longer a great monolithic and uniformly hierarchical force against which various liberatory cultural forces might be aligned (even were one to accept that such was ever the case). On the contrary, the challenge now, by my conception, is how to theorize capital as *simultaneously diversifying culturally, and segregating economically and spatially.* The abstract apparatus of such a theory might take some work, but its concrete instantiation can be experienced in a brief walk through the privileged spaces of upper Manhattan, where the beneficiaries of flexible accumulation happily consume the music, cuisine, film, art, clothing, writing—dare one add "identities"?—of the most diverse and incommensurate cultural sources.

Such a state of affairs militates against another commonality between many cultural studies approaches to music and that of Adorno, namely the desire to locate liberatory force in expressive culture. The foregoing should render obvious the need for skepticism about such a project, but that does not require refusing it completely. Indeed, the moment of truth in postmodern cultural studies may well lie in the mapping of how discourse and expressive culture can contaminate the symbolic registers of domination in a given social formation. Quite clearly, some forms of domination *do* occur largely, if not principally, in symbolic realms, and expressive culture would no doubt embody some of the more emotive, not to mention unidentified, experiences of a hegemonic order. Whether the more purely production-based forms of domination and segregation that accompany the weakening of ethnic- and gender-based hegemony constitute a preferable state of affairs might be left aside as a moral question of little heuristic value.[32] But too exclusive a focus on such quagmires may blind us as to how the mode of production, including the regime of accumulation, sets possibilities and limitations for such discursive practices and may even interact with them in ways that are not often considered. Such interactions do not stem magically from new processes of capital accumulation but rather attain the realm of representation (including, but not limited to, music) through mediation. Given not only the focus of this book but also the tendency of major cities in the developed world to concentrate and spatialize the workings of capital, the instance of mediation, whose discussion will occupy the rest of this chapter, will naturally be the contours of urban space, as it shapes and limits representation within the genre system of rap music.

Reality Rap, Knowledge Rap, and the Urban Ethos

The discussion so far has argued that both the "Adorno question" in popular music scholarship and cultural studies-inspired validations of some popular music cannot adequately consider contemporary music, because both are based on a conception of culture inconsistent with the present state of capitalism; relying as they do on at least partially inaccurate premises, they not surprisingly lead in directions that ultimately impede, rather than enable, critique. But, despite Adorno's usual association with Marxism in popular music studies, the basic project of Marxist analysis in the humanities, as conceived here—namely, the tracing of the systematic aspects of capitalism in the production, circulation, and reception of expressive culture—nevertheless retains its vital significance. In fact, this is all the more so, as capitalism comes to characterize our societies on an ever broader scope and in deepening cycles. With the Adornan premises cast aside, including cultural studies validations, the question becomes: What would a non-Adornan Marxism look like in music theory? The remainder of this discussion outlines and exemplifies a Marxism after Adorno, positing at least one direction such an effort could take.

As in previous chapters, the focus now shifts to urban geography and the changes wrought on city environments by the restructuring of capitalism under post-Fordist regimes of accumulation. Such a focus naturally departs from models of mass production and standardization and thus avoids at least that particular drawback of Adorno's vision. Cities focus and intensify certain aspects of capital, including one described by David Harvey: "The interweaving of simulacra in daily life brings together different worlds (of commodities) in the same space and time. But it does so in such a way as to conceal almost perfectly any trace of origin, of the labor processes that produced them, or of the social relations implicated in their production" (*Condition*, p. 102). The task of the following discussion of rap music and the urban ethos will be to suggest one way to uncover the hidden social relations within a development in genres of rap music, tracing flexible accumulation in the very sound of the musical tracks.

It almost need not be specified that American rap music and video have always taken as a crucial locus the inner city, or that the social force of rap music has depended on this.[33] But though most scholars underline this point and it also looms large in the popular imagination, it does not necessarily follow that the "inner city" or "ghetto" image remains static throughout time. On the contrary, as many fans but few scholars have remarked (the former often complaining), images and ideas of "the urban" in rap music and video, in fact, change drastically over time, and those changes are inseparable from the development of rap music as a genre system. My earlier study of rap music describes, among other things, two musical genres that I label "reality" rap and "knowledge" rap. Reality rap subsumes what is often called "gangsta rap" and some related genres, and until fairly recently it focused on a musical strategy that I labeled the "hip-hop sublime."[34] In music-analytical terms, the "hip-hop sublime" deploys dense combinations of musical layers; all of the layers reinforce the quadruple meter, but in the domain of pitch they comprise a sharply dissonant combination, even by the standards of jazz, or soul, harmony. In fact, the layers tend not even to be "in tune," so to speak: instead, they are separated by intervals that can only be measured in terms of fractions of well-tempered semitones. The result is that no pitch combination may form conventionally representable relationships with the others; musical layers pile up, defying aural representability for Western musical listeners. In many cases (e.g., Mobb Deep's "Drop a Gem on 'Em"), a listener will not even be able to locate a normative or "principal" pitch level against which the others can be heard as deviating.[35] The hip-hop sublime is achieved using a procedure that, following Tricia Rose, I call *layering*.[36] Layering results from the superposition of several different tracks, using either preexisting recordings and/or new studio-produced recordings, to form a complex texture that serves as the musical complement to the MC's performance. The technique figures crucially in constructing the hip-hop sublime, as the source for each layer, if not already out of tune with the other layers, may be manipulated to play at an incommensurate pitch level.

Raekwon's "Can It Be All So Simple (Remix)," from *Only Built 4 Cuban Linx*, can serve well to illustrate the hip-hop sublime; fellow Wu-Tang Clan member RZA, one of the pioneers of the technique, produced the track.[37] Example 4.1 transcribes the layers that produce the effect in question. The first of them, labeled layer (a), is sampled from a preexisting recording, namely Gladys Knight and the Pips' 1974 cover recording of "The Way We Were"[38]; the sample is excerpted from the bridge of the earlier song and provides Raekwon's title (the relevant lyrics being "Can it be that it was all so simple then?"). The original setting of the Knight recording, in G major, sets the melody first to IV (first measure), then to ii^7 (second measure); that harmonic progression provides consonant support for that melody, which descends from an initial G5 through a passing F#5 to a final E5. Also, exactly at the beginning of the third beat in the second measure, Knight releases the final note by aspirating heavily the "-n-" (in a performance gesture common in both African-American charismatic religious preaching and gospel-related musical styles, such as soul). The gesture ends up being prominent in the layer's overall texture.

Such conventional melodic and harmonic behavior, however, does not survive its radical recontextualization as a layer in the RZA's setting, though the aspirated ending does. The other layers are all composed and added in the studio by the RZA. The second layer in Example 4.1, labeled layer (b), comprises a synthesizer line that also projects a melodic third, but in this case a minor third rather than the major third of layer (a). What is more, the melody changes both timbre and register in the middle of the line. The timbre transforms from a reedy synthesizer sound in the first measure (though without the attack of a reed instrument, as the melody is played legato throughout) to a synthesized string sound an octave higher in the second half of the measure. The effect enjoys some prominence in the overall texture, because the vocal sample (i.e., layer [a]) decrescendos

Example 4.1 Musical Layers in Raekwon/The R2A's "Can It So Simple (Remix)."

in the second measure and then drops quickly out of the texture (with the aspirated "-n-" mentioned above) on the third beat. The combination of the octave transfer in the synthesizer, together with the quieting and ending of the vocal line, results in layer (b)'s replacing to a large extent layer (a) texturally in the second measure.

Layer (c) consists simply of two block chords played on an electric keyboard (sounding like a Fender Rhodes electric piano, though that sound can easily be mimicked electronically). The first chord projects ii (an a-minor triad), the second iii (a b-minor triad); the layer therefore clashes somewhat with the vocal sample, whose original harmonization, it will be recalled, had been IV in the first measure, followed by ii.^{7} The contrast between the two would perhaps only be relevant to someone with an aural memory of the original setting (and some interest in the matter); more salient, the new harmonic context renders the final E5 in layer (a) an incomplete dissonant lower neighbor to the preceding F#5 in the second measure. Although the resulting unresolved dissonance in the voice does not constitute the phenomenon referred to here as the "hip-hop sublime," as it does not involve incommensurable tunings, it increases the degree of harmonic tension in the mix.

Layer (d) is played by a bass guitar, loud and prominent in the mix (as is common in rap recording). The first measure accompanies the ii^7 harmony formed by layers (a), (b), and (c)—that is, the aggregate ii^7 formed by the addition of the chord-members of ii and IV—with arpeggiation from the third to the root of the chord.[39] The second measure initially supports the prevailing iii harmony projected in the electric piano. On the whole, though, the interaction of the bass with the other layers never achieves stability. For while the bass indeed supports the iii harmony of the piano in the first half of the second measure, the voice and synthesizer (i.e., layers [a] and [b]) together highlight the pitch-classes A and E, thus themselves suggesting a possible ii harmony. That suggestion, in turn, finds reinforcement as a prospective continuation of the first measure's harmony. So harmonically, while the bass in layer (d) reinforces the harmony of layer (c), it conflicts with the (at least implied) harmony of layers (a) and (b). On the second half of beat 3 in the second measure, the relationship reverses: the E2 struck by the bass dissonates with the iii chord in layer (c), while reinforcing the suggested ii of layers (a) and (b).[40] Thus, there is never a time at which all the layers consonate; rather, (a) and (b) together constantly exist in a state of tension with (c), while (d) alternates between the two conflicting harmonies.

But harmonic ambiguity is one thing (not uncommon in many popular styles), and the hip-hop sublime is another: for the defining aspect of these layers is that they are dramatically *out of tune*.[41] Whereas layers (a) and (b) are roughly in tune with each other (mirroring their harmonic proximity), layer (c) plays conspicuously sharp (roughly a quarter tone) of layers (a) and (b), while layer (d) plays conspicuously flat (again, roughly a quarter tone) of layers (a) and (b). Thus, even though the layers may sometimes form a stable harmonic combination within their own pitch levels, they clash at a much more fundamental level; they are simply not from the same well-tempered universe. It is the radical disparity in their composition—their incommensurability—that comprises the hip-hop sublime being discussed here.

It should be noted that the layers just discussed do not by any means constitute the only musical sounds in the song; they are foregrounded here as the ones that contribute to the hip-hop sublime. A drum machine, of course, beats out the 4/4 rhythm, and furthermore, in certain parts of the song there are other musical layers. As is common in rap production (especially from the time of hip-hop history in which the song was produced), certain "basic" layers are deployed throughout much or most of the song, whereas others are reserved for special events or effects. The MCing, of course, forms a crucial aspect of the musical fabric, often creating cross-rhythms with the more regular occurrences in the (other) musical tracks. Layers (a), (b), (c), and (d), however, form the basis for the refrains in the song.

The 'detuning' of musical layers just described has figured widely as a production technique of reality rap, and its sublimity stems from the musical layering's defeating the conceptual boundaries and unifying descriptions in our categories of pitch combination. It thus partakes of the dynamics required for at least postmodern versions of the sublime (i.e., unrepresentability, giving rise both to pleasure and to terror).[42] The resulting aesthetic effect may account for the widespread impression that rap music soundscapes sound menacing and aggressive, quite apart from the lyrical content: Many (usually more casual) listeners may be attuned more to the fear than the pleasure. But more important for present purposes, the hip-hop sublime had constituted at the time of the production of "Can It Be So Simple (Remix)," since roughly the early 1990s, musical "hardness" in reality rap music, and indexically, for artists and consumers, it encoded musically the urban conditions of community devastation and danger that the lyrics in the genre most described. The force with which that encoding developed into a classic case of musical semiosis can be seen both in interviews with rap producers and in the consistent pairing of the musical technique with semantic references to urban dangers and devastation. Producers, print media, and fans alike policed the purity of that semiosis, often with a ferocity and to a degree that would probably not be recognizable in the present, far more eclectic and playful hip-hop climate (Krim, *Rap Music*, 71–75). The hip-hop sublime framed for the listener at that time the fears and pleasures of the black, inner-city ghetto that both fascinated and horrified rap fans and our popular culture generally. In other words, this particular musical strategy had served, in rap music culture, as a figure for the view of inner-city menace and despair from the point of view of a trapped underclass. It had also served that function in the music of commercially prominent artists such as the Wu-Tang Clan, Dr. Dre, Nas, and Mobb Deep, among many others. A heady mixture of social knowledge and obscene enjoyment, the hip-hop sublime for some time anchored in sound the "reality" of "reality rap," a sonic shorthand for urban conditions inseparable from publicly projected identities of the underclass and the inner city.

The other pertinent genre in the present story is so-called "knowledge" rap, which presented a critical and contrasting view of the social function of rap music. Knowledge rap continued in hip-hop culture (and in some quarters does to this day) the centuries-old African-American tradition of music as oral history and pedagogy. More important, it had formed a locus of popular critique against hardcore reality rap since the emergence of the gangsta figure in the latter. A central and consistent musical aspect of knowledge rap had thus been an *avoidance* of the hip-hop sublime and a deployment, instead, of playful invocations of jazz, R&B, and other popular, mainly black, musical styles. The song "1nce Again" of A Tribe Called Quest

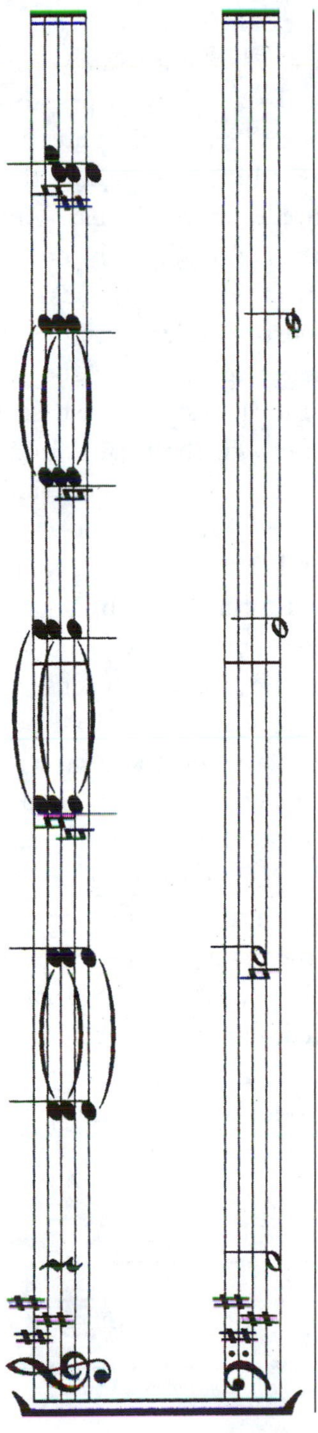

Example 4.2 Musical Layers in A Tribe Called Quest's "1nce Again".

provides an informative example, as the layers (combining samples and live instruments) not only are in tune with each other, but also form a fairly conventional jazz (or pop) progression.[43] Example 4.2 transcribes the basic repeated harmonic material of the song, namely I / bIII / bVII / V^7. Two things complicate the harmony, but only mildly. First, as the example shows, the bass guitar (lower staff) and keyboard line (upper staff) are staggered by one beat, with the former attacking on strong beats and the latter attacking on weak beats. This results, then, in some fourth-species dissonant blending of adjacent harmonies. But such staggering does not stand out as at all unusual in jazz style or, indeed, in many pop styles; the basic progression remains quite clearly projected. Second, the final dominant seventh receives color from the presence of an added minor sixth, which dissonates especially audibly with the adjacent perfect fifth of the chord (and prominently in the mix); but this, too, lies well within the range of jazz harmony, even constituting something of a characteristic gesture. In short, then, the song projects nothing of the hip-hop sublime, instead repeating a harmonic progression consistent with mainstream (especially) jazz harmonic practices, and all perfectly in tune. The situation described in my earlier portrait of the rap genre system thus consisted of the reality genre, with its hip-hop sublime, and a contrasting knowledge genre, with its sampling and emulation of older musical forms. (Not only the knowledge genre contrasted reality rap; but in the present discussion, the two may be usefully isolated.) And in the semantic realm, the reality genre, as its name implies, staked a claim to projecting bleak conditions of inner-city life, while the knowledge genre critiqued, sometimes even ridiculed, the luridness of the purported reality, positing its own counter-story of the richness of ghetto life. Figure 4.1 models schematically this generic relationship, as it existed previous to the mid-1990s.

REALITY RAP	KNOWLEDGE RAP
Hip-hop sublime; ghetto realism	*Standard pitch combinations; education and humor*

Figure 4.1 Reality Rap vs. Knowledge Rap Before c.1996.

But by roughly the end of 1996, aspects of that same reality genre had begun shifting, with only rare exceptions, to a blatantly contrasting view of urban life. In the newly configured genres, the transgressive wealth that had formerly characterized a third genre, namely pimp rap, seemed to infuse the reality genre, foregrounding fantasy and nearly obliterating any trace of the devastated inner-city surroundings. Instead of "signifyin'" marginalized subjects or street hoods from a devastated inner-city neighborhood, reality rap artists had become crime bosses decked out in illicit finery, heroes in narratives inspired by comic books or popular film, or, less commonly, triumphant survivors in a postapocalyptic urban future. Although Puff Daddy (or P-Diddy) arguably provided some pivotal examples before the trend had become widespread, the 1999 video for the song "It's Mine," starring Mobb Deep and guest-starring Nas, provides an even more informative example, as Mobb Deep and Nas had already achieved, at that time, status as central figures in reality rap.[44] The visual situations of the video draw from the set of images often called "Big Willy," referring to representations of lavish (and highly masculist) lifestyles and object worlds: in this case, the object world involves expensive speedboats, a lavish mansion in a tropical setting, multiple bottles of expensive champagne, MCs decked out in fine and costly clothing, and (of course) large numbers of women dressed in scanty bathing suits, moving provocatively. All the imagery supports the mainly "Big Willy" semantic content of the lyrics, a reality-style mixture of fantasy and gangster imagery.[45] Although the emergence of "Big Willy" style—or "bling-bling"—has been much recognized and discussed in popular media, fan magazines, and websites (many of the latter decrying what they see as "selling out" in its open embrace of consumer capitalism) as a phenomenon of visual representation, such commentary has not yet captured the sonic characteristics that mark this video as a new conception of urban life.

In particular, "It's Mine" instantiates the new kind of reality rap that tends to preclude the hip-hop sublime, the musical strategy that had previously anchored the genre sonically; instead, many of the song's features borrow the poetics of other rap genres. The refrain of the song tropes the highly successful duet of Brandy and Monica, "The Boy Is Mine," substituting for its refrain the lyrics "Y'all need to give it up / We don't give a fuck / What y'all niggaz want? / Thug, life, is, mine" (repeated once).[46] The singing, like much MC singing in rap music, is purposefully, even joyously, out of tune, thus retaining hardcore rap's traditional refusal of singing as comfort or human communication: Mobb Deep and Nas retain the detachment and carefree contemptuousness so crucial to the personage of reality MCs during the era of classic gangsta rap. But although the singing itself may retain that feature of older reality rap, the musical tracks themselves project a newer situation, confining themselves to a strong and harmonically conventional alternation between iv and i (in g minor). In older reality rap such harmonic alteration would not have been precluded, and in fact it appeared in songs like Raekwon's "Ice Cream";[47] but in that previous style, the detuning tracks of the hip-hop sublime would simultaneously destabilize the harmonic design, imposing the menacing character that keeps even R&B progressions "hard"—as indeed happens in "Ice Cream," which, despite its lyrical allegiance to the pimp (or seduction and macking-related, as described in *Rap Music*, 62–65) genre, maintains a hardcore sound. No such imposition troubles "It's Mine," however, which suggests itself as the reverse of "Ice Cream": whereas the latter, through the hip-hop sublime, retained a hard sound despite lyrical invocations of mack rap, "It's Mine" draws on the soft, consonant harmonic alternation of R&B traditionally associated with pimp rap to set lyrics reminiscent of the defiant "signifyin'" of classic gangta style. What previously, in the reality genre, presented a musical backdrop of stunningly unassimilable and immobile layers of sound—and it is worth noting that Nas and Mobb Deep had both been exemplary for the consistent sublimity of their production in their earlier careers—now became a fairly conventional soul or R&B progression.

Writing at the end of the 1990s, I mentioned this shift in persona and musical style in the context of the decline of classic gangsta rap, or at least its displacement to Atlanta and New Orleans (*Rap Music*, 83). Although that decline seems indeed to have been happening, and now may show itself as more or less complete, a significant complementary development may now be added, namely the transfer of the project of 'realist' ghetto representation to the knowledge genre. Rather than disappearing, reality rap's earlier project of a "hardcore" ghetto realism had been taken up within the knowledge genre that formerly had so assiduously disowned or critiqued it. Rather than project the realist project musico-poetically, as the reality genre had formerly done, the knowledge genre now began to take its representational cues mainly in the semantic reference of the lyrics and the visual settings of cover art and videos.[48] A contrasting video by three exemplary figures in the "knowledge" genre, Mos Def and Talib Kweli (known jointly as "Black Star") and their Native Tongues colleague Common (formerly known as Common Sense), can serve to illustrate the then-new arrangement. The video to their song "Respiration" adopts much of the project of ghetto realism in its lyrics and visual codes.[49] In particular, one can find there a blatant deployment of many of the music video codes that have come, within and outside rap music, to connote the project of urban ghetto realism: the video presents the architecture and street spaces of decaying neighborhoods, the brownstone stoops that connote at the same time earlier black community life and its still recent devastation, the struggling abject classes and decaying transportation infrastructure, and even the black and white photography which, in the music video world, encodes the idea that one is viewing the starkly real. The musical tracks, on the other hand, maintain the knowledge genre's previously existing jazz orientation, not significantly detuned but rather (by jazz-harmony standards) fully consonant. In other words, the hip-hop sublime does not anchor the ghetto realist project of "Respiration," as it had done in the reality genre.[50] More generally, the knowledge genre has, since roughly the mid- to late 1990s, hosted much of the remaining deployment of ghetto realism, from groups such as Company Flow, the Jurassic Five, the Black-Eyed Peas, and Black Star to groups on the periphery of the genre such as the Beatnuts (whose music often crosses over into the party genre).

All of this is to say that after all, the project of mapping inner-city devastation had not disappeared from rap music but, rather, had shifted from reality to knowledge rap. Given the intimate connection of genre to views of the ghetto, in hip-hop production and reception (*Rap Music*, 68–79), such a shift constituted a major change in the shape and workings of rap music. The two genres certainly retained their identity: public reception of their work (for instance in the fan

REALITY RAP	KNOWLEDGE RAP
Standard pitch combinations; fantasy characters and situations	*Greater variety of pitch combinations (not limited to the hip-hop sublime); ghetto realism*

Figure 4.2 Reality Rap vs. Knowledge Rap Since c.1996.

media and album reviews) retained their separation and continuity, while simultaneously marking the changes in musical style and semantic reference of the lyrics.

Figure 4.2 models graphically the new generic relationship in place by the end of the 1990s. There one can see what, in the context of hip-hop culture, constituted nothing short of a striking reversal; in an earlier state of the rap genre system, the reality genre prompted Nelson George's neologism "ghettocentricity," while the more explicitly didactic knowledge rap emphasized afrocentrism and even, as in the case of De La Soul, suburban spaces as loci of critique often aimed directly at reality rap itself (though just as often, sometimes equivalently, at society as a whole).[51] By the time of the release of the two videos in question (i.e., by the end of the 1990s), in the new state of the genre system, it is precisely the avoidance of ghetto realism that characterizes the mainstream reality genre to be critiqued, while the knowledge genre presses to restore its visibility. But in terms of the musical poetics, the two genres did not exchange roles or characteristics; instead, as reality rap abandoned the hip-hop sublime for more differentiated (and arguably, more radio- and crossover-friendly) musical strategies, the knowledge genre maintained its jazz-oriented and largely consonant musical tracks (though it should be specified that it also, shortly after the time of the two videos in question, expanded its musical strategies to encompass the abundance of dance styles in output of artists like Q-Tip and the Jungle Brothers—again, arguably in a gesture toward greater audience appeal). The genres still worked differentially, with the social signification only comprehensible in each with respect to the other; but the shifting of the project of ghetto realism denoted significant mutations in rap music's overall orientation toward the African-American inner city. And as long as reality rap lays the claim (whether justified or not) to representing the "real" or "hardcore" hip-hop music, its sidelining nothing short of the ghetto itself—sonically and imagistically—cannot be taken as anything less than a seismic shift. Thus, such a shift constitutes far more than fodder for popular music trivia, an aesthetic mutation among many in the constantly shifting world of musical aesthetics, even taken alone.

These developments in the genre system of rap music constitute, in fact, part of a much larger changing field not only of popular music, but of changing popular cultural representations of urban life in the mid- to late 1990s. In other words, one returns here to the rubric of the urban ethos at precisely that time, and from which, of course, the changes within rap music's genre system cannot be separated. But rather than return to that field of representation already outlined earlier in Chapter 1, one might more usefully focus on a specific social process whose force would be felt in the same landscape at the same time: Neil Smith describes a middle- and upper-class reconquest of the American metropolis of the mid-1990s, coining the term "revanchist city" to indicate the processes by which those classes have forcibly reconquered urban terrain previously thought to be threatened by the presence of more economically marginal residents.[52] Although such activity has always gone on in major cities, Smith identifies and documents a wholesale and coordinated concentration and acceleration ranging from the early through the mid-1990s, following a period of declining property values. Focusing on New York City, he outlines the colonizing of previously low-rent districts in Manhattan amid a general rise in housing costs (a dynamic familiar to any current resident of the island) (*Frontier*, 3–30, 140–164). Hallmarks of that acceleration, and the style of its progression throughout the urban United States, include the proliferation of gated communities, aggressive enforcement of vagrancy laws, loosening of building and planning regulations, and highly publicized jail terms for previously minor offences (all of these, of course, facets of New York City's much-vaunted "renewal") (*Frontier*, 210–231). Such measures have worked to increase spatial segregation and transfer marginal inner-city residents from low-income properties (or streets) to newly built and overcrowded jails and prisons; that, in turn, has reduced the mobility and visibility of the underclasses and their perceived threat to urban existence, along with the widely touted drops in violent crime rates. The reconquest of Western cities by the propertied classes has changed substantially the experience of urban life for all classes, some for the better, and some for the worse. Such developments were not random in their timing; after all, the middle and upper classes have always had an interest in securing the city for themselves. But the revanchist city acquired an urgency and salience, starting in the early 1990s, for reasons comprehensible only from a broader view of urban economic development, one that distinguishes between the 1990's economic boom and that of the 1980s, because that difference turns out to have everything to do with cultural representations of urban life.

Economic growth bears consequences not simply for those who profit from it but also for those who are left behind; and differing sorts of urban development host varying ways in which the prospering society deals with those who are left behind. Such factors precisely distinguish the 1980s from the 1990's economic growth spurts. The earlier economic boom of the 1980s had been publicly conspicuous for how it had left behind the black underclass of America, in the wake of the final devastations of central-city industry already mentioned above as one of the hallmarks of flexible accumulation. Sociologists and economic geographers like William Julius Wilson, John Kasarda, and Mark Alan Hughes have documented just how this happened.[53] The increasing crime and devastated physical and social infrastructure in such areas attracted enough media attention to shock the public consciousness (articulated, of course, with long-standing racist discourses about the largely African-American and Hispanic people living in such areas). Suddenly, the ghetto loomed large in the American, even to some extent the global, public imagination in the 1980s and early 1990s, and its notoriety, spilling over into the very notion of urban life itself, threatened the viability of gentrified neighborhoods established in the inner city earlier in the 1980s—the very neighborhoods that had supported the culture of the yuppie. Not coincidentally, popular culture registered this mutation in urban life with well-known musical and filmic representations of what one might call the "dangerous city." Cultural productions like NWA (Niggaz With Attitudes), *Boyz 'N the Hood* (1991), and *South Central* (1992) seemed to proliferate through popular culture, not caused by the deteriorating inner cities so much as staging them for a shocked (and fascinated) public consciousness.

But Smith's revanchism manifested itself not solely in the real-world property speculation that he details in Manhattan (and elsewhere); its expressive-culture vision manifested itself across popular-cultural forms, beginning about the time in the early 1990s when the US media environment discovered and romanced (what was in image, more than in reality) a city with sufficient social and spatial distance from the decaying cities of the Midwest and Northeast corridor, namely Seattle. Seattle then quickly attracted cathexes as a site for adventure, romance, and hipness on the part of young, (almost always) white adults. Fed by combinations of the burgeoning computer economy (and its attendant educated bourgeois economy of consumption) with the popularization of grunge music, Seattle's new allure and visibility in American media culture manifested itself with movies like *Singles* (1992) and, of course, *Sleepless in Seattle* (1993). But crucially, perhaps more through accidental prescience than through any direct causal relationship, the symbolic recathexis of urban life announced a broader development embracing a great many North American cities, especially the larger ones, and affecting the real lives carried on there; the economic boom of the 1990's Clinton era had then began to achieve visibility, with its own characteristic consequences for urban life. The 1990's boom actually much resembled the 1980's boom in record-high levels of corporate profits and stock prices, but it differed in the far more dramatic rise in employment, which was widely represented as fulfilling the trickle-down promise of Reaganism, a softer form of capitalist prosperity that purportedly did, indeed, raise all boats. A second major difference between the 1980's and 1990's economic expansion, inseparable from the first difference, stems more from intentional policy, namely the unprecedented crackdown on inner-city "deviance" that involved three-strike laws, mandatory minimum sentences, anti-immigrant fervor, and skyrocketing rates of incarceration for petty crimes.

Rudolph Giuliani's "renaissance" in New York City proved emblematic for conditions of the new city life, especially Times Square, which provided a prominent cultural confirmation for the American public that the underclass was then out of the way and, furthermore, had run out of excuses in the newly flourishing economy. The revanchist city was in full swing. At the same time, job statistics showed that many groups (such as inner-city African-Americans) enjoyed little, if any, more access to jobs and education than ten years previously. More to the point of flexible accumulation, many of the new jobs being formed were designed for the so-called "flexible workplace," offering less than full-time employment and little or no benefits. In other words, that "recovery" since the mid-1990s had instantiated the characteristics discussed above of flexible accumulation, solidifying the stagnation, if not the outright subjugation, of the lower end of the labor pool and the unprecedented agility of capitalism in extracting surplus value out of labor. Such does not imply that flexible accumulation had nothing whatsoever to do with the 1980's economic expansion, but rather that it was the subsequent decade's economic growth that solidified the spatial effects in the metropolis, in effect cleaning up the underclass problem for the more prosperous urban residents and workers. The black underclass in particular, having loomed as America's cultural nightmare and morbid fascination, had lost that cultural status, as its impact on city life had been largely neutralized for the middle and upper classes. Rather than imposing a threat, the impacted ghettoes now quietly shifted away from the center stage of cultural representation. Of course, as Friedrich Engels famously noted, capitalist urban housing "reform" does not solve problems so much as shift them;[54] but the clearing of urban space for more privileged subjects sufficed for the purpose of media representations.

Such expressive-cultural effects of the revanchist city arise not as aspects of a crude mass psychology but, rather, as assumed backgrounds to the literal and representational spaces all around those who inhabit the changing metropolis. They figured new contours of a naturalized daily life for urban inhabitants. And, indeed, it must be granted that the enforcement of spatial boundaries, mass incarcerations, and absorption of marginal labor into the flexible labor pool had, in fact, worked wonders for popular representations of urban life. One can note the visible and audible rehabilitation of the American metropolis just about anywhere in the great telescoping sweep from economic geography back to rap music, figured in anything from the new (and newly sanitized) family entertainment complexes in New York's Times Square to the romanticized urban settings of television shows like (the American) *Queer as Folk* (2000-2005), whose cozy streets, diner scenes, and intimate, renovated interiors conjure the urban libidinal investments of white youth in a manner reminiscent of the early 1980s. Music videos outside the genre of rap could more easily embrace the now-sanitized city, as Bjork's "Big Time Sensuality," the Corrs' "So Young," and Beck's "Devil's Haircut" all deployed varied visual and music-poetic strategies for imaging a contained and reconquered urban landscape.[55] Of one piece with the burgeoning return to large cities by educated bourgeois professionals, and the city's concomitant erection of barriers to segregate them from other urban subjects, the new regime of representation sidelined the very same impacted black ghetto that had loomed so large from the mid-1980s through the very beginning of the 1990s. As always (including, of course, during the days of ghettocentric reality rap), the prevailing representations of city life were partial, and tellingly so. Of course, the impacted ghetto was still there *materially*, but its relation to the dominant consumers of popular culture, and thus the culture industry, had been transformed. Hence the suggestion offered here that the sidelining of the hip-hop sublime, and the corresponding playing down of the impacted ghetto in hip-hop culture, was not a mere musicological detail of "It's Mine" but, rather, formed part of a much larger cultural mutation, an altered urban ethos imaging a newly sanitized city.

In another historical twist with happy commercial value, rap music participated in that shifting urban ethos at a crucial point in its fortunes: in the biggest market for CDs, the U.S., rap music had, by the beginning of the twenty-first century, overtaken country music to become the second best-selling genre (after rock); its commercial reach had been steadily improving throughout the late 1990s.[56] Thus, rap's turning away from the former configuration of the reality genre and its "ghettocentricity" figured in a significant development within the sphere of popular music, even popular culture generally, by dint of sheer market share, if nothing else. The corresponding adoption of the ghettocentric project by knowledge rap formed most certainly a less commercially visible development; but, conceived systematically, it was inseparable from the fortunes of all rap and hip-hop music, whose explosion into the mainstream of popular music bespoke a cultural significance that scholars who confine their research only to hip-hop purism tend to miss. As reality rap—in its new incarnation led by not only Mobb Deep and Nas but also Puff Daddy (or whatever one might want to call him), Jay-Z, and other venerable figures—abandoned ghettocentricity and celebrated fun, pleasure, and consumption, the more lurid, playful, and celebratory pleasures of the revanchist city found their comically exaggerated expressions there. With reality rap cleared of ghetto threat (even if knowledge rap strained to maintain it), genres outside of rap music could celebrate other urban subjects and areas of the city in their newfound liberation. Such systematic workings, between genres and also between expressive culture and other social relations, exemplify the urban ethos and its proximity to broader aspects of city life.

Conclusion

Given the ambitiousness of the arguments in this chapter, and the distance that the discussion has covered since the original focus on Adorno, it will be helpful to make most explicit in what sense the scenario and musical examples just outlined constitute a non-Adornan Marxism. Pursuing such a project of course also encompasses avoiding the cultural studies mode of "resistance" validation already argued here to be part and parcel of the problematic inherited from Adorno. In no way should one venture to suggest, for example, that the more commercialized reality genre represents domination and the knowledge genre the subaltern voice mustering resistance; such textualist and utterly symbolic struggles may have their place but hide the continuity between expressive culture and other cultural practices (including urban production). If anything, one might do better to trace the force of capital itself in the representation of inner-city devastation. The earlier centrality of the ghetto in reality rap had offered its own form of surplus value for these cultural products. That surplus value, in the wake of the shift in the urban ethos, had then been channeled into the knowledge genre, while the more commercially prominent reality rap merged increasingly with other aspects of (especially male) teen popular culture, such as sexual fantasy, skateboarding, video games, comic books, action fantasy, and wrestling.[57] The representational shift in the genre system had everything to do with changes in objective relations of production in North American society (and others), including what has to transpire in cities like New York to protect the expansion of its communications, financial, and entertainment infrastructure into areas like Times Square.[58] None of the present scenario relies on notions of cooptation or resistance, nor would it be significantly enriched by such a problematic. Furthermore, and equally important for a non-Adornan Marxism, nowhere in the situation described here must one try to map stylistic, representational, or formal homogenization to industrial centralization or integration (i.e., the mass production and standardization model outlined by Adorno). On the contrary, one of the more imposing developments in rap music since the mid-1990s has been a proliferation of new styles and generic hybrids, ranging from the Caribbean hip-hop of Wyclef Jean through the southeastern eclectic style of Outkast to well-known metal/rap hybrids of groups like Limp Bizkit and Kid Rock, not to mention crunk and other styles internal to hip-hop. All of this, one must hasten to add, unfolded against a background of increasing centralization in the music industry, as even majors like EMI continued to be gobbled up in communications mergers of record size. One could thus not posit any significant parallel between the structures of ownership and the character of the products (form or content). Therefore, something well beyond the Adornan problematic must be advanced to map all these developments. The lesson, as so often, comes from a return to Marx himself, for whom the relations of production, in their various forms (be it company ownership or musical production), remain always thoroughly historical. Nobody who has learned this lesson from Marx should be surprised to see many of Adorno's observations, as insightful as they had been for a certain period, fall out of sync with later stages of capitalism.

Tracking shifts in musical poetics and representation, and tracking their placement within capital and the social requirements of its accumulation, involves abandoning the monolithic and inflexible models of capitalism that music scholars (and others) have inherited (or interpreted) from Adorno. It also involves at least a critical eye toward the cultural-studies-inspired validations of the subaltern voice and its cultural praxis. Indeed, one of the hallmarks of flexible accumulation remains its stunningly successful deployment of subaltern subjects, both for new forms of labor like back-office organization and for low-level services—and, as Christopher Mele has shown, for cultural outputs like "world music," "ethnic" restaurants, and cultural festivals.[59] One need not extend this argument to the point of arguing that analyses from cultural studies must be set aside; in fact, they may still prove enormously valuable in mapping battles of representation in popular music. But an argument that embeds expressive culture in the cultural practices called production and accumulation requires a more detailed accounting of the term *capitalism*, whose specific meaning in scholarly analyses must change with the social system itself. Adorno's critiques have proven useful and could still do so, perhaps, with some major tinkering and updating; but popular music studies, and music theory and musicology overall, must track the profound changes in capital and its urban forms in order to get past the ghost of Adorno into a more versatile, complex, and, above all, contemporary Marxism.

5

Music for the Design-Intensive City

Much of the discussion in this book so far has consciously modified or avoided altogether the cultural studies paradigm that has now found such dominance in cultural musicology. The previous chapters have consistently urged, instead, a consideration of expressive culture that integrates it with other aspects of human life. The notion has been not so much that any instance (including "the economic") in itself determines the course of character of musical expression but, rather, that music occurs within, and is conditioned by, a wide range of activities and circumstances that are not in themselves "artistic" (though they may, including the economic, take on many aspects of artistic design). One would have to suspect that most musicologists who would characterize their work as "cultural musicology" would endorse such a notion, stated in such a generalized fashion, although in practice, even those rare musicological works that integrate cultural theory about music with discussions of society overall do so with the latter more as background to the former as foreground. In part, those approaches represent something of a strategic essentialism, as previous studies of art and society have often tended to underestimate the power of music in shaping culture. Also, the foregoing chapters have, of course, singled out urban change and conditions as particularly tied to musical developments, including the characteristics of much music per se; at least, they have argued that those aspects of human life particular to urban geography have been a heretofore neglected set of instances. Some music theorists and musicologists may well agree with that, too, or at least not be theoretically predisposed to challenge it. But at the same time, one of the more abstract, yet quite pressing, purposes of this book is also to establish a specifically Marxist approach to music theory and musicology; that approach would see the production and reproduction of human life and culture (the latter taken in the broadest possible sense) as irreducibly integrated to music (even if necessarily separated out for the purpose of examination), and it would also treat capitalism as a fundamental and systematic force. It is this last purpose that may meet with more skepticism from the music-theoretical and musicological community at large, given both the images (or rather loaded keywords, like "totalizing") that have attached themselves to Marxism and the lineage of cultural musicology in what are presumably post-Marxist paradigms. So in this chapter I will illustrate why such an integrated approach—one that looks, as it were, through both ends of the telescope—can alone offer, if not an adequate, at least a particularly rich account of contemporary musical culture. Furthermore, that integrated approach will constitute, by its nature, a challenge to the dominant cultural studies paradigm in cultural musicology.

One common critique aimed at that paradigm (including in popular music studies) has been that it tends to favor atypical examples of presumably "resistant" culture, foregrounding such examples at the expense of a thorough characterization of the mainstream; such skewing, in turn, may mischaracterize the cultural field at any given time, painting, in effect, a smiley face over a far more richly characterized historical moment.[1] Although the selective privileging of disruptive representations may have, at one point, formed an understandable reaction against the nightmarish vision of mass culture perpetuated in Adorno's writings (see Chapter 4), they now, according to this argument, offer a glorified picture of the present, portraying an overwhelming resistance to an absent dominant force. Indeed, a survey of the cultural studies inspired scholarship on music, "high" and "low," at the advent of cultural musicology would seem to reveal precisely such a scenario, in which "resistance" appears nearly everywhere and the few ordinary practices addressed find themselves redressed as secret rebellion (against dominant practices somehow nowhere exactly visible, or at least constantly vulnerable). Thus, for example, heavy metal really turns out to upset dominant constructions of gender, among other things.[2] Meanwhile, more recently the dominant sound of "Americanness" in the art music of the twentieth-century United States turns out ineluctably to encode queerness at its heart.[3]

Indeed, looking through the musicological scholarship inspired by cultural studies approaches over the past couple of decades, one could be forgiven for seeing resistance absolutely everywhere and wondering what exactly was "out there" being resisted! Surely, by now, the subaltern voice, according to these approaches, has so long and so thoroughly pervaded what we used to think was the great bulk of cultural production that it has now found itself transformed into our new dominant. And yet, of course, that would simply be impossible: the notion of resistant culture depends structurally on a great, looming normalizing mainstream, whose composition, however, must always remain fundamentally vulnerable to the heroic attacks that it is the cultural studies practitioner's task to document. Once such scholarly procedures constitute a mainstream—which surely has been the case in cultural musicology almost, if not fully, since its inception in the 1980s—one encounters the ironic result that the scholarship ends up creating the illusion of resistance everywhere and yet seems less fully to document precisely against what that resistance plies its force. Such endless—truly endless—vistas of the rebellion of the dispossessed and despised may well be comforting; indeed, the sneaking suspicion arises that such comfort provides the true function of such analyses, by which middle-class university intellectuals may feel engaged in genuine social critique and yet embrace a totality whose analytical description they have been instructed is a thought error. In any case, at its best, an approach stemming from cultural studies underlines the subtlety of the cultural world around us, emphasizing its vulnerability to the upsetting of hierarchies, the breaking through of boundaries. But, in the collective force of an accumulation of such scholarship, one eventually finds a sparkling sameness and a seeming ethical coercion to embrace cultural practices, at the risk of being (inevitably) identified with a (presumably immoral) condemnation of mass culture and a simplicity of thought that cannot see the subtly textured nature of culture. In the face of such intellectual pressure, often materially embodied in academic publishers or other professional organizations, even the best scholarly minds find it difficult to resist the resistance industry. One purpose of the present chapter is to present an alternative to such a virtual intellectual freeze-out, offering ways of analyzing commercially proffered cultural practices without the obligatory preemptive embrace but also without the categorical condemnation often identified with the absent figure of Theodor Adorno.

One of the great insights of cultural studies must be maintained, namely its view of expressive culture as a locus of struggle, rather than a reflection of the outcomes of struggles on other fronts (the latter a position often incorrectly identified with Marxism). Cultural studies comprises, to a great extent, an agonistic story about representational struggle. In other words, it addresses the right to construct possibilities for subjectivity and identity, about which kinds of subjects will be hegemonic and which ones will be subaltern—in other words, which ones will rule and which ones will struggle for recognition. Musicology and music theory came late to this eminently postmodern field, and, as suggested above, one cannot reasonably disclaim the exciting results in work ranging from Monteverdi through Schubert to the Village People and Ice Cube; however formulaic the matters of queering this or that, boosting this-or-that subaltern voice, and so forth, may become, some of the more imaginative ventures break such molds or present substantial intellectual matter despite their somewhat rigid outlines. And although such musicological and music-theoretical studies may have been, so far, more theoretically derivative and uniform than innovative, the adoption (or adaptation) of cultural studies nonetheless has proffered a problematic equally crucial to a genuinely Marxist approach, namely the close examination of the relation between the music we listen to and how that music helps to form the kinds of people we become and the kind of world we will live in.

Apart from the critiques enumerated above, cultural studies approaches in musicology and music theory may suffer less theoretically basic, but still pervasive, lapses. One such lapse appears, quite simply, in a missing term from the scenario of the kinds of music we listen to and their cultural effects, namely, the whole problematic of how it is that we listen. Although the modality of listening has attracted some attention in recent years, it nevertheless, in most accounts of music's cultural force, remains the hidden mediator.[4] Now, the manner of listening could also be a proper object of cultural studies: Shuhei Hosokawa arguably marries the two in his discussion of the Walkman phenomenon, although much of his discussion is structured by philosophical elaboration that, for much of the field, might be regarded as quaint.[5] And while that philosophical bent constitutes one of the essay's strengths, allowing it to range across some basic forms of social activity, it also highlights a conceptual ambitiousness that sometimes evades cultural studies itself. The latter could conceivably have much to say about the difference in demeanors expected of concert audiences, who are to maintain a respectful silence between movements of a symphony at a concert hall but cheer wildly at a concert of Jay-Z. Optimistically, one would hope that any investigation into such a differentiation of "high" and "low" genre behavior would begin by historicizing it, as it is surely just as historical in music as it is in other media. Lawrence Levine, for instance, shows that even when such categories applied for a long time in the U.S., they intermixed and aimed at audiences not associated, more recently, with them.[6]

Once established, distinctions between high and low genres do not disappear readily, despite some assessments that may in retrospect have overstated some recent twists and turns;[7] such distinctions certainly do change, intermingle, and modify each other, but cultural memory and even contemporary representations maintain the separation, even often in blended forms (such as chamber ensembles like Bond). Thus, whereas one crucial purpose of examining urban change in both classical and popular recordings remains to trace common developments across both, they will often operate as different fields (and, of course, there will be many internal differentiations as well). So for the moment, it will be useful to confine the discussion to the high genre of classical music, drawing out parameters of urban change before looking for comparable, if different, parameters in popular music. Classical music, after all, offers in many ways a well-outlined case for examining historical difference, comprised as it is of (relatively) unchanging texts set against changing traditions of interpretation. Thus, the performance of at least the existing classical canon—still the dominant basis of classical music culture—always involves a merging of older cultural practices with contemporary conditions.[8] In the case of the present discussion (unlike in most discussions of changing performance practice), those contemporary conditions are what Ellen Meiksins Wood calls the "force field" of new relations of production, and they have much to do with how changes in the material world, and relations of production, contribute to shape our experience of culture.[9] A close observation of such a productive clash of historical frames promises to contextualize the more text-oriented efforts from literary and cultural studies within a careful and nuanced look at the changes imposed on our world by the social effects of capitalism itself. As the following discussion, naturally, focuses on one particular aspect of those effects—namely, urban restructuring—it may be taken as only a partial glimpse of the far greater historical forces of that clash. It will also be argued that it is both a crucial and a generally overlooked determination of the changing character of classical recordings. Finally, some of those same shaping forces can be seen to open across genres into the character of music recordings more generally.

Glimpsing this process, however, requires a look through, beyond, and sometimes around the kinds of music production that tend to occupy the attention of music scholars. For by far the majority of discussions of musical performance tend to address the canonical repertory of Anglophone academia—Beethoven, of course, Mahler, perhaps Sibelius or Prokofiev, and similar staples of the overlap between concert-hall canon and those pieces (and composers) respectable enough to find a place at the table of musicology.[10] Although it will eventually be helpful to turn back to music recordings within that canonical repertory, beginning in a more eccentric place can prove instructive as well, by highlighting a paradoxical state of affairs, namely the remarkable gap between the standard objects that music professors study and the bulk of production and consumption of classical music in the world around them. Scholars tend to flesh out the cultural significance of classical music in the venerable scholarly canons of a mainly Germanic mainstream or in the new scholarly traditions of women composers, avant-garde excursions, or previously undervalued national or ethnic traditions; and complaints published about this canon are commonplace enough and surely constitute legitimate critiques in themselves. In the meantime, the world of classical music performance and recordings mutates with less scholarly investigation, and it would be instructive to begin in one of those mutating places: the burgeoning world of crossover classical. Crossover titles in classical catalogues increasingly have provided for the commercial survival of classical divisions of the major recording labels;[11] with their evidently more robust sales and greater media coverage, they also constitute to a great extent the public face of classical music (regardless of whether one thinks that they should). In their arguably more malleable character as well, classical crossover titles may more blatantly manifest trends that appear in subtler (but still pronounced) fashion in more 'legitimate' classical repertory.

It would make sense, then, to start with one of the phenomenon's greatest successes: the Welsh singer Charlotte Church's commercial impact suggests that her recordings struck a raw cultural nerve. Her debut album rendered her the youngest solo artist with a Top 30 album in the (n.b.) Billboard pop charts;[12] and yet in the U.K., with the same album, she became the youngest artist ever to produce a no. 1 album in the *classical* charts, as well as the youngest to have a top 5 hit in the UK album charts. Indeed, Church's designation as "Artist of the Year" at the first annual Classical Brit Awards (May 2000) suggests that despite her obvious crossover characteristics, her commercial identity remained firmly tied to classical music. Great anticipation (not the least by Sony Classical) attended Charlotte Church's eponymous second album, and it arguably represents a cultural event whose force suggests serious study.[13] Yet investigations by music scholars (or rather, their lack in this respect) suggest little better than a puzzled, or more commonly indifferent, silence. It was released not only to unprecedented expectations from a "classical" artist but also with a single ("Just Wave Hello") that already participated in a multimillion-dollar television advertising campaign by Ford Motor Company.[14] Indeed, Church's popular embrace has at times surpassed those of Pavarotti, Bocelli, and Domingo, but unlike those singers, most of whose performances and recordings continue an old tradition of potboiler arias and seasonal favorites, Charlotte Church represents a conjunction of that tradition with something else, a new social force observable in the vocal qualities, musical soundstage, and visual imagery of her CDs. Those vocal qualities can be observed on the track "*Voi Che Sapete* (Tell Me What Love Is)," which furthermore provides a useful handle on her sound world. Drawing as it does on "traditional," canonical classical repertory (the well-known aria from Mozart's *Le Nozze di Figaro,* K.492), it also may serve to represent a place in which her generic identity as a classical artist finds a (relatively) firm foundation. Set (unlike some tracks from the album) in a conventional orchestration and sung in English (hence the subtitle), the track floats her trademarked "angelic" voice above the orchestral background in a manner that is characteristic of her other recordings. Indeed, to a mainstream classical listener not familiar with her distinctive vocal sound, the juxtaposition of her singing style with the aria and the orchestral playing may initially be shocking. But the voice in itself promises to tell a great deal, and a more conventional cultural studies approach could go some way toward mapping it as a collective phenomenon. One could imagine, for example, that the recently hot field of white studies should have a field day with her, so to speak, "pure" and "uncolored" tone, and with her cross-pollination of classical material with that racialization of whiteness that the music industry has come to label "Celtic" (in this case, Welsh) music. A cultural studies approach could also reveal a great deal about the desexualized purity of her supple lines (since then rounded with maturity) and innocent pose, and on the other hand, that white female adolescence that acts simultaneously as our culture's beauty standard and as its stigmatized perversion. But notably, all these rubrics of analysis would remain within the realm of what scholars traditionally label as *culture*, i.e., would relate representation to representation, perhaps across history but always within that rubric.

One indication that theories of representation might sometimes encounter limits arises when one recognizes large numbers of similar representations developing similar characteristics at the same time. In this case, we need only turn our heads slightly to see similar gender dynamics behind the stunning success of Sarah Brightman. Brightman's commercial fortunes are among the few that can rival those of Charlotte Church in the classical genre: her 1997 album *Time to Say Goodbye* sold more than twelve million copies, while her successive albums *Eden* and *La Luna* then enjoyed congruent sales success.[15] With a similarly light, vibrato-free 'angelic' tone often set against more traditional classical orchestration (though also frequently paired with more popular instrumentation), and an ethereal, distant femininity (without such overt pedophilic overtones), Brightman, although she more obviously crossed over into Broadway, occupied similar spaces of sonic and visual representation to those of Church.

The meteoric rise (by classical standards) of similar stars like Charlotte Church and Sarah Brightman may not in itself be remarkable; after all, trends are just that—trends—and by definition they do not come in singletons. But far more notably, many of the sonic characteristics underpinning the two star crossover artists at roughly the same time found their way into the heart of legitimate, utterly mainstream classical recording: Anonymous 4, the American all-female *a cappella* group founded in 1986, became one of the star classical recording ensembles of the 1990s and early twenty-first century. Releasing *An English Ladymass* as their first recording on the quite legitimate label Harmonia Mundi (which remained their exclusive label throughout their existence), and taking their name from the eponymous music theorist, Anonymous 4 immediately established a signature sound.[16] Indeed, while many critics enthusiastically endorsed their recordings, others complained that their sound remained constant across what should have sounded like a varied repertory. Whatever the merits or demerits of their style, Anonymous 4 found a robust and committed audience—importantly, without adopting a crossover repertory or the sexy rock-star imagery often reproached in more successful classical artists—that did not substantially lapse throughout their career (whose end they announced in 2003). Appealing to mass phonogram buyers and critics alike, they won numerous record awards and sold close to 1,500,000 CDs (an enormous number for a classical ensemble). Their *American Angels* CD spent more than one year on the Billboard Classical Top 20 list, peaking at no. 1.[17] Their subsequent Hildegard von Bingen *The Origin of Fire* recording (their second Hildegard CD) debuted in the top ten of the Billboard Top Classical Chart,[18] and once their immanent (though oft-postponed) dissolution had been announced, their concert tour ignited loud choruses, in the critical press, of eulogies. Their new releases were major events for the classical media, their performances covered in the popular press to an extent largely unmatched by noncrossover ensembles. In short, from the time of their first release, Anonymous 4 represented, in public classical music culture, music-making of the highest order, uncompromisingly serious early music performance—presumably the opposite end of the spectrum from figures such as Charlotte Church.[19]

And yet one may observe in their sound some by now familiar characteristics, which in turn place Anonymous 4 uncomfortably close to Church and Brightman, namely their timbre and its framing in the overall soundstage. In other words, the collective sound of Anonymous 4 largely replicates the timbral aspects of Charlotte Church and Sarah Brightman, their vibrato-free purity, the "angelic" aspects that, in the case of the overt crossover singers, became prominent aspects of the marketing language. Indeed, it also figures regularly in their album titles, which stress images of angels and light. And whereas Church's and Brightman's pure timbres hovered over a contrasting traditional orchestral sound, Anonymous 4 performed "early" music, according to their authentic aspect, *a cappella*—and yet their recordings arguably found their equivalent effects, not in a contrast with orchestration, but rather in the acoustic space of the recording itself. Those recordings tended to frame the voices in a highly resonant space, in which the voices seem to float ethereally, losing their traces of corporal production: breaths, any reedy timbre, the shaping by bodily production of vocal sound effects, often against the singer's will—all recede in the beautified haze of floating, resonant sound. Naturally, much sacred music throughout the history of classical recordings has been set in resonant spaces to imitate church environments and, of course, are often recorded in churches themselves. However, in the case of Anonymous 4, rather than simply establishing authenticity or suggesting a sacred environment, the recorded space decorporealizes (if one may excuse the neologism) the singer's voices. The difference finds its constitution not only in the type of space deployed, but also in Anonymous 4's own vocal production, the vibrato-free, deadly accurate intonation, as well as the uniformity of their voices, which in turn projects the image of a single musical source. Although such a unified sound production constitutes, of course, the aesthetic goal of many vocal ensembles, in the case of Anonymous 4, combined with the kind of vocal production and the recorded soundstage, the result further erases the corporal presence of the singers. No one body under any circumstances could produce the three- and four-part textures normal to their repertory; but once the bodies of the singers seem to have been removed from the recording, the high timbre and resonant space offer a replacement suggestion; the figures of angels and lightness suggested by their album titles arise insistently in public discourse about the group (for instance, in many reviews of their recordings). An anonymous reviewer for the *Seattle Times* quoted in many of their biographical blurbs cites their "four pure voices whom many consider our best argument for the existence of angels."

Floating, disembodied female voices, contrasting any earthly existence (like that, in the case of Charlotte Church, of orchestral instruments), images of angels and light—one might be forgiven for forgetting that the discussion here centers on Anonymous 4, rather than on Ms. Church herself. And yet that is precisely the point: the highly gendered and specific cultural images—sonic, visual, and discursive—remain remarkably consistent between the 'high' and 'middle' music of Anonymous 4 and Charlotte Church (respectively). But at the same time, this gendered niche of classical music in recent years has attracted surprisingly little attention from music scholars, especially given the breakaway success of gender studies in music scholarship. The feminine angel as bearer of classical music will return (as do all good angels) later in this discussion.

Other remarkable trends of recent classical recordings that tempt analysis from cultural studies are not so explicitly gendered. One development that seems to have escaped the disciplinary grasp of musicology is the proliferation of recordings that blend classical music and environmental, especially nature, sounds. While maintaining generic connections to other products that feature nature sounds alone, such recordings often tout the specific identity of classical music to produce distinctive commodities: some prominent features of those recordings appear in *Dan Gibson's Solitudes series*, of which the CD *Beethoven: Forever by the Sea* can be taken as an illustration.[20] Each track reproduces a movement of a Beethoven composition, either arranged for synthesized keyboards, or (as in the third track, "Spring Sonata for Violin and Piano," reproducing the second movement of the named composition) performed in the original arrangement, in both cases with ocean-related sounds added. Indeed, in the case of the "Spring Sonata" track, the slow movement of Beethoven's Op. 24 sonata is played through completely, if blandly, with added sounds of ocean waves and chirping birds. As bizarre or comical as such an object may seem to scholars of concert music, it partakes of broader trends that together constitute some of the great new frontiers within the classical music industry; titles like *Bach for Relaxation*, and other recordings that gather back items in a company's catalogue under "lifestyle" labels, for instance, now constitute some of the preeminent vehicles of classical recordings to the general public.[21] The latter format differs from Gibson's titles in that it simply involves repackaging existing (usually older) recordings of standard repertory under lifestyle-related titles. Such recordings more typically flow from the classical departments of the major labels and significantly, the industry maintains a distinction in artistic character between the repackaged lifestyle titles and those, like Church's and Brightman's, that inscribe their crossover ambitions directly to the musical poetics. Such a distinction becomes most visible in classical departments' and labels' public relations messages—for example in 2005, when Gilbert Hetherwick assumed the presidency of Sony BMG Masterworks (the product of a merger like those discussed in Chapter 4) and assured consumer publication *Gramophone* magazine that his department would maintain artistic integrity: "I think that making records that are basically pop records and calling them classical is in some ways surrendering. We should look at the actual music and figure out ways to sell it. That will mean that we'll do lifestyle compilations, but we're not going to do anything to the music. We don't want to dumb the music down—we just want to bring the music to people in different ways."[22]

The "dumb[ing] down," of course, refers to Church's and Brightman's brands of crossover, whereas the "bring[ing] the music to the people in different ways" refers, at least in part, to the lifestyle compilations that he affirms will continue. Such distinctions carry, of course, heavy ideological baggage, and they remain all the more revealing for doing so, for they show to what extent musical poetics, in this case within the commercial culture of classical recordings, carries potent ideological force. Hetherwick relies here on the weight that consumers, and the classical media, will ascribe to the integrity of the score, the value of "the music itself," as distinguished from its packaging, the presumably insignificant manner in which record companies and retailer embed the music in the lives of consumers. Like any good ideology, the value claimed for repackaged lifestyle recordings helps to obscure something else as well—namely, their similarity to titles like

Beethoven: Forever by the Sea, in which music finds its marketing not in the notion of autonomous masterwork (despite Hetherwick's ironically relying on the force of such older notions in his publicity), but rather in its forming an accoutrement for a certain kind of quintessentially urban existence. Nothing explicitly urban intrudes in the imagery, of course; on the contrary, such recordings, whether repackaged mainstream repertory or specially manufactured to purpose, normally offer (like Gibson's titles), if anything geographically specific, the imagery of natural environments. But at the same time, such recordings rejoin the urban practice of design-intensive production, and this time, instead of the commercial process described in the Introduction, one encounters the *design-intensive production of the self*. Such design deploys classical recordings (among others) strategically, to emphasize either situations (e.g., the numerous titles associated with "relaxation") or even basic traits of humans (e.g., the numerous titles associated with the so-called Mozart effect). Whereas the design-intensive production of the self may, of course, take place anywhere, it takes its pattern from the total cross-marketed environment of urban retailing, the Borders book/music/café megastores that offer music as part of a totally controlled and designed environment. As the foregoing discussion implied, recordings aimed at such cross-marketing often mix "lifestyle" goals such as relaxation with religious and/or vaguely transcendent imagery such as that of angels. The musical poetics themselves may convey a generalized sense of transcendence, as when Yo-Yo Ma plays Bach chorales on his retro-authenticated cello.[23] Or sometimes, as with the case of Charlotte Church, even vocal timbre can translate into privileged cultural identities and identifications. Indeed, nothing elucidated so far about new functions of classical recordings necessarily implies that the properties of existing classical compositions make no difference whatsoever; it is probably safe to say, for example, that we are far more likely to encounter *Bach for Relaxation* than *Shostakovich for Relaxation* in the process of shopping for scented candles and "deep spirituality," and surely some properties of J. S. Bach's musical scores contribute to that likelihood.

Such recordings have found, by classical standards, an enormous success, proliferating, importantly, in points of sale that were unimaginable just fifteen to twenty years ago, such as houseware stores, bookstores, tourist shops, coffeehouses, interior design shops, and those businesses that market ranges of stylized products and are known as "lifestyle stores." And as Hetherwick's remarks suggest, such musical products, both his more respectable kind and the more scandalous products of Gibson, carry enormous importance in the industry. Although sales figures are difficult to obtain because of the scattered geography of the market, my interviews with classical distributors, and those in other genres, consistently indicate that a growing proportion of phonogram units are heading for these new points of sale. That information which is available indicates the prominence of the lifestyle (or "life-design") classical CD, especially in the mid- and low-price ranges of the classical recordings market. Billboard's Year-End Charts for 2004, for example, lists, among the fifteen top mid-price classical albums for that year, *The Most Relaxing Piano Album in the World … Ever!*, *The Most Romantic Classical Music in the Universe*, and *More of the Most Relaxing Classical Music in the Universe.*[24] In addition, a Gregorian chant compilation (in fact, reissues of the classic CDs that touched off the "Gregorian Chant revival" of the mid-1990s) marked a clearly related phenomenon of using chant for "contemplative or, indeed, relaxing life states.[25] In the budget chart, *Classics for Relaxation* topped the list, which also featured *The Most Relaxing Classical Music in the Universe*, *Classics for Meditation*, and *Moonlight Classics.*[26] Such figures at least informally suggest the power of this phenomenon within the classical recording industry. Unlike other less-studied subgenres of classical recording that nevertheless enjoy considerable commercial success—such as the operatic aria potboilers that essentially represent nothing new whatsoever, dating back at least to the days of Enrico Caruso—such recordings for design represent a relatively recent phenomenon, at least on the large scale that predominates recently.

The novelty of recordings like *Beethoven: Forever by the Sea* may also be underlined by observing the kinds of places where such things are purchased. The following table provides the relevant statistics, namely the volume of phonogram units for different points of sale in the United States between 1990 and 1999—the period in which much of the retail market for classical recordings began to show signs of dispersion.[27]

Table 5.1 Points of Sale for Phonograms, 1990–1999

POINTS OF SALE	1990	1991	1992	1993	1994	1995	1996	1997	1998	1999
Record store	69.8	62.1	60.0	56.2	53.3	52.0	49.9	51.8	50.8	44.5
Other store	18.5	23.4	24.9	26.1	26.7	28.2	31.5	31.9	34.4	38.3
Tape/ record club	8.9	11.1	11.4	12.9	15.1	14.3	14.3	11.6	9.0	7.9
Mail order	2.5	3.0	3.2	3.8	3.4	4.0	2.9	2.7	2.9	2.5
Internet	na	na	na	na	na	na	na	0.3	1.1	2.4

Note: na = not available.

Source: Recording Industry Association of America.

Most salient in the present context are the two top rows that measure points of sale, labeled "record store" and "other store." A remarkable trend emerges: while the category of "other stores" increased from 18.5% to 38.3% of purchases over that period, record stores as points of sale declined from 69.8% to 44.5%. In other words, what one can witness is a major shift in the geography of points of sale for phonograms; specialized CD stores, although still important, rapidly lost ground to retail sites in which CDs are not segregated, but rather cross-marketed. Some of that shift may reflect phenomena such as Wal-Mart's CD marketing, but the brunt of the effects of that development was not felt until shortly after the period represented here. Instead, the trend indicated by these figures can still be visible to anyone who patronizes the local supermarket, or souvenir shop, or interior design shop; in such places, one could hardly miss, for instance, the little free-standing shelf with a display of CDs and the miniature built-in speakers for sonic sampling. And whereas such a display surely marks the hosting section of the store as a musical space, recordings (mainly CDs) sold in places like these receive their marketing in relation to the other merchandise on display: perhaps a bag of gourmet pasta in the supermarket, or some decorative candles in the houseware shop, or jewelery that marks the wearer, like the *Beethoven: Forever by the Sea*, as a "spiritual" person. In other words, such recordings find their retail geography in cross-marketing; understanding such an aspect of them both underlines their place in design intensity and more generally highlights a change in how a good number of people buy classical music. Classical music thus takes its place in the world not only with coffee, gifts, and books, but also with kitchen utensils, gourmet food products, lamps, and furniture. And commodities like *Beethoven: Forever by the Sea* are not only destined for different points of sale from more commonly researched classical recordings, but also are more explicitly destined to different kinds of consumption from those normally assumed by scholars for more "legitimate" products. These recordings openly embrace their usage as music less for concentrated listening than for ambience and interior design. Such a function corresponds to the means of marketing, alongside the books one might read while such music is playing, the interior decor such music might enhance, or the kitchen implements with which one might be preparing a meal. Of course, music as a background for other activities is not in itself new, as anyone familiar with lounge jazz or Telemann's *Tafelmusik* knows perfectly well; what is new and worth remarking is the successful cross-marketing of these recordings with interior decor and "lifestyle" accessories for the design-intensive self.

It is not, however, simply the self that classical recordings may design, but also interior spaces. Here, again, the novelty lies not in the act itself but in its context and characteristics: music, classical and otherwise, has, of course, long held at least the potential to characterize an interior environment, and its deployment to enhance both domestic and commercial spaces enjoys a long and rather well-known history. What changes, in the period of the post-Fordist city, is the extent to which its deployment eases into interior design, and the extent to which its presentation openly and consistently embraces such a role. Here, one can begin with Yo-Yo Ma's successful ventures for Sony Classical, including the ultra-gentle Bach chorales of his two *Simply Baroque* CDs, which topped the noncrossover charts for quite a while—a phenomenon not quite equivalent to *Appalachian Journey*, or other titles overtly claiming the status of classical crossover.[28] Here, the cello claimed the softness of authentic timbre for ease of sound, while the very (well-publicized) fact of its retro-fitting simultaneously elicited a respectability that may attract traditional classical recording purchasers; the accompaniment of the Amsterdam Baroque Orchestra, conducted by their long-time music director and authentic stalwart Ton Koopman, of course reinforced the same dynamic. At the same time, the conversion of vocal music into lighter instrumental arrangements and selection of well-known Bach favorite movements outside their larger contexts promised a synergy with the already-established practice of "greatest hits" albums and their more overt invocation of lifestyle activities and situations. It worked: both recordings figured prominently in the Billboard Top Classical Albums chart (notably not the crossover chart), even together figuring in the top ten slots during 2000.

On first brush, such a phenomenon can appear quite distant from what progressive music scholars construct as the objects of study, namely the closely observed and highly articulated structural and stylistic aspects of music that form gender identity, ethnicity, and so on. But the examples discussed so far are arguably closer to that world than one might infer from the academic silence that envelops them, and another example can be invoked to illustrate that. Released in 1997, organist Christine Schornsheim's CD of Carl Philipp Emanuel Bach's *Organ Concerto* Wq. 34, with the Akademie für Alte Musik, falls firmly into the territory of legitimate classical recording, not even partaking of the open attempt at broad appeal embraced by the *Simply Baroque* releases.[29] That particular recording is, in fact, by all critical accounts a marvel of closely read and deeply thought classical performance; not just the gut strings and authentic-style organ, but also the careful, energetic phrasing, detached keyboard runs, and well-publicized attention to period style have imprinted on this recording a comfortable position within legitimate classical culture.[30] From one perspective, such a title would seem to be the antithesis of those Charlotte Church, Sarah Brightman, or for that matter recordings featuring Beethoven sonatas mixed with recorded ocean waves. Designed for close listening and thoughtful concentration, it hardly caters to cross-marketing with track lighting and kitchen serving bowls.

But from another perspective, the C. P. E. Bach recording falls closely alongside Yo-Yo Ma's relaxing and widely consumed Bach CDs, namely, in its deployment of musical soundstage. The soundstage of a musical recording arguably constitutes the most unfortunately overlooked aspect of professional discussions of classical music and culture, and of course it is completely missed in analyses that confine themselves to details of the musical score. The *Organ Concerto* on this recording did not differ significantly from that played on recordings by Klaus Kirbach with the Carl Philipp Emanuel Bach Chamber Orchestera and by Martin Haselbock with the Vienna Academy Orchestra, and other artists, from the standpoint of the published score;[31] yet in important respects it constitutes nevertheless a new type of object. The combination of the close microphone placement, spacious stereo imaging, and highly resonant space offers a telling illustration of precisely how this recording serves specifically contemporary purposes. The activity of each instrument jumps out in unprecedented detail, complementing the highly articulated phrasing and instrumental projection, but the acoustic resonance opens out a performance space behind and around the instrumentalists, in a dramatic contrast to the more consistent acoustic space favored in most earlier organ concerto recordings. The microphone placement alongside each instrument group would seem to place the listener directly in front of the instrumental players simultaneously, but the proportional volume of the reverberation implies a greater distancing, suggesting that the listener lies farther from the performing body as a whole. The two perspectives, one within inches of the players and the other set back within a cavernous space and listening to the orchestra as a whole, together impose on the listener a spatial experience not available in any imaginable live performance. All of this is to describe an *abstract musical soundstage*, not mimetically referring to any achievable live concert experience and not audible outside the mediating presence of the recording itself. But whereas at one point in the history of classical recording such attributes would have constituted flaws by falling short of the goal of concert realism, this abstract soundstage has, in fact, become an extremely successful and highly coveted recording technique. Such a playback space suggests a new manner of conceiving and constructing the recorded-music listening situation, diverging from the traditional notion of concert realism (which, however, in a continuation of older discourses, continues occasionally in classical-recording advertising to this day). It invokes the goal of private, indoor listening and takes that situation as its exemplary location.

The private-playback sound has achieved such prominence in classical recording that published reviews of classical CDs in such magazines as *Gramophone* to *Fanfare* and the *New York Times* tellingly often tend to avoid judgments of concert realism altogether, instead offering more generalized comments on the properties of the playback space. Such an abstract spatial arrangement marks the coming into its own of the interior playback space as a cultural and commercial goal; now where the listener sits down to consume the music becomes the salient reference location, rather than any putative concert hall or church. The designing of sound properties subsumes the (in any case, ideologically loaded) goal of imitating collective listening situations—a development not significant so much for any moral scolding of "selfishness" as for its indication of moving targets in the social destination of recordings.

One can see the force of the playback-location reference reflected across other developments in the classical music industry. For instance, it is observable in the commercial success of classical radio stations that deploy the so-called "wallpaper format," whose very name stresses its function as decor for an interior space. The relative appeal of music as wallpaper has transformed the classical radio industry: to take just one prominent example, the UK commercial Classic FM station has occasionally topped the ratings among commercial stations in Britain.[33] Significantly, that station conspicuously and repeatedly announces the function of its programming for relaxation, even naming one program (*Relaxing Classics at 2*) for the purpose. With such deployment, classical recording here rejoins much repertory that we think of as crossover, such as, for instance, not only the Charlotte Church, Sarah Brightman, and Beethoven/nature excerpts already discussed, but also albums such as *The Most Relaxing Classical Album in the World … Ever!*[34] The similarity, in this case, has to do not with repertory, or even necessarily recorded sound—in fact, many of the selections played on Classic FM are standard repertory recorded long before the period under discussion here—but rather with the goal of a certain interior playback space. However, although the argument in the case of Classic FM hinges on a certain repackaging of existing materials (as in many, if not most, of the compilation recordings cited here), those recordings destined, in the first place, for the abstract playback space indicate more forcefully a new conception of music and space.

Grasping the significance of that abstract space requires thinking it simultaneously with the cross-marketing of CDs in retail spaces, because the two phenomena bear intimate connections. The link of cross-marketing to the specific character of the playback sound lies not simply in the object world of commodities, but also more specifically in the *function of classical recordings to characterize and design an interior space.* Classical recordings of the type being discussed here serve much the same function that music does more generally in those houseware stores or gift shops: it is used to add certain characteristics to a desired space, i.e., as an element of design. It should not be surprising, then, to find that the characteristics of the playback area become, in this scenario, the predominant cultural and commercial force. To recognize such changes in the social deployment of music does not amount to mourning the loss of music's autonomy or greatness; rather, it follows the thick and often rather tangled set of cultural practices called "music" into a (in some respects) new totality, at some historical remove from the initial conditions in which that autonomy was conceived.

But exactly which processes of urban life suggest music's role as an element of overall place design? That question calls for a more thoroughgoing consideration of urban geography, and Figure 5.1 provides the beginning of that process, offering an initial glimpse of the kind of locations where these new cross-marketings take place. It shows an area of Lace Market in Nottingham, United Kingdom, a design-intensive and upscale area of that city that combines tourism with specialized shopping, entertainment, and restaurants catering largely to single young urban adults. Although Nottingham is surely a provincial city of moderate scale, it suffices to demonstrate that even secondary cities develop according to the trends described in this book. As a combination of entertainment and tourist destination, combining the two with retailing, Lace Market instantiates the political economy of contemporary developed cities, which have increasingly been turning to such downtown development as economic stimuli.[33] John Hannigan, in particular, focuses specifically on North American instantiations of such districts (*Fantasy City*, 51-100), although he indicates their

Figure 5.1 Lace Market, Nottingham.

growing prevalence as far away as East Asia (*Fantasy City*, 175-88), and one can readily identify a great number of European examples, from Amsterdam's Eastern Docklands to London's Camden Town. And, in fact, those two European examples both suggest an integral role for music, as both districts rely crucially on music as attractions and/or activities, with the Eastern Docklands partially anchored by its grand Muziekgebouw ann't IJ ("music building on the Ij [river]") and Camden Town a featured location for the purchase of "alternative" music recordings. Places like Lace Market, the Eastern Docklands, and Camden Town (and, of course, many similar ones) arose as relatively recent phenomena, having constituted significant aspects of urban space only over roughly the last twenty to twenty-five years. Although Hannigan has arguably documented this specific phenomenon most thoroughly, David Harvey supplied the classic description of the recent replacement of heavy industries in (especially North American) cities with centers that combine entertainment, tourism, and retail districts.[35] And, in particular, both Harvey and Hannigan describe the making over of inner-city areas as entertainment centers for those with higher levels of disposable income, mixing architectural innovation with entertainment venues and destinations, often also mixing highly stylized restaurants with small- (or large-) scale and specialized retail establishments. Such destinations enjoy characteristic physical attributes, usually either purpose-built (e.g., Amsterdam's Arena Boulevard, anchored by a large Pathé Arena Multiplex Cinema and the Heineken Music Hall, paired with the smaller Pepsi Stage) or exploiting existing, often 'classic,' buildings initially built for other purposes. The latter case often has occupied the focus of canonical discussions in urban geography, for instance, in David Harvey's description of the making over of Baltimore's waterfront as an entertainment, tourism, and shopping destination. In virtually all such districts, however, whether purpose-built or redesigned, some design-intensive structure mixes entertainment, (often) food consumption, and retailing into a cross-marketed urban interior. The FNAC building of central Barcelona, for instance, offers a modest proprietary café on its ground floor, through which shoppers must pass from the main entrance on the way to the selling points for visual and audio materials; the phonogram displays of the second floor, then, highlight the interior-décor-oriented materials, whereas more traditional titles can also be found in the less prominent displays to the side. Tourists and locals alike constitute the customer base, as the store's location in one of the prime tourist areas (the Plaça de Catalunya) suggests. Such retail locations not only market food, books, movies, and so on; they also market a new urban conception of space itself.[36] After all, one can find much the same music, food, and so on, in any number of other retail points around Barcelona, or many other major cities of Europe, North America, or East Asia, but the unique draw of such stores remains their character as configurations of urban space. One may visit them for an extended period, consuming a light meal and strolling through displays that not only market music as an aspect of the store's design but also market that music for use in domestic space. The transfer of design aspects from the retail location to the domestic playback space often may remain implicit, but the musical recordings, with their abstract space achieved in sound, offer precisely the needed mediation. Also, in the most fully achieved domestic urban design, the design intensity already pervades the space, as Sharon Zukin has been indicating as early as 1982, when she described for the first time the "loft lifestyle" (at that time identified with New York City's SoHo neighborhood), not materially wealthier than many of those that had been lived in some North American suburbs, but aesthetically and ideologically distinct in its embrace of urban space and new aspects of urban interior design.[37] Once that particular instance of domestic design intensiveness had been embraced it was commodified, in her analysis. However, far more crucial to the current context, such an embrace of interior design for urban living now extends to sonic design, cross-marketed with other commodities more readily identified as central to the "lifestyles." Such highly elaborate and controlled urban interiors constitute one of the significant mediating instances of the overall cultural and political economy of contemporary cities, in which production itself increasingly focuses on design, information, and cultural content.[38] Living in them, socializing in them, and experiencing other aspects of "everyday life" in them, the new cultural intermediaries see the habits of production that they develop at work realized in sight and sound, in the forms of habitation and leisure.

And precisely these hotbeds of artistic and cultural production form and disseminate the practice of music as interior décor.

The urban inhabitants of such spaces, then, frequently deploy music as part of the sonic design of their residential, automotive, or even working space. The integration of music with other aspects of design finds its retail equivalent in the cross-marketing of music in places like the Barcelona FNAC, or the many thousands of equivalent retail spaces in cities all over the developed world. It is toward such a deployment of music that the classical recordings being considered here seem to be moving. And, of course, the dynamic does not confine itself to retail environments explicitly dedicated to phonograms: those houseware, gift, and décor stores, not to mention supermarkets, which feature racks of CDs exploit the same cultural dynamic in slightly different ways, as part of a comprehensive package of design.

A great number of these classical recording titles, both those targeted to abstract listening spaces and those simply repackaged for sale in the new cultural environment, come to parallel other products that one might more commonly conceive as aspects of domestic design and personal style—art, painting, wallpaper, stylized lamps and bowls, and even clothing. As an example of the last-named item, one could recall that the two best-selling classical albums of all time, before the release of the *Titanic* soundtrack in 1997, were collections produced and marketed by the lingerie company Victoria's Secret.[39] That company started with their 1988 *Classics by Request*, custom-produced with the London Symphony Orchestra, which sold ten million copies—a then-unprecedented number for classical recordings of any type.[40] The success of that title, and subsequent Victoria's Secret classical titles that boasted sales of about 15 million, spawned similar measures and a specialized music industry, pioneered by Billy Straus and his Rock River Communications company. That company has produced compilations for, among others, Pottery Barn, the Gap, Eddie Bauer, Polo/Ralph Lauren, Restoration Hardware, Williams Sonoma, Structure, Lane Bryant, W Hotels, and Volkswagen. Although some of the latter compilations do not feature classical music, the classical titles of this variety share characteristics attributable to any such compilations, namely, the cross-marketing with consumer products and aspects of "lifestyle" marketing, and its blending into more aspects of design.

And such cross-marketed branding and design strategies often dwarf the rest of the classical music industry in scale: of the 16 classical albums that have sold more than 1 million copies in the U.S. since 1988, five were introduced by Victoria's Secret.[41]

But cross-marketing and branding do not form necessary conditions for the changing deployment of classical recordings. More ordinary symptoms can be seen even from standard points of sale, on classical sales charts, in which collections such as *Mozart on the Menu: A Delightful Little Dinner Music* vie with Andrea Boccelli and André Rieu—the more traditional crossover material—for best-selling status.[42] Named for an activity, time of day, or state of mind, such collections are targeted by manufacturers, and purchased, for the design and lifestyle aspects of those activities, times, and mental states. There certainly exists a political economy driving the wide marketing of such titles, as classical music divisions of large record companies find them an inexpensive way of recycling older performances otherwise difficult to sell, while saving themselves the expense of hiring musicians and producers for a new recording. However, in the present context, the more significant political economy is the one that drives the overall design intensity of contemporary urban life and music's fit within that dynamic.

A changing function for classical recordings need not be confused with their outright degradation, and a historicizing, rather than moralizing, narrative would insist on sidestepping what one might call the "Adorno mode." In other words, nothing being elucidated here need be understood as a narrative of decline, the inevitable car-crash of capitalist culture. And in particular, the loss of a presumed autonomy, in the face of greater integration in the object world of commodities, need not be mourned. Nor should one assume, if one inherently values attentive listening, that consumers of classical music in the forms described here necessarily listen less attentively to the music. Furthermore, the developments being described do not constitute the first mutation in the social deployment of the musical tradition we now call classical, and it seems vanishingly unlikely that they have ushered in a permanent new state. A romantic yearning, either for earlier stages of capital accumulation or for the feudal world, could itself constitute an interesting symptom but would be quite beside the point being drawn here. Instead, it would be productive to look back over the ground covered so far in this chapter and ask the question: Why could such cultural and social developments not have been adequately mapped by cultural studies–based approaches?

One of the principal weaknesses that would hinder a cultural studies approach to this material remains its inability to capture the intimacy of aesthetic and cultural developments (which in themselves it can map quite well) with the wider world of production and social organization. As a result, "culture" becomes separated from the rest of the social body, essentializing both rather than capturing their dynamic relations and dependence on each other for definition. Ironically, essentializing remains one of the faults often attributed to approaches (such as Marxist ones) that integrate culture with broader social organization, particularly when the latter focus on developments tagged as "economic." In truth, not only is culture economic, but also economics is cultural. One need look no further than the rich ways of life exemplified in economic organizations like Google or, for that matter, General Motors to conclude that the register of "the economic" begins its life in culturally shaped entities, through and through. Grasping the mutual dynamic, even the equation, of production with culture leads to the opposite of essentialism, a wholly relational view that locates essence nowhere. Although many cultural studies–inspired approaches totalize "culture" so that it may describe just about any aspect of any society, such a leveling, in fact, obscures the true ubiquitousness of culture, whose significance can only be grasped at the moment of surprise, when one believes that one is examining something not cultural and finds it, instead, quite saturated with collected human constructions and representations.

For this reason, there is no impoverishment of imagination when one considers seriously the determining force of objective relations (including music) in society. Now, of course, a great deal of postmodern theory is designed specifically to erode the notion of objective relations, even to portray such an idea as epistemologically barbaric, and (ironically) ideologically retrograde. A very long story lies behind this condition of postmodern theory, in which progressive politics has been equated with a certain epistemological and aesthetic avant-gardism, and Marxist notions like "objective relations of production" end up being as philosophically naive as, perhaps, the idea of philosophy itself. Peter Starr most likely argues correctly that the reaction against Marxism, and the framework of objective conditions, largely stems from the early French post-structuralists and the failure of the revolution of May 1968 in Paris.[43] But one could take the argument even further to suggest that the cultural studies emphasis on cultural struggle obscures just how changes in the objective relations of production themselves connect to musical practice and experience. The present discussion relating urban change to the abstract recording space proposes bringing that connection back into view and theorizing that how that set of relationships operates requires, among other things, getting past the venerable caricature that associates Marxist viewpoints with the Second International base/superstructure dichotomy, pitting the "purely" economic against the "purely" cultural and allowing the former to determine the latter. Although there have been some strands of Marxism that have at least approached such a view, most operate with quite different theoretical premises (and there is certainly no evidence that Marx himself thought in such a blunt or mechanistic way). Nor are they an instance of superstructure following base, as such a conception (let alone what "base" or "superstructure" might mean) models base and superstructure as primordially separate entities whose relation must then be coordinated, as cause to effect. Instead, it is more helpful to conceive of changing classical recordings and changing urban environments as mutually conditioning, each essential to the other. Rather than conceiving events normally deemed "cultural" as somehow determined by some mutation in the means of production, one might more usefully think of them as completing some kind of cultural unity—since, after all, the base is "cultural," too—not in principle different from the changes, say, in musical phrasing that accompanied new instrument design (the latter, of course, incorporating aesthetic priorities). Musical instrument design stands, after all, as simultaneously cultural and material practice; the fact that it owes its existence in the first place to the field of "culture" matters less than its embodiment of priorities, beliefs, and traditions in its very form. Precisely the same may be said about a bank, a computer, or for that matter, a city.

Explanations from cultural studies that isolate "culture" also tend to obscure the dynamism of capitalism, and the influence it can exercise on the character, and equally significant, the pace, of the object world that surrounds us on a daily basis. Capitalism since its inception has wrought frequent and far-ranging cultural changes, particularly noticeable at times of change in methods of capital accumulation. Most famously, Marx observed that in his world of quickly developing industrialization "[a]ll that is solid melts into air."[44] Despite the fact that scholars in the humanities tend to discuss capitalism as if its social force were ineluctably conservative, capitalism also nurtures, and at times quite dramatically unleashes, a revolutionary force, constantly transforming social relations at virtually, if not fully, every level. Cultural practices, including those of expressive cultures like music, do not tag along behind economic production, eventually being transformed by it, as in some caricatures of (Second International style) Marxism. On the contrary, they represent crucial means by which people of all classes operate in constantly and quickly changing new social conditions. Socially, one might consider eccentric, if not in some ways incompetent, a subject of our times living in a city like London or New York who knows only late nineteenth-century English as a language and whose musical knowledge ends with late Liszt orchestral poems. Such an example locates its hypothetical subject in cities from two advanced societies, precisely because cities tend to lead new developments in capital accumulation and cultural innovation, often owing their very existence and character to the particular advantages that they offer for such activity (or analogous activity in an earlier mode of production).[45] So the force of change, in the character of the object world as well as the speed of life, tends to concentrate especially in precisely such locations, where at the same time cultural innovators practice their vocations on products for both localized consumption and also distribution to more remote places. It should not be surprising, then, that the present discussion of musical (and other) developments in classical recordings focuses on the character of those cities, intentionally sidelining the fact that the people and conditions described here do not exist throughout the contemporary world; such cultural transformations eventually touch just about every place in the world, varying in speed and character with local conditions and local histories.

Music scholars do sometimes read across the variegated texture of social life and connect musical expressive culture to the wider totality—for example, in linking certain forms of instrumental music to the rise of the bourgeoisie in much of Europe during the late eighteenth and early nineteenth centuries. That truism of music history even goes so far (in most forms) as to isolate the rise of a certain (Weberian) class as a driving force in musical development. But regardless of the veracity of such an explanation—at a minimum, it remains incomplete and in itself offers no sense of mediation—it suggests the possibility of thinking music across greater scales of social organization, focusing on what was, after all, a fundamentally urban development (involving Vienna, London, Paris, and so on). Nor do music scholars who recount this story seem to hesitate on the grounds that the non-musical content of the explanation slights the integrity or continuity of musical logic; on the contrary, both accounts that treat intramusical developments during this period (e.g., Charles Rosen's) and those that propose more properly cultural or political stories (e.g., Stephen Rumph's) tend to borrow freely from the other historiographic style.[46] Nor should one be tempted to condemn such borrowings: to imagine some kind of inviolable line between musical poetics and other aspects of social life would be precisely again to hypostasize one or both terms. But such felt freedom to interpret jagged lines across the social totality too often remains oddly confined to this and perhaps a few other moments in Western music history. At other times, those who care in the first place to examine culture in the context of broader social organization normally separate the two, with culture somehow reacting to social structure (and in the case of cultural studies, often against it). In the meantime, our glimpses of music and its interaction with urban form remain sporadic, as if the changes wrought on cities by capitalism only occasionally burst into visibility, by fiat. But changes in cities continue to produce spaces in which music continues its own transformations.

The molding of many classical recordings into roughly interchangeable modular designs for urban interiors would then constitute only one of the most recent mutual conditionings between changing urban space and musical practice. As the discussion until now strongly implies, that development would carry little force, were it confined to music alone. On the contrary, music's value in stylizing and designing interior space may be increasing, but it does so simply in the context of increasingly stylized space for urban interiors across the board. In fact, the cross-marketing of music already mentioned in connection with Rock River Communications most likely enjoys the status of symptom: the newer sales strategies reflect the use of both music and the other commodities to design (principally domestic) interiors. Of course, one will find variations in how precisely the music and the other commodity (or commodities) contribute to the design. The music itself most likely bears most of the weight of that process in the case of Victoria's Secret collections mentioned earlier (perhaps enhanced by the preexisting product's association with the bedroom), while in the case of Starbucks' well-known and highly successful jazz CDs, customers may well have transferred (so to speak) some aspects of the design-intensive (if highly standardized) shops to their own domestic environment.[47] But whatever the particular combination, such often high-selling recordings project music out of the world of disinterested listening into the object world of not only commodities, but also of changing urban spaces of habitation and the consumption of products and services.

Viewed from the perspective of urban space, these processes spread music across the spaces of new urban shopping and entertainment districts, more closely associating the character of that music with mental/physical states (like relaxation), particular activities, districts, and even urban spatial configurations. In relation to this last item, one might recall the racks of CDs prominently displayed in many houseware stores, marketing a full range of branded "lifestyles" for consumption in the privileged urban surroundings of luxury condominiums in renovated abandoned factories, wharves, and warehouses. Of course, such CDs can be consumed in other spaces, but their partnership with interior design finds its nascent forms in developing practices of urban design: large urban centers form, develop, and distribute the recordings and marketing strategies.[48] Even in cases where such a musical product emanates from outside a major urban center, one can easily recognize a cultural practice originating elsewhere: just as music-compositional styles such as twelve-tone composition may originate in an urban context and eventually find dissemination to the most distant, sometimes rural, regions, so might a deployment of music endemic to large urban centers be replicated in other spaces—the Schornsheim/Carl Philipp Emanuel Bach recording thus was produced by French Harmonia Mundi, whose headquarters lies just outside the small Provençal city of Arles.

Although classical recordings arguably most clearly reflect the new function, such a shift in music's deployment would not likely be confined to that genre. In fact, the gradual incorporation of various traditional and "world" musics to the category of "high" art would suggest that, at a minimum, one may find closely related developments there. But the growth of music as interior design arguably has pervaded quite a few musical genres, high and low alike. Certain kinds of popular music, for instance, may be deployed as means to characterize a space: producers of some kinds of electronica, for instance, quite often work with explicit concepts of opening up musical space, while at the same time designing the music to stylize a dance club. Hip-hop producers sometimes also speak of effects like vinyl surface noise as a way of opening up the sound of space between playback speakers. At the same time, the danger looms of overgeneralizing: popular music has its own ideological histories and meanings, less suited to the spatial deployments that are coming to characterize many classical recordings. For instance, the old ideology of direct, emotional communication by the performer has probably helped to secure the many popular genres from a lot of the social change being detailed in this discussion. Nevertheless, some popular music genres also help to provide a soundscape for design-intensive urban interiors, and they do so, arguably, just as classical recordings do, by targeting a soundscape to the design or desired ethos of the private playback space. In contrast to traditional uses like that of Muzak, which attempts to set a mood through the conscious or unconscious attention of the listener to the music,[49] and which of course enjoys a long history in elevators, dentists' offices, and supermarkets, popular soundscape music attempts a closer assimilation to physical space. Given the developing urban deployments of space discussed in the Introduction to this book, those playback spaces would most likely include private and highly isolated interiors, be it highly stylized and differentiated dance clubs or clothing stores, or, for that matter, automobiles or living rooms. Symptomatic of the growing significance of soundscape, the star producer has risen to prominence since roughly the early 1990s, the Goldies and the Dr. Dres of the musical world. Here, history does not repeat itself: the star producer does not recycle the Phil Spector phenomenon, in which a single innovative sound strategy transforms the whole genre system and sets a widely imitated trend. Although that does occur now (and the RZA illustrated this well in the mid-1990s), the system of star producers rather proffers a range of different soundscape strategies, branded with the names of favored production specialists. Unlike the classical recordings just discussed, the recordings of the star producers almost never label themselves for a particular environment or "lifestyle" activity. Instead, they rely for their marketing on star-texts and other systems of fandom and publicity not nearly as well established in the classical music world. But in many cases, those soundscapes prove no less crucial than those of the classical genre in branding urban interiors and spaces. It can be recalled here, too, that not only jazz but also many other kinds of popular music found themselves featured in Rock River Communications releases, not to mention those of Starbucks (self-produced in conjunction with the jazz label Concord Records). The new marketing strategies and points of sale for popular releases cannot be dismissed as statistically insignificant: it was none other than Starbucks' Hear Music label (again in conjunction with Concord Records) that issued Ray Charles' final release, *Genius Loves Company*, which achieved triple-platinum status and won eight Grammy awards.[50] None of Charles' previous albums had achieved even single-platinum status, and the CD was thus by far the best-selling of his career, reaching second place on the Billboard Album charts (the first time that Charles had reached that chart since 1964). Such a development does not simply constitute an instance of a beverage retailer's expanding into a new product line but, rather, illustrates the present argument concerning new points of sale: Starbucks itself sold approximately 25% of those copies.[51] So pivotal have music sales become to Starbucks that they have begun to stand their cross-marketing strategy on its head: Starbucks is presently opening Hear Music cafés in the U.S., in which music shoppers may sip their coffee while purchasing existing CDs or customizing their own from the Hear Music collection. In the meantime, a Hear Music channel was initiated on XM Satellite Radio in 2004. The traditional cross-marketing from Starbucks itself, however, continues to anchor its sales, especially appealing to older buyers not well served by traditional music retailers and urban professionals whose schedules and habits encourage one-stop, lifestyle-driven shopping. The repertory of such releases, predominantly light jazz, acoustic song, and older rock, consistently (and explicitly) suggests the adult sophistication that Starbucks takes care to project in their retail locations, so that the recordings, as mentioned earlier, suggest a transfer of that one indoor environment to the playback location—the often heavily secured living rooms and cars of the more privileged urban subjects.

Companies like Rock River Communications and Hear Music, not to mention the classical labels already discussed earlier, form conditions of possibility behind new patterns of musical consumption that take music as an aspect of private decor for an interior space. More speculative questions could and do surround whether such patterns necessarily imply equally new ways of listening. One could certainly at least reasonably infer that in such a mode of listening, aspects of spatial projection, as already mentioned, would occupy a crucial role. More speculatively, timbre, texture, phrasing, pace, and other aspects that contribute to an overall 'atmosphere' may play a greater role in the music's appropriateness to interior design than musical form, as commonly conceived (i.e., intramusical, mainly pitch- and rhythm-based relations that unfold over time). It may, at some time, prove useful as well to inquire whether, just as in classical music, the abstract musical soundstage has, to a large extent, displaced the mimesis of live performance as a standard of judgment. The spatial properties of some popular recordings may themselves have achieved a similar autonomy. Of course, that autonomy of the playback space has always existed to some extent, especially after unabashed studio-oriented releases like the Beach Boys' *Pet Sounds* and the Beatles' *Sgt. Pepper's Lonely Hearts Club Band*.[52] So the transfer from mimetic to intrinsic judgments about the recorded soundscape may not be nearly as palpable as in the case of classical recordings; nonetheless, one may argue that many of the forms of popular music that have emerged in the last decade or two represent a quantitative and qualitative change. Electronica's spatializing tendencies have already been mentioned, as well as the constraint that the ideology of direct communication may exercise on the spatializing of popular genres; but in fact, even those two apparently opposed worlds may come together, under the right conditions. A close listening to the musical poetics of songs like Bjork's "Hunter" may capture both the urgent communication impressed on the listener as well as that relatively recent sense of autonomous soundscape.[53] Quite a few of Bjork's soundscapes, in fact, exemplify what is being described here, and the artist herself often discusses her recordings in such terms, as with *Vespertine*: "I needed this album to explore what we sound like on the inside ... worshipping the home and finding that paradise underneath the kitchen table."[54] Indeed, in the majority of the publicity that I have seen for this album, Bjork mentions prominently its theme of domestic space.

Bjork's highly emotive, emotionally vulnerable music thus, perhaps surprisingly, shares a cultural field with a good deal of recorded rap music, in which the manner of a recording's filling the playback space remains so crucial, culturally and commercially, that it is not at all uncommon for CDs to advertise guest producers, assuring the consumer that the "beats" on the CD will fill the playback space in trademarked ways. The beat, of course, occupies a crucial position in hip-hop production and reception, and its appreciation could never be reduced to interior décor.[55] But, for that matter, even the classical recordings used for that purpose cannot entirely be reduced to a matter of spatial design; they do, after all, benefit from the historical prestige of the genre, the musical poetics of (usually) tonal or modal composition and appreciation, and so on. But in the case of hip-hop, the embrace of the producer's art, his or (rarely) her ability to create a spatialized sound world, blends with the commodifying tag of that producer's name (as also in electronica) in a particularly conspicuous manner. The rap/hip-hop producer Timbaland, for example, has long formed a branded value added to quite a few rap and hip-hop albums. The high-selling MC Nas drew on Timbaland (Tim Mosley) to brand the song "You Owe Me" on Nas's album *Nastradamus*, and for the initial release of the album, a sticker on the front of the CD advertised Timbaland's presence.[56] Of course, by now, such promotion has become standard and not only within the context of hip-hop (though it most often appears in the case of hip-hop–associated producers). In such cases, the advertising in no way suggests that the musical soundscape imitates any possible live performance; in fact, in many live situations such music sounds quite different, as anyone who has attended a rap performance quickly finds. But the star producers maintain their value not for anything they could perform in a concert but rather for the way that their beats fill the room that they are played in—or as is often the case with rap music, the way they fill a car, a jeep, or a club dance floor. One could certainly argue some specificity to the history of rap music in this case: Los Angeles car culture nurtured the so-called "jeep beats," tracks mixed specifically for playback in car audio systems. Jeep beats occupy something of a special case, an urban interior playback space deserving a discussion of its own in both the contexts of rap music and of Los Angeles.[57]

The similarity of developments between classical and popular recordings also undermines the disciplinary separation that often exists in contemporary musicology and music theory between popular and classical music, which may itself stymie observations and explanations that require a more totalizing view. Of course, taking both high and low genres together would stem, in any case, from the generality of the theses in this book: surely, if the changes affecting contemporary developed cities are as drastic as I (and many urban geographers) claim, it would have to be odd indeed were such changes to affect only one category of music and not the other. Although Robert Fink may well have been premature in announcing the demise of classical music as a distinct genre (or set of genres), his vista of intermingling surely complements the similar tendencies already observed in this chapter.[58] Differences among kinds of sounds providing interior design abound, of course, in their types, deployment, and additional social uses, and cultural studies illuminates such differences particularly well. However, in the present context, the similarities remain more revealing, whether one examines Timbaland, Bjork, or, more surprisingly, the C. P. E. Bach organ concerto, Sarah Brightman, Charlotte Church, or even the CD of the Beethoven "Spring" sonata by the ocean. All these commodities, taken together, suggest a proliferation in our culture of recordings that may legitimately be tagged as interior design, and by implication new urban spaces in which those recordings are marketed and consumed.

Taken together, the changing face of musical recordings generally and classical recordings in particular suggests that when considering how listening takes place, in the very concrete sense of material circumstances, one may discover culturally significant aspects of music not generally conveyed by a cultural studies examination of the music or discourses that surround it. The changes shared between musical culture and urban spaces by no means separate themselves entirely from the properly postmodern intersection of discourse, power, and the subject; on the contrary, postmodern theories of culture have at times proven indispensable for understanding music's role in identity formation. But such a rubric less successfully captures, and sometimes might even obscure, other kinds of social organization, particularly those that bridge discourse and more mundane operations of social organization like working, stopping for coffee and a CD on the way to work, or relaxing to *Classical Chillout*.[59] Such daily activities—the real stuff of Marxism, or at least its equivalent of the now-too-fashionable and often mystifying concept of "daily life"—may often shape discourse but are not themselves discursive. They also form some of the less often examined content of urban restructuring. Such restructurings, after all, do not simply partake of abstractions or economic determinism, but rather inscribe themselves in lived experience, that is, the places in the city where one encounters the jagged edges of discourse and the spatial effects of social relations on a daily basis.

Notes

Introduction

1. Population Reference Bureau, Human Population: Fundamentals of Growth Patterns of World Urbanization, at http://www.prb.org/Content/NavigationMenu/PRB/Educators/Human_Population/Urbanization2/Patterns_of_World_Urbanization1.htm (accessed November 8, 2005).
2. Allen Scott, *The Cultural Economy of Cities*, Thousand Oaks, CA: Sage, 2000 (hereafter cited in text as *Cultural Economy*).
3. Saskia Sassen, *The Global City: New York, London, Tokyo*, Princeton, NJ: Princeton University Press, 1991 (hereafter cited in text as *Global City*).
4. Derek Wynne, *The Culture Industry: The Arts in Urban Regeneration*, Aldershot: Ashgate, 1992.
5. Scott Lash and John Urry, *Economies of Signs and Space*, Thousand Oaks, CA: Sage Publications, 1994 (hereafter cited in text as *Economies*); David Harvey, *The Condition of Postmodernity: An Enquiry into the Origins of Cultural Change*, Oxford: Blackwell, 1989 (hereafter cited in text as *Condition*).
6. Lawrence Kramer, *Music as Cultural Practice, 1800–1900*, Berkeley, CA: University of California Press, 1990, provides an example of the former; Susan McClary, *Feminine Endings: Music, Gender, and Sexuality*, Minneapolis, MN: University of Minnesota Press, 1991, provides an example of the latter (along with, of course, many works since).
7. Derek Sayer, *The Violence of Abstraction: The Analytic Foundations of Historical Materialism*, Oxford: Blackwell, 1987, pp. 50–82 (hereafter cited in text as *Violence*).
8. Karl Marx, *A Contribution to the Critique of Political Economy*, 1859; London: Lawrence and Wishart, 1975.
9. Gerald Cohen, *Karl Marx's Theory of History: A Defence*, Oxford: Oxford University Press, 1978.
10. Karl Marx, *Grundrisse: Foundations of the Critique of Political Economy*, 1858; Harmondsworth: Penguin Books, 1993.
11. The 1846 work that Sayer quotes is Karl Marx and Friedrich Engels, *The German Ideology*, Amherst, NY: Prometheus Books, 1998.
12. Andy Merrifield, *Metromarxism: A Marxist Tale of the City*, New York: Routledge, 2002, proceeds along similar lines to those being advocated here.
13. Michael Piore and Charles Sabel, *The Second Industrial Divide: Possibilities for Prosperity*, New York: Basic Books, 1984.

14. John Tomaney, A new paradigm of work organisation and technology?, in *Post-Fordism: A Reader*, Ash Amin, Ed., Oxford: Blackwell, 1994, pp. 157–194.
15. Sharon Zukin, in her classic study penned before the coining of "post-Fordism," traces Manhattan's de-industrialization back to the 1950s (and its planning all the way to the 1920s). She specifies, however, that Manhattan formed a vanguard in this respect. Sharon Zukin, *Loft Living: Culture and Capital in Urban Change*, Baltimore, MD: Johns Hopkins University Press, 1982 (hereafter cited in text as *Loft Living*).
16. "Youngstown" appears in Bruce Springsteen, *The Ghost of Tom Joad*, Columbia 67484, 1995.
17. William Julius Wilson, *When Work Disappears: The World of the New Urban Poor*, New York: Random House, 1996.
18. Mark Alan Hughes, Formation of the impacted ghetto: evidence from large metropolitan areas, 1970–1980, *Urban Geography*, 11(3), 265–284, 1990.
19. Allen Scott, *Regions and the World Economy: The Coming Shape of Global Production, Competition, and Political Order*, Oxford: Oxford University Press, 1998.
20. Manuel Castells, *The Rise of the Network Society*, Oxford: Blackwell, 1996.
21. Justin O'Connor, Left loafing: cultural consumption and production in the postmodern city, in *From the Margins to the Centre: Cultural Production and Consumption in the Post-Industrial City*, Justin O'Connor and Derek Wynne, Eds., Aldershot: Ashgate, 1996, pp. 49–90.
22. Mike Davis, *City of Quartz: Excavating the Future of Los Angeles*, London: Verso, 1990, pp. 221–264 (hereafter cited in text as *City of Quartz*).
23. John Hannigan, *Fantasy City: Pleasure and Profit in the Postmodern Metropolis*, New York: Routledge, 1998 (hereafter cited in text as *Fantasy City*).
24. Charles Euchner, Tourism and sports: the serious competition for play, in *The Tourist City*, Dennis Judd and Susan Fainstein, Eds., New Haven, CT: Yale University Press, 1999, pp. 215–232.
25. Saskia Sassen and Frank Roost, The city: strategic site for the global entertainment industry, *The Tourist City*, Dennis Judd and Susan Fainstein, Eds., New Haven, CT: Yale University Press, 1999, pp. 143–154.
26. Derek Wynne and Justin O'Connor, Consumption and the postmodern city, *Urban Studies*, 35(5–6), 841–864, 1998.
27. Scott, *Regions and the World Economy*, pp. 76–97.
28. Richard Peterson, Understanding audience segmentation: from elite and mass to omnivore and univore, *Poetics*, 21, 243–258, 1992; Richard Peterson and Albert Simkus, How musical tastes mark occupational status groups, in *Cultivating Differences: Symbolic Boundaries and the Making of Inequality*, Michele Lamont and Marcel Fournier, Eds., Chicago, IL: University of Chicago Press, 1992, pp. 152–186; Koen van Eijck, Social differentiation in musical taste patterns, *Social Forces*, 79(3), 1163–1185, 2001.

29. Anastasia Loukaitou-Sideris and Tridib Banerjee, *Urban Design Downtown: Poetics and Politics of Form*, Berkeley, CA: University of California Press, 1998.
30. Bruce Ehrlich and Peter Dreier, The New Boston discovers the old: tourism and the struggle for a liveable city, in *The Tourist City*, Dennis Judd and Susan Fainstein, Eds., New Haven, CT: Yale University Press, 1999, pp. 155–178.
31. Jonathan Raban, *Soft City*, London: Hamilton Press, 1974. David Harvey's *Condition* famously opens with a critique of Raban's study.
32. Fredric Jameson, Postmodernism, or the cultural logic of capitalism, *New Left Review*, 146, 53–92, 1984.
33. Postmodern theory might nevertheless be described as a historically urban phenomenon, developed by intellectuals in urban centers like Paris, New York, and Los Angeles, and arguably describing phenomena more specifically urban than is often acknowledged in the canonical writings. So perhaps the tag "postmodern" *does* convey the specificity of urban experience after all, but as a hidden and unacknowledged premise.
34. Neil Smith, *The New Urban Frontier: Gentrification and the Revanchist City*, New York: Routledge, 1996, pp. 3–29, 210–231 (hereafter cited in text as *New Urban Frontier*). Davis, *City of Quartz*, 221–264.
35. Edward Blakely, *Fortress America: Gated Communities in the United States*, Washington, DC: Brookings Institution Press, 1997.
36. Jonathan Sterne, Sounds like the mall of America: programmed music and the architectonics of commercial space, *Ethnomusicology*, 41(1), 22–50, 1997.
37. Adam Krims, Marxism, urban geography, and classical recording: an alternative to cultural studies, *Music Analysis*, 20(3), 347–363, 2001.
38. Adam Krims, *Rap Music and the Poetics of Identity*, Cambridge, Cambridge University Press, 2000 (hereafter cited in text as *Rap Music)*.
39. Lawrence Kramer, *Musical Meaning: Toward a Critical History*, Berkeley, CA: University of California Press, 2001; Lawrence Kramer, *Franz Schubert: Sexuality, Subjectivity, Song*, Cambridge, Cambridge University Press, 2003.
40. Robert Fink, Orchestral corporate, *Echo: A Music-Centered Journal*, 2(1), June 2000, http://www.echo.ucla.edu/Volume2-Issue1/fink/fink-article.html (accessed February 6, 2005).
41. Jean Baudrillard, *The System of Objects*, trans. James Benedict, London: Verso, 1996 (originally published in 1968).
42. This is not to suggest that Fink commits this error: on the contrary, his concerns lie elsewhere, especially in the construction of the masculine business subject and its musical lineages.
43. Kelly Ritter, Spectacle at the disco: Boogie Nights, soundtrack, and the New American musical, *Journal of Popular Film and TV*, 28(4), 166–175, 2001.

Chapter 1

1. Petula Clark, *Downtown/You'd Better Love Me*, Warner Brothers 5494, 1964.
2. Petula Clark, *Who Am I?/Love Is a Long Journey*, Warner Brothers 5863, 1966.
3. Martha and the Vandellas, *Dance Party*, Motown 915, 1965; Jan and Dean, *Dead Man's Curve*, Liberty 55672, 1964.
4. 50 Cent, *The Massacre*, Shady/Aftermath/Interscope 4092, 2005.
5. 50 Cent, *Get Rich or Die Tryin'*, Interscope 493544, 2003.
6. Krims, *Rap Music*, 73–78 (hereafter cited in text as *Rap Music*).
7. Here, as in the rap book, I divide the lines with slashes such that the beginning of each new line represents the first syllable uttered after the start of the 4/4 measure.
8. Elvis Costello and Burt Bacharach, *Painted from Memory*, Mercury 80022, 1998.
9. Robert Alter, *Imagined Cities: Urban Experience and the Language of the Novel*, New Haven, CT: Yale University Press, 2005.
10. Grandmaster Flash and the Furious Five, *The Message*, Sugarhill 584, 1982 (hereafter cited in text as *Message*).
11. Tom Wolfe, *The Bonfire of the Vanities*, New York: Farrar, Straus and Giroux, 1987; Madonna, *True Blue*, Sire 2–25442, 1986; The Association, *Insight Out*, Warner Brothers 1696, 1967.
12. Andrew Goodwin, *Dancing in the Distraction Factory: Music Television and Popular Culture*, Minneapolis, MN: University of Minnesota Press, 1992.
13. Roland Barthes, *Mythologies*, Paris: Éditions du Seuil, 1957.
14. Chaka Khan, *I Feel for You*, Warner Brothers 2–25162, 1984.
15. William Julius Wilson, *The Truly Disadvantaged: The Inner City, the Underclass, and Public Policy*, Chicago, IL: University of Chicago Press, 1987.
16. Nelson George, *Hip-Hop America*, New York: Viking, 1998, pp. 42–49.
17. Tina Turner, *Private Dancer*, Capitol C2-46041, 1984.
18. Wyclef Jean, *We Tryin' to Stay Alive*, Sony 78602, 1997.
19. Geto Boys, *The Resurrection*, Rap-A-Lot/Noo Trybe 41555, 1996.
20. Krims, *Rap Music*, 79.
21. Kylie Minogue, *Can't Get You Out of My Head*, Capitol 77685, 2002.
22. Tricia Rose, *Black Noise: Rap Music and Black Culture in Contemporary America*, Middletown, CT: Wesleyan University Press, 1994, pp. 32–33.
23. Susan Crafts, Daniel Cavicchi, Charles Keil, and the Music in Daily Life Project, *My Music: Explorations of Music in Daily Life*, Hanover, NH: University Press of New England, 1993, p. 26. As the Introduction to this book indicated, the work of Richard Peterson and others adds the important caveat that such genre straddling may have its class determinations. Peterson, "Understanding Audience Segmentation"; Peterson and Simkus, "How Musical Tastes Mark Occupational Status Groups"; van Eijck, "Social Differentiation in Musical Taste Patterns."

24. Alanis Morissette, *Supposed Former Infatuation Junkie*, Maverick 47094, 1998; Sarah McLachlan, *Surfacing*, Arista 18970, 1997.
25. Mike Davis, *Dead Cities: And Other Tales*, New York: W.W. Norton & Co., 2002, pp. 127–142.
26. Alanis Morissette, Interview with Carson Daly, www.mtv.com (accessed February 15, 2002; emphasis added).
27. Charles Kaiser, *The Gay Metropolis: 1940–1996*, Boston, MA: Houghton Mifflin, 1997.

Chapter 2

1. Scott, *The Cultural Economy of Cities*, pp. 113–128 (hereafter cited in text as *Cultural Economy*).
2. Justin O'Connor, Adam Brown, and Sara Cohen, Local music policies within a global music industry: cultural quarters in Manchester and Sheffield, *Geoforum*, 31, 437–451, 2000; Harvey, *The Condition of Postmodernity* (hereafter cited in text as *Condition*); Hannigan, *Fantasy City*, (hereafter cited in text as *Fantasy City*).
3. Susan Fainstein and Dennis Judd, Global forces, local strategies, and urban tourism, in *The Tourist City*, Dennis Judd and Susan Fainstein, Eds., New Haven, CT: Yale University Press, 1999, pp. 1–20.
4. Tony Mitchell, *Popular Music and Local Identity: Rock, Pop, and Rap in Europe and Oceania*, London: Leicester University Press, 1996, best exemplifies this tendency.
5. Sassen, *The Global City* (hereafter cited in text as *Global City*).
6. Essay collections evincing this trend include *Mapping the Beat: Popular Music and Contemporary Theory*, Thomas Swiss, John Sloop, and Andrew Herman, Eds., Malden, MA: Blackwell, 1998; *Music, Space, and Place: Popular Music and Cultural Identity*, Sheila Whiteley, Andy Benett, and Stan Hawkins, Eds., Aldershot: Ashgate, 2004 (hereafter cited in text as *Music, Space, and Place*); and *The Place of Music*, Andrew Leyshon, David Matless, and George Revill, Eds., New York: Guilford, 1998. Relevant monographs include John Connell and Chris Gibson, *Soundtracks: Popular Music, Identity, and Place*, New York: Routledge, 2002 and George Lipsitz, *Dangerous Crossroads: Popular Music, Postmodernism and the Poetics of Place*, London: Verso, 1994.
7. Manuel Castells, *End of Millennium*, Malden, MA: Blackwell, 2000 (hereafter cited in text as *End*).
8. Houston A. Baker, Jr., *Black Studies, Rap, and the Academy*, Chicago, IL: University of Chicago Press, 1993, pp. 33–60.
9. Arif Dirlik, Globalisation and the politics of place, *Development*, 41(2), 7–13, 12, 1998.
10. Joanne Hollows and Katie Milestone, Welcome to Dreamsville: a history and geography of northern Soul, in *The Place of Music*, Leyshon,

Matless and Revill, Eds., pp. 83–103. Their brief mention of south-eastern domination occurs on pp. 87–88.

11. Through an unfortunate misunderstanding of (tellingly uncited) Marxist approaches, Hollows and Milestone claim that their study corrects those approaches' focus on production (89). But, of course, such a view narrows the meaning of "production" in ways wholly inconsistent with at least the better-informed Marxist treatments of culture.
12. Mitchell, *Popular Music and Local Identity*, again provides the most blatant example.
13. Most often the term "place" is indeed used as described here; its opposed term is sometimes tagged as "space" but just as often left unlabeled or marked by a number of other, related terms (such as "capitalist structuring," "economic development," "globalization," "homogenization," etc.)—all serving as equivalents for space, as described at the beginning of this chapter.
14. In contrast to such discussions, however, it is always worth noting the much more convincing argument advanced by Scott, *Cultural Economy*, that, in fact, globalization does not so much homogenize as rediversify, through new agglomerations based on local cultures of production.
15. Murray Forman, *The 'Hood Comes First: Race, Space, and Place in Rap and Hip-Hop*, Middletown, CT: Wesleyan University Press, 2002.
16. That is, space becomes place in the sense of functional equivalence, under the conditions described below: they do not literally become the same phenomena. My thanks to James Buhler for insisting on maintaining this distinction.
17. Lash and Urry, *Economies of Signs and Space* (hereafter cited in text as *Economies*); Harvey, *Condition*, 66–98; Michael Sorkin, *Variations on a Theme Park: The New American City and the End of Public Space*, New York: Hill and Wang, 1992.
18. Roger Wallis and Krister Malm, *Big Sounds from Small Peoples: The Music Industry in Small Countries*, Stuyvesant, NY: Pendragon, 1984, provides an example of the former tendency; Sara Cohen, Sounding out the city: music and the sensuous production of place, in *The Place of Music*, Leyshon, Matless and Revill, Eds., pp. 269–290, provides an example of the latter.
19. Jocelyne Guilbault, The politics of calypso in a world of music industries, in *Popular Music Studies*, David Hesmondhalgh and Keith Negus, Eds., London: Arnold Publishers, 2002, pp. 191–204.
20. It is perhaps useful to keep in mind how closely the (presumably) agonistic struggle between dominant and subaltern locations resembles, in description, the classic cultural studies struggle between dominant and subaltern identities. Such a striking parallel may go some way toward suggesting that the way was greased for "place" to attain its current popularity among music scholars.
21. Edward Soja, *Thirdspace: Journeys to Los Angeles and Other Real-and-Imagined Places*, Cambridge: Blackwell, 1996, p. 20, advocates

conceptualizing through space, rather than place, though on significantly different grounds from my own.

22. The Netherlands Antilles also contains the Dutch-speaking region of Sint Maarten (Saint-Martin) and the small islands of Saba and Sint Eustatius.
23. Johannes Hartog, *Curaçao: From Colonial Dependence to Autonomy*, Aruba: De Wit, 1968.
24 The statistics used here are taken from the CIA World Factbook, http://www.cia.gov/cia/publications/factbook/print/nt.html (accessed June 4, 2004).
25. Rita Giacalone, Venezuela's relationship with Curaçao and Aruba: historical linkages and geopolitical interests, in *The Dutch Caribbean: Prospects for Democracy*, Betty Sedoc-Dahlberg, Ed., New York: Routledge, 1990, pp. 219–240.
26. Polly Pottullo, *Last Resorts: The Cost of Tourism in the Caribbean*, London: Cassell, 1996.
27. Felio Colinet, *Ensiklopedia Tumba di Karnaval 1971–2002*, Willemstad: Kas di Kultura, 2004.
28. Lynyrd Skynyrd (pronounced "Leh-nerd Skin-nerd") (MCA 363, 1974); Led Zeppelin, *Led Zeppelin IV*, Atlantic 7208, 1971. A helpful formal and historical overview of common rock forms can be found in John Covach, Form in rock music: a primer, in *Engaging Music: Essays in Music Analysis*, Deborah Stein, Ed., Oxford: Oxford University Press, 2004, pp. 65–76.
29. Interest in developing areas of Asia provide a case in point: Sarah Turner and Phuong An Nguyen, Young entrepreneurs, social capital and *Doi moi* in Hanoi, Vietnam, *Urban Studies*, 42(10), 1693–1710, 2005; Eric Harwit, Telecommunications and the Internet in Shanghai: political and economic factors shaping the network in a Chinese city, *Urban Studies*, 42(10), 1837–1858, 2005. Those looking for news on urban development in Curaçao often have to look to official reports of governments or NGOs, or to press reports such as Gobièrnu ke yega na un sektor industrial mas inovativo, *La Prensa*, July 13, 2005.
30. Ministerio di Asuntonan Economico ta organiza un mision entreprearial pa Antiyas Hulandes y Aruba, *La Prensa*, August 12, 2005.
31. PNP na Megapir a atraé kantidat grandi di hende, *La Prensa*, March 27, 2005.
32. The new Howard Johnson hotel, introduced with much fanfare, has not always fit comfortably into the densely settled and popularly used Brionplein. For example, it recently found itself engaged in conflicts with locals playing music in Brionplein at decibel levels that disturbed its guests. After some conflicts, public dispute, and political response by the island's government, a compromise limited public musical activity in Brionplein for the benefit of hotel clientele. A yega na solushon pa kontroversia Brionplein, *La Prensa*, March 2, 2002.

33. Jane Jacobs, *The Death and Life of Great American Cities*, New York: Random House, 1961; O'Connor, Brown, and Cohen, "Local Music Policies."
34. Theodor Adorno and Max Horkheimer, The culture industry: enlightenment as mass deception, in *Dialectic of Enlightenment*, 1944; repr. London: Verso, 1979. In Chapter 4, I question the relevance of Adorno and Horkheimer's vision to present-day music.
35. Zukin, *Loft Living*, 111–125; Pierre Bourdieu, *Distinction: A Social Critique of the Judgement of Taste*, trans. Richard Nice, Cambridge: Harvard University Press, 1987 [originally pub. 1979], pp. 310–311; Mike Featherstone, *Consumer Culture and Postmodernism*, Thousand Oaks, CA: Sage Publications, 1991.

Chapter 3

1. Fredric Jameson, Periodizing the 60s, in Fredric Jameson, *The Ideologies of Theory: Essays 1971–1986*, Vol. 2, Minneapolis, MN: University of Minnesota Press, 1988, pp. 204–208.
2. Richard Dyer, In defense of disco, *Gay Left*, 8, 20–23, 1979.
3. Nelson George, *The Death of Rhythm and Blues*, New York: Pantheon Books, 1988, pp. 147–170.
4. Walter Hughes, In the empire of the beat: discipline and disco, in *Microphone Fiends: Youth Music and Youth Culture*, Andrew Ross and Tricia Rose, Eds., New York: Routledge, 1994, pp. 147–157.
5. Robert C. Sickels, 1970s disco daze: Paul Thomas Anderson's *Boogie Nights* and the last golden age of irresponsibility, *Journal of Popular Culture*, 35(4), 52, 2002.
6. The Emotions, *The Best of My Love*, Columbia 10544, 1977.
7. The Chakachas, *Jungle Fever*, Polydor 2480 084, 1972.
8. Eric Burdon and War, *Spill the Wine*, MGM K144118, 1970.
9. Ritter, "Spectacle at the Disco," 168.
10. Andrew Gold, *Lonely Boy*, Elektra-Asylum 13-082, 1976; Elvin Bishop, *Fooled Around and Fell in Love*, Capricorn 39635, 1976.
11. Hot Chocolate, *You Sexy Thing*, EMI 5592, 1975.
12. KC and the Sunshine Band, *(Shake, Shake, Shake) Shake Your Booty/Boogie Shoes*, TK 8, 1976.
13. Not all music in the film receives the same treatment; there are instances of more conventional soundtrack usage. For example, (Fleetwood Mac member) Walter Egan's "Magnet and Steel" appears first ambiguously, then becomes unambiguously nondiegetic, then perhaps becomes ambiguous again, after Diggler delivers his impassioned acceptance speech for his Best Actor (Adult Film Award) prize. Viewers with the most knowledge of 1970's music history will have known all along that the music could not have been diegetic, as the single was released in 1978, and the scenes that the song accompanies are all set in 1977 (though, tellingly,

1978 is announced just as the music fades). Walter Egan, *Magnet and Steel*, Columbia 3-10719, 1978.

14. The Commodores, *Machine Gun*, Motown M1307F, 1974.
15. Beach Boys, *Wouldn't It Be Nice/God Only Knows*, Capitol 5706, 1966.
16. The Four Aces, *Mr. Sandman*, Decca 29344.
17. For example, to take one of the more extreme cases, Three Dog Night's "Mama Told Me Not to Come" was released, and a Top 40 hit, in 1970, well before the action of the film takes place. The obvious pun with the film's subject matter no doubt contributes to the song's aptness. Three Dog Night, *It Ain't Easy*, Dunhill 50078, 1970.
18. Andrew Gold, *Lonely Boy*, Elektra-Asylum 13-082, 1976; Eric Burdon and War, *Spill the Wine*, MGM K144118, 1970; Silver Convention, *Save Me*, Midland International 1129, 1976.
19. This is roughly what Kelly Ritter refers to as musical "spectacle" in the film. On the other hand, the argument being made here would clearly differ from her contention that "film follows a clear progression from diegetic sound/image harmony to diegetic dissonance" (*Spectacle*, 173).
20. Hal Foster, *Design and Crime (and Other Diatribes)*, London: Verso, 2003; Lash and Urry, *Economies*.
21. KC and the Sunshine Band, *(Shake, Shake, Shake) Shake Your Booty/Boogie Shoes*, TK 8, 1976.
22. Wyclef Jean, *We Tryin' to Stay Alive*, Sony 78602, 1997. The video of this song is also discussed in Chapter 1.
23. Representations in hip-hop culture, such as not only Wyclef Jean's mentioned above, but also in roughly contemporary songs and videos by artists such as Snoop Dogg, Smoothe Tha Hustler, and quite a few others, are often more ambiguous than the rest. This most likely stems from the happy coincidence of some of the more outlandish 1970's fashion trends with pimp or mack images. I describe this in *Rap Music*, 62–65.
24. Michel Foucault and Noam Chomsky, Human nature: justice vs. power, in *Reflexive Water: The Basic Concerns of Mankind*, Fons Elders, Ed., London: Souvenir Press, 1974, pp. 135–197.
25. This is not to say that the shifting view of cities was the *only* factor that led to changing receptions of disco: of course, homophobia, racial tensions (as in the "disco sucks" slogan), and more localized social movements such as punk also contributed and perhaps were necessary. The present discussion posits the urban ethos as a previously unrecognized and crucial ingredient in the reception of disco.
26. Fredric Jameson, *The Seeds of Time*, New York: Columbia University Press, 1994, pp. 24–32.
27. Fredric Jameson, *Signatures of the Visible*, New York: Routledge, 1992, pp. 175–177.
28. Kim Campbell, Disco music—what were we thinking?, *The Christian Science Monitor*, C24, February 18, 2005.
29. A *Gedanken* experiment might help to establish the urbanness of the scenario discussed here: one might imagine the modality of a possible

film representation of a rural disco. Such a scene would most likely be received as comic or ironic—or would at least call attention to its own unusual location.

30. It can be noted in passing that the soundtrack to *Saturday Night Fever* (Various artists) not only became a best-selling album but also, in the mind of many pop historians, stands at the beginning of the current practice of cross-marketing films with soundtrack albums. *Boogie Nights*, of course, continued that practice with not one but two successful associated soundtrack CDs, which in turn reinforce the significance of music in the cultural life surrounding the film. Various artists, *Saturday Night Fever* [soundtrack] (RSO 2658123, 1977); Various artists, *Boogie Nights* [soundtrack] (Capitol 55631, 1997); Various artists, *Boogie Nights, Volume 2* [soundtrack] (Capitol 93076, 1998).
31. Wilson, *The Truly Disadvantaged*; Hughes, "Formation of the Impacted Ghetto."
32. Figure 3.1 is adapted from information found in Barry Bluestone, *The Polarization of American Society: Victims, Suspects, and Mysteries to Unravel*, New York: Twentieth Century Fund Press, http:/epn.org/tcf/xxblue.html (accessed April 9, 1995).
33. The one significant exception to this is the small-group scene of (then) Eddie's confrontations with his aggressive mother and hapless father early in the movie—a contrast that, if anything, underlines the celebratory weight of crowds and Eddie's new "family."
34. Though the film's simplistic contrast of 1970s versus 1980s finds wide resonance in our media culture generally, there are some accounts that find seeds the urban degeneration of the 1980s already in the heart of the late 1970s, such as Jonathan Mahler's *Ladies and Gentlemen, the Bronx is Burning*, which also correctly specifies New York City as the source for many impressions of cities generally in Anglophone media culture. Jonathan Mahler, *Ladies and Gentlemen, the Bronx is Burning: 1977, Baseball, Politics, and the Battle for the Soul of a City*, New York: Farrar, Straus and Giroux, 2005.
35. The loss of great pornographic film is, in fact, a singular focus of the director Paul Thomas Anderson, who makes a point, in interviews about the film, of underlining how the transition from film to video degraded the artistic quality of the movies. Paul Thomas Anderson, interview with Henri Behar ["Video Killed Porn"], at http://www.filmscouts.com/scripts/proj.cfm (accessed July 15, 1999).
36. Snoop Dogg, *Tha Last Meal*, Priority 23225, 2000.

Chapter 4

1. Richard Leppert, Introduction, in Theodor Adorno, *Essays on Music*, Richard Leppert, Ed., trans. Susan H. Gillespie, Berkeley, CA: University of California Press, 2002, pp. 1–84.

2. Steven Best and Douglas Kellner, *Postmodern Theory: Critical Interrogations*, New York: Guilford Press, 1991; Martin Jay, *Adorno*, Cambridge, MA: Harvard University Press, 1994; Henry Klumpenhouwer, Commodity-form, disavowal, and practices of music theory, in *Music and Marx: Ideas, Practice, Politics*, Regula Qureshi, Ed., New York: Routledge, 2002, pp. 23–44.
3. Max Paddison, *Adorno's Aesthetics of Music*, Cambridge: Cambridge University Press, 1993.
4. Lipsitz, *Dangerous Crossroads*; John Fiske, *Television Culture*, London: Routledge, 1987.
5. Keith Negus, *Popular Music in Theory: An Introduction*, Middletown, CT: Wesleyan University Press, 1996.
6. Dominic Strinati, *An Introduction to Theories of Popular Culture*, New York: Routledge, 1995; Peter Manuel, *Cassette Culture: Popular Music and Technology in North India*, Chicago, IL: University of Chicago Press, 1993.
7. Lenin is quoted in Valeriu Marcu, *Lenin: 30 Jahre Russland*, Leipzig: List, 1927.
8. Davis, *City of Quartz*, 15–88.
9. Debates have raged on the scale, characteristics, and historical significance of post-Fordism. Such debates are beyond the scope of this book; some useful summaries of the major issues can be gleaned from Mark Elam, Puzzling out the post-Fordist debate: technology, markets, and institutions, in *Post-Fordism: A Reader*, Ash Amin, Ed., Oxford: Blackwell, 1994, pp. 43–70.
10. Harvey, *The Condition of Postmodernity* does this; hereafter cited in text as *Condition*.
11. Lash and Urry, *Economies of Signs and Space*, pp. 111–144; Scott Lash and John Urry, *The End of Organized Capitalism*, Cambridge, MA: Polity, 1987.
12. Timothy Taylor does attribute significance to post-Fordism in the advent of postmodernity (though he mistakenly refers to flexible accumulation as a "mode of production"); Timothy Taylor, Music and musical practices in postmodernity, in *Postmodern Music/Postmodern Thought*, Judy Lochhead and Joseph Auner, Eds., New York: Routledge, 2000, pp. 93–118.
13. Alfred Chandler with the asssistance of Takashi Hikino, *Scale and Scope: The Dynamics of Industrial Capitalism*, Cambridge, MA: Belknap Press, 1990.
14. In the only other study so far addressing post-Fordism and the music industry, David Hesmondhalgh argues against centralizing the notion of post-Fordism in discussions of the popular music industry. The conception of post-Fordism against which he argues, however, is the optimistic "New Times" version, in which the term is proffered as an index of liberatory cultural force. Against such a notion, Hesmondhalgh observes that the industry still moves principally through historically dominant circuits. His argument, in other words, is consistent with what is being argued in this chapter, while his objections are marshalled against

the more optimistic assessments of post-Fordism that range the latter against the organized force of capital. David Hesmondhalgh, Flexibility, post-Fordism and the music industries, *Media, Culture and Society*, 18(3), 469–488, 1996 (hereafter cited in text as "Flexibility").

15. Peter J. Alexander, Peer-to-peer file sharing: the case of the music recording industry, *Review of Industrial Organization,* 20, 151–161, 2002; Steve Jones, Music that moves: popular music, distribution, and network technologies, *Cultural Studies,* 16(2), 213–232, 2003.
16. Roger Wallis, Business as Usual or a Real Paradigm Shift? The Music Industry's Response to E-Commerce Technology and Ideology, paper presented at the Key Action II annual conference, 2001.
17. Stephen Lee, Re-examining the concept of the 'independent' record company: the case of *wax-trax!* records, *Popular Music*, 14(1), 13–31, 1995 (hereafter cited in text as "Re-Examining"); Keith Negus, *Music Genres and Corporate Cultures*, New York: Routledge, 1999 (hereafter cited in text as *Genres*).
18. Robert Burnett, *The Global Jukebox: The International Music Industry*, London: Routledge, 1996, pp. 44–63.
19. Peter Wood, Flexible accumulation and the rise of business services, *Transactions of the Institute of British Geographers*, 16, 160–172, 1991.
20. Jameson, *Postmodernism*, 88–92.
21. Theodor Adorno and Max Horkheimer, The culture industry: enlightenment as mass deception, in *Dialectic of Enlightenment*, 1944; repr. London: Verso, 1979, p. 120.
22. Oliver Boyd-Barrett, Media imperialism: towards an international framework for the analysis of media systems, in *Mass Communication and Society*, James Curran, Michael Gurevitch, and Janet Woollacott, Eds., London: Edward Arnold, 1977, pp. 116–135, provides an example of the earlier disparagement; Lipsitz, *Dangerous Crossroads*, 173–181, offers an account consistent with more recent trends.
23. Vladimir Ilyich Lenin, *Imperialism: The Highest Stage of Capitalism*, trans. Norman Lewis and James Malone, 1916, London: Pluto, 1996.
24. Gayatri Chakravorty Spivak, Can the subaltern speak?, in *Marxism and the Interpretation of Culture*, Cary Nelson and Lawrence Grossberg, Eds., Urbana and Chicago, IL: University of Illinois Press, 1988, pp. 271–313.
25. The figures here are adapted from Bluestone, *The Polarization of American Society.*
26. Michael Hardt and Antonio Negri, *Empire*, Cambridge, MA: Harvard University Press, 2001, pp. 139–146, in fact, theorizes just such a dependence.
27. Peterson, "Understanding Audience Segmentation."
28. A thoroughly standard example from musicology can be found in Renée Coulombe, Postmodern polyamory or postcolonial challenge? Cornershop's dialogue from west, to east, to west, in *Postmodern Music/Postmodern Thought*, Judy Lochhead and Joseph Auner, Eds., New York: Routledge, 2000, pp. 177–195.

29. Fiske, *Television Culture*; Iain Chambers, *Border Dialogues: Journeys in Postmodernity*, London: Routledge, 1990; Lisa Lewis, *Gender, Politics and MTV: Voicing the Difference*, Philadelphia, PA: Temple University Press, 1990.
30. Dick Hebdige, *Subculture: The Meaning of Style*, New York: Methuen, 1979. Don Robotham, *Culture, Society, and Economy: Bringing Production Back In*, New York: Routledge, 2005, pp. 36–42, offers a withering and utterly convincing critique of such a view of Gramsci, via a detailed reconstruction of the context of his writings.
31. Iain Chambers, *Urban Rhythms, Pop Music and Popular Culture*, London: Macmillan, 1985.
32. Such shifts in ethnic and gender dynamics are documented in John Bound and George Johnson, What are the causes of rising wage inequality in the United States?, *Economic Policy Review*, 1(1), 18–25, 1995.
33. Robin Kelley, *Yo' Mama's Disfunktional!: Fighting the Culture Wars in Urban America*, Boston: Beacon Press, 1998, pp. 15–42; Charles Kubrin, Gangstas, thugs, and hustlas: identity and the code of the street in rap music, *Social Problems*, 52(3), 360–378, 2005.
34. Krims, *Rap Music*, 73–79 (hereafter referred to in text as *Rap Music*).
35. The song can be found on Mobb Deep, *Hell on Earth*, Loud 66992, 1996.
36. Rose, *Black Noise*, 21–61. Krims, *Rap Music*, 46–92, discusses layering in a great deal more detail.
37. Raekwon, *Only Built 4 Cuban Linx*, Loud 66663, 1995.
38. The song can be found on Gladys Knight and the Pips, *I Feel a Song*, Buddah 5612, 1974.
39. It could be argued that the initial C3 in the bass suggests an opening IV harmony. Such a contention, though, would have to be tempered by the fact that the electric piano already sounds a ii triad. In either case, the harmony unambiguously projects ii^7 by the second eighth-note of beat 3, when the bass guitar plays A2.
40. If one relies on harmonic theory derived from classical music, the reinforcement of layers (a) and (b) is somewhat compromised by the position of the purported harmony. However, that chord position does not bear the same ambiguous status in many popular styles, including rap, which it does in classical music.
41. In professional conversations I have had since the publication of *Rap Music*, the question has occasionally arisen whether it is purposeful or not. The question itself probably reveals a good deal about assumptions that some audiences make concerning the character of the musicians involved in rap music. The answer is that no hip-hop producer I have encountered is unaware of this effect, and that the ability to detune layers in effective ways is much prized among rap producers, at least those interested in this particular effect (which is, obviously, less fashionable now than during the period that I was then describing).
42. Jameson, *Postmodernism*, 34–36.

43. The song may be found on A Tribe Called Quest, *Beats, Rhymes, and Life*, Jive 41587, 1996.
44. Mobb Deep, *It's Mine*, Sony 79265, 1999.
45. Krims, *Rap Music*, 83–86, foreshadows and briefly discusses the emergence of this new generic hybrid.
46. Brandy and Monica, *The Boy Is Mine*, Atlantic 84118, 1998.
47. Raekwon, *Ice Cream*, RCA 64426, 1995.
48. This is not to say that the ghetto itself had disappeared from reality rap, so much as that the tragic-realist version of that ghetto shifted its center of gravity to the knowledge genre.
49. The song comes from their eponymous debut album Black Star, *Black Star*, Rawkus 11581, 1998.
50. The present discussion refers to the album version of the song, not the two remixes released separately as a vinyl single; it is the album version that provides the soundtrack for the video discussed here.
51. Nelson George, *Buppies, B-Boys, Baps and Bohos: Notes on Post-Soul Black Culture*, New York: HarperCollins, 1992, pp. 95–97.
52. Smith, *The New Urban Frontier* (hereafter cited in text as *Frontier).*
53. Wilson, *The Truly Disadvantaged*; John Kasarda, Structural factors affecting the location and timing of urban underclass growth, *Urban Geography*, 11(3), 234–264, 1990; Hughes, "Formation of the Impacted Ghetto."
54. Friedrich Engels, *Condition of the Working Class in England*, 1845; London: Penguin, 1984, p. 368.
55. Bjork, *Big Time Sensuality*, Elektra 66244, 1994; The Corrs, *So Young*, Atlantic 00571, 1998; Beck, *Devil's Haircut*, Geffen 22222, 1996.
56. Record Industry Association of America, http://www.riaa.com/news/marketingdata/facts.asp (accessed June 5, 2003).
57. Similar ideas are explored in Adam Krims, The hip-hop sublime as a form of commodification, in *Music and Marx: Ideas, Practice, Politics*, Regula Qureshi, Ed., New York: Routledge, 2002, pp. 63–80.
58. Hannigan, *Fantasy City*, pp. 129–138, discusses Times Square in the context of more general trends in urban restructuring.
59. Christopher Mele, Globalization, culture, and neighborhood change: reinventing the lower east side of New York, *Urban Affairs Review*, 32(1), 3–22, 1996.

Chapter 5

1. David Morley, Active audience theory: pendulums and pitfalls, *Journal of Communication*, 43(4), 13–19, 1993; Jacqueline Warwick, Review of Theodore Gracyk's rock music and the politics of identity and Lori Burns and Mélisse Lafrance's disruptive divas: feminism, identity, and popular music, in *Journal of the American Musicological Society*, 57(3), 702–712, 2003.

2. Robert Walser, *Running With the Devil: Power, Gender, and Madness in Heavy Metal Music*, Hanover, NH: Wesleyan University Press, 1993.
3. Nadine Hubbs, *The Queer Composition of America's Sound: Gay Modernists, American Music, and National Identity*, Berkeley, CA: University of California Press, 2004.
4. Anahid Kassabian, Ubiquitous listening, in *Popular Music Studies*, David Hesmondhalgh and Keith Negus, Eds., London: Arnold, 2002, pp. 131–142.
5. Shuhei Hosokawa, The Walkman effect, *Popular Music*, 4, 165–180, 1984.
6. Lawrence Levine, *Highbrow/Lowbrow: The Emergence of Cultural Hierarchy in America*, Cambridge, MA: Harvard University Press, 1988, pp. 11–82.
7. Robert Fink, Elvis everywhere: musicology and popular music studies at the twilight of the canon, *American Music*, 16(2), 135–179, 1998.
8. Naturally, the extent to which texts change may vary greatly (as in, say, the case of much trouvère music); and perhaps more important, it can often become impossible to distinguish a changing musical text (i.e., score) from a changing performance tradition (as in the case of Baroque music). Nevertheless, as long as music from a given era remains an active area of the canon, performances will address at least a substantially continuous body of written information.
9. Ellen Meiksins Wood, *Democracy against Capitalism: Renewing Historical Materialism*, Cambridge: Cambridge University Press, 1995, p. 24.
10. *The Practice of Performance: Studies in Musical Interpretation*, John Rink, Ed., Cambridge: Cambridge University Press, 1995.
11. Marin Cullingford, Sony BMG Announce New Classical Division, http://www.gramophone.co.uk (accessed April 15, 2005).
12. Charlotte Church, *Voice of an Angel*, Sony Classical 60957, 1999.
13. Charlotte Church, *Charlotte Church*, Sony Classical 64356, 1999.
14. Charlotte Church, *Just Wave Hello*, Sony Classical 6685312, 1999.
15. Sarah Brightman, *Time to Say Goodbye*, Angel 56511, 1997; Sarah Brightman, *Eden*, Angel 67692, 1998; Sarah Brightman, *La Luna*, Angel 56968, 2000.
16. Harmonia Mundi does have nonclassical lines of recordings; the company, however, segregates them strictly into its non-Western and folk series (like *Le Chant du Monde* and *HM Iberica*).
17. Anonymous 4, *American Angels*, Harmonia Mundi 907326, 2004. *American Angels* also became Harmonia Mundi's first Billboard Classical no. 1 album.
18. Anonymous 4, *The Origin of Fire*, Harmonia Mundi 907327, 2005.
19. Anonymous 4, *An English Ladymass*, Harmonia Mundi 907080, 1993. Anonymous 4 did also produce one CD of contemporary music, Richard Einhorn's *Voices of Light*, which spent seven weeks on the Billboard classical charts, and did sing some contemporary music in many of their concerts. However, even these were generally works of composers associated with reviving early-music styles in their music, e.g., John Tavener (whose

works they interspersed with twelfth- to fourteenth-century hymns on their *Darkness into Light*), Henryk Górecki, and Einhorn himself. Like many classical artists, they also ventured into traditional music on some releases (including *Darkness into Light* and the *American Angels* disc discussed above). All these ventures, of course, remain firmly within the territory associated with "serious" classical artists, and none of them changed the group's principal association with "early" music. Richard Einhorn et al., *Voices of Light*, Sony 62006; Anonymous 4, *Darkness into Light*, Harmonia Mundi 907274, 2000; Anonymous 4, *American Angels*, Harmonia Mundi 907326, 2004.

20. Dan Gibson, *Beethoven: Forever by the Sea*, Solitudes 14135, 1997.
21. Various artists, *Bach for Relaxation*, RCA 68697, 1998.
22. Cullingford, Sony BMG Announce New Classical Division.
23. Yo-Yo Ma, *Simply Baroque*, Sony Classical 60680, 1999; Yo-Yo Ma, *Simply Baroque II*, Sony Classical 60681, 2000.
24. Various artists, *The Most Relaxing Piano Album in the World … Ever!*, EMI 67526, 2003; Various artists, *The Most Romantic Classical Music in the Universe*, Denon 17334, 2004; Various artists, *More of the Most Relaxing Classical Music in the Universe*, Denon 17266, 2003.
25. The Benedictine Monks of Santo Domingo de Silas, *Chant: The Anniversary Edition*, EMI/Angel 62943, 2004. The retailing website Amazon.com, in fact, paired this CD as a "Better Together" offer with various artists, *Lost in Meditation: Meditative Gregorian Chants*, Laserlight 14157, 1994.
26. Various artists, *Classics for Relaxation*, Madacy 24349, 2004; Various artists, *The Most Relaxing Classical Music in the Universe*, Denon 17232, 2003; various artists, *Classics for Meditation*, Madacy 25289, 2004; various artists, *Moonlight Classics*, Madacy 23329, 2004.
27. The numbers here represent US dollar values in millions; the Internet numbers do not reflect record-club purchases made over the Internet. Statistics here are taken from the Recording Industry of America's *1999 Consumer Profile*, available at http://www.riaa.com/news/marketingdata/pdf/1999consumerprofile.pdf (accessed on November 5, 2001).
28. Yo-Yo Ma, *Simply Baroque*, Sony Classical 60680, 1999; Yo-Yo Ma, *Simply Baroque II*, Sony Classical 60681, 2000; Yo-Yo Ma, Edgar Meyer, and Mark O'Connor, *Appalachian Journey*, Sony 66782, 2000.
29. Christine Schornsheim, *C. P. E. Bach: Symphonies, Concerto pour Orgue et Orchestre*, Harmonia Mundi, France 901622, 1997.
30. By the time of the album's release, an energetic playing style implying improvization and passionate expression, along with certain technical practices such as hard bow strokes for string instruments, had become hallmarks of "authentic" instrumental performance, with the Akademie für Alte Musik among the most visible practitioners.
31. Martin Haselbock, *CPE Bach: Sonatina II D-Dur; Concerto per l'Organo G-Dur; Concerto doppio*, Novalis 150025, 1994; Klaus Kirbach, *C. P. E. Bach: Organ Concertos*, Capriccio 10135, 1995.

32. Caroline Parry, Classic FM set to woo musical youth: Britain's most popular commercial radio station is rebranding to attract a younger audience, *Marketing Week*, 43(49), 32–33; BBC Radio One Loses Listeners, http://news.bbc.co.uk/1/hi/entertainment/tv_and_radio/3110667.stm, accessed August 12, 2003.
33. Various artists, *The Most Relaxing Classical Album in the World ... Ever!*, Virgin 44890, 1999.
34. Hannigan, *Fantasy City*; *The Tourist City*, Dennis Judd and Susan Fainstein, Eds., New Haven, CT: Yale University Press, 1999 (hereafter cited in text as *Tourist City*).
35. Harvey, *The Condition of Postmodernity*, p. 88–98.
36. The essays collected in *Variations on a Theme Park: The New American City and the End of Public Space*, Sorkin, Ed., and in *Tourist City* demonstrate precisely this point about such areas of contemporary cities, along with their function in broader economic and cultural transformations of (especially Western) cities.
37. Zukin, *Loft Living*, 58–81.
38. Guy Julier, *The Culture of Design*, Thousand Oaks, CA: Sage, 2000, pp. 117–142.
39. James Horner, *Titanic* soundtrack, Sony 63213, 1997. Source: "Harper's index," *Harper's Magazine*, 295, 13, July 1997.
40. Nancy J. Kim, House blends: like its coffee, Starbucks picks and mixes its own music, *Puget Sound Business Journal*, December 8, 1997.
41. Independent Music Source, http://www.independentmusicsource.org/why_choose_ims.htm (accessed June 4, 2005).
42. Various artists, *Mozart on the Menu: A Delightful Little Dinner Music*, Philips 46762, 1995. This particular title comes from a series produced by Philips called "Set Your Life to Music."
43. Peter Starr, *Logics of Failed Revolt: French Theory after May '68*, Stanford, CA: Stanford University Press, 1995, pp. 24–37.
44. Karl Marx, *The Communist Manifesto*, 1848; London: Verso, 1998, p. 42.
45. Peter Hall, *Cities in Civilization*, New York: Pantheon, 1998.
46. Charles Rosen, *The Classical Style: Haydn, Mozart, Beethoven*, New York: Norton, 1972; Stephen Rumph, *Beethoven after Napoleon: Political Romanticism in the Late Works*, Berkeley, CA: University of California Press, 2004.
47. BMG Special Products, *Starbucks Jazz CD* (no serial number given, 1999).
48. Rock River Communications originated in New York City and is now located in San Francisco.
49. Joseph Lanza, *Elevator Music: A Surreal History of Muzak, Easy Listening, and Other Moodsong*, London: Picador, 1995.
50. Ray Charles, *Genius Loves Company*, Concord/Hear Music 1033, 2004. Interestingly, Concord itself has acquired a profile in the "legitimate" classical recording repertory, having acquired the label Telarc in late 2005.
51. Manuel Duarte, Starbucks Shuns Springsteen CD for Racy Lyrics, *All Headline News*, May 7, 2005.

52. Beach Boys, *Pet Sounds*, Capitol 2458, 1966; Beatles, *Sgt. Pepper's Lonely Hearts Club Band*, Parlophone 46442, 1967.
53. Bjork, *Hunter*, Polygram 567199, 1998; the song can be found on her album *Homogenic*, Elektra 62061, 1997.
54. Michael Paoletta, Bjork paints from new palette, *Billboard*, 20, July 23, 2001.
55. Joseph Schloss, *Making Beats: The Art of Sample-Based Hip-Hop*, Middletown, CT: Wesleyan University Press, 2004.
56. Nas, *Nostradamus*, Columbia 63930, 1999.
57. Brian Cross discusses the jeep beat in the context of a more closely argued history of rap in Los Angeles; Brian Cross, *It's Not About a Salary: Rap, Race, and Resistance in Los Angeles*, London: Verso, 1993, pp. 42–45.
58. Fink, "Elvis Everywhere."
59. Various artists, *Classical Chillout*, Angel 67737, 2002.

Bibliography

Adorno, Theodor, *Essays on Music*, Richard Leppert, Ed., trans. Susan H. Gillespie, Berkeley, CA: University of California Press, 2002.

Adorno, Theodor and Max Horkheimer, The culture industry: enlightenment as mass deception, in *Dialectic of Enlightenment*, 1944; repr. London: Verso, 1979, pp. 120–167.

Alexander, Peter J. Peer-to-peer sharing: the case of the music recording industry, *Review of Industrial Organization*, 20, 151–161, 2002.

Alter, Robert, *Imagined Cities: Urban Experience and the Language of the Novel*, New Haven, CT: Yale University Press, 2005.

Amin, Ash, Ed., *Post-Fordism: A Reader*, Oxford: Blackwell, 1994.

Anderson, Paul Thomas, *Interview with Henri Behar ["Video Killed Porn"]*, at http://www.filmscouts.com/scripts/proj.cfm (accessed July 15, 1999).

A yega na solushon pa kontroversia Brionplein, *La Prensa*, March 2, 2002.

Baker, Houston A., Jr., *Black Studies, Rap, and the Academy*, Chicago, IL: University of Chicago Press, 1993.

Barthes, Roland, *Mythologies*, Paris: Éditions du Seuil, 1957.

Baudrillard, Jean, *The System of Objects*, trans. James Benedict, London: Verso, 1996.

BBC Radio One Loses Listeners, http://news.bbc.co.uk/1/hi/entertainment/tv_and_radio/3110667.stm (accessed August 12, 2003).

Best, Steven and Douglas Kellner, *Postmodern Theory: Critical Interrogations*, New York: Guilford Press, 1991.

Blakely, Edward, *Fortress America: Gated Communities in the United States*, Washington, DC: Brookings Institution Press, 1997.

Bluestone, Barry, *The Polarization of American Society: Victims, Suspects, and Mysteries to Unravel*, New York: Twentieth Century Fund Press, http://epn.org/tcf/xxblue.html (accessed April 9, 1995).

Bound, John and George Johnson, What are the causes of rising wage inequality in the United States?, *Economic Policy Review*, 1(1), 18–25, 1995.

Bourdieu, Pierre, *Distinction: A Social Critique of the Judgement of Taste*, trans. Richard Nice, London: Routledge, 1989.

Boyd-Barrett, Oliver, Media imperialism: towards an international framework for the analysis of media systems, in *Mass Communication and Society*, James Curran, Michael Gurevitch, and Janet Woollacott, Eds., London: Edward Arnold, 1977, pp. 116, 135.

Burnett, Robert, *The Global Jukebox: The International Music Industry*, London: Routledge, 1996.

Campbell, Kim, Disco music—what were we thinking?, *The Christian Science Monitor*, February 18, 2005.

Castells, Manuel, *The Rise of the Network Society*, Oxford: Blackwell, 1996.

Castells, Manuel, *End of Millennium*, Malden, MA: Blackwell, 2000.

Chambers, Iain, *Urban Rhythms, Pop Music and Popular Culture*, London: Macmillan, 1985.

Chambers, Iain, *Border Dialogues: Journeys in Postmodernity*, London: Routledge, 1990.

Chandler, Alfred, with the asssistance of Takashi Hikino, *Scale and Scope: The Dynamics of Industrial Capitalism*, Cambridge, MA: Belknap Press, 1990.

Cohen, Gerald, *Karl Marx's Theory of History: A Defence*, Oxford: Oxford University Press, 1978.

Cohen, Sara, Sounding out the city: music and the sensuous production of place, in *The Place of Music*, Andrew Leyshon, David Matless, and George Revill, Eds., New York: Guilford, 1998, pp. 269–290.

Colinet, Felio, *Ensiklopedia Tumba di Karnaval 1971-2002*, Willemstad: Kas di Kultura, 2004.

Connell, John and Chris Gibson, *Soundtracks: Popular Music, Identity, and Place*, New York: Routledge, 2002.

Cooper, James C. Technology and Copyright Protection: The Effect of Digital Recording on the Music Industry, Unpublished doctoral dissertation, University of Melbourne, 2002.

Coulombe, Renée, Postmodern polyamory or postcolonial challenge? Cornershop's dialogue from west, to east, to west, in *Postmodern Music/Postmodern Thought*, Judy Lochhead and Joseph Auner, Eds., New York: Routledge, 2000, pp. 177–195.

Covach, John, Form in rock music: a primer, in *Engaging Music: Essays in Music Analysis*, Deborah Stein, Ed., Oxford: Oxford University Press, 2004, pp. 65–76.

Crafts, Susan, Daniel Cavicchi, Charles Keil, and the Music in Daily Life Project, *My Music: Explorations of Music in Daily Life*, Hanover, NH: University Press of New England, 1993.

Cross, Brian, *It's Not about a Salary: Rap, Race, and Resistance in Los Angeles*, London: Verso, 1993.

Cullingford, Marin, Sony BMG Announce New Classical Division, http://www.gramophone.co.uk (accessed April 15, 2005).

Davis, Mike, *City of Quartz: Excavating the Future of Los Angeles*, London: Verso, 1990.

Davis, Mike, *Dead Cities: And Other Tales*, New York: W.W. Norton and Co., 2002.

Dirlik, Arif, Globalisation and the politics of place, *Development*, 41(2), 7–13, 1998.

Duarte, Manuel, Starbucks Shuns Springsteen CD for Racy Lyrics, *All Headline News*, May 7, 2005.

Dyer, Richard, In defense of disco, *Gay Left,* 8, 20–23, 1979.

Ehrlich, Bruce and Peter Dreier, The New Boston discovers the old: tourism and the struggle for a liveable city, in *The Tourist City*, Dennis Judd and Susan Fainstein, Eds., New Haven, CT: Yale University Press, 1999, pp. 155–178.

Eijck, Koen van, Social differentiation in musical taste patterns, *Social Forces*, 79(3), 1163–1185, 2001.

Elam, Mark, Puzzling out the post-Fordist debate: technology, markets, and institutions, in *Post-Fordism: A Reader*, Ash Amin, Ed., Oxford: Blackwell, 1994, pp. 43–70.

Engels, Friedrich, *Condition of the Working Class in England*, 1845; London: Penguin, 1984.

Euchner, Charles, Tourism and sports: the serious competition for play, in *The Tourist City*, Dennis Judd and Susan Fainstein, Eds., New Haven, CT: Yale University Press, 1999, pp. 215–232.

Fainstein, Susan and Dennis Judd, Global forces, local strategies, and urban tourism, in *The Tourist City*, Dennis Judd and Susan Fainstein, Eds., New Haven, CT: Yale University Press, 1999, pp. 1–20.

Featherstone, Mike, *Consumer Culture and Postmodernism*, Thousand Oaks, CA: Sage Publications, 1991.

Fink, Robert, Elvis everywhere: musicology and popular music studies at the twilight of the canon, *American Music*, 16(2), 135–179, 1998.

Fink, Robert, Orchestral corporate, *Echo: A Music-Centered Journal*, 2(1), June 2000, http://www.echo.ucla.edu/Volume2-Issue1/fink/fink-article.html (accessed February 6, 2005).

Fiske, John, *Television Culture*, London: Routledge, 1987.

Flaherty, Julie, Music to a Retailer's Ear, *The New York Times*, July 4, 2001.

Forman, Murray, *The 'Hood Comes First: Race, Space, and Place in Rap and Hip-Hop*, Middletown, CT: Wesleyan University Press, 2002.

Foster, Hal, *Design and Crime (and Other Diatribes)*, London: Verso, 2003.

Foucault, Michel and Noam Chomsky, Human nature: justice vs. power, in *Reflexive Water: The Basic Concerns of Mankind*, Fons Elders, Ed., London: Souvenir Press, 1974, pp. 135–197.

George, Nelson, *The Death of Rhythm and Blues*, New York: Pantheon Books, 1988.

George, Nelson, *Buppies, B-Boys, Baps and Bohos: Notes on Post-Soul Black Culture*, New York: HarperCollins, 1992.

George, Nelson, *Hip-Hop America*, New York: Viking, 1998.

Giacalone, Rita, Venezuela's relationship with Curaçao and Aruba: historical linkages and geopolitical interests, in *The Dutch Caribbean: Prospects for Democracy*, Betty Sedoc-Dahlberg, Ed., New York: Routledge, 1990, pp. 219–240.

Gobièrnu ke yega na un sektor industrial mas inovativo, *La Prensa*, July 13, 2005.

Goodwin, Andrew, *Dancing in the Distraction Factory: Music Television and Popular Culture*, Minneapolis, MN: University of Minnesota Press, 1992.

Gottdiener, Mark, *The Theming of America: Dreams, Visions, and Public Spaces*, New York: HarperCollins, 1997.

Guilbault, Jocelyne, The politics of calypso in a world of music industries, in *Popular Music Studies*, David Hesmondhalgh and Keith Negus, Eds., London: Arnold Publishers, 2002, pp. 192–204.

Hall, Peter, *Cities in Civilization*, New York: Pantheon, 1998.
Hannigan, John, *Fantasy City: Pleasure and Profit in the Postmodern Metropolis*, New York: Routledge, 1998.
Hardt, Michael and Antonio Negri, *Empire*, Cambridge, MA: Harvard University Press, 2001.
Hartog, Johannes, *Curaçao: From Colonial Dependence to Autonomy*, Aruba: De Wit, 1968.
Harvey, David, *The Condition of Postmodernity: An Enquiry into the Origins of Cultural Change*, Oxford: Blackwell, 1989.
Harwit, Eric, Telecommunications and the Internet in Shanghai: political and economic factors shaping the network in a Chinese city, *Urban Studies*, 42(10), 1837–1858, 2005.
Hebdige, Dick, *Subculture: The Meaning of Style*, New York: Methuen, 1979.
Hesmondhalgh, David, Flexibility, post-Fordism and the music industries, *Media, Culture and Society*, 18(3), 469–488, 1996.
Hollows, Joanne and Katie Milestone, Welcome to Dreamsville: a history and geography of northern Soul, in *The Place of Music*, Andrew Leyshon, David Matless, and George Revill, Eds., New York: Guilford, 1998, pp. 83–108.
Hosokawa, Shuhei, The Walkman effect, *Popular Music*, 4, 165–180, 1984.
Hubbs, Nadine, *The Queer Composition of America's Sound: Gay Modernists, American Music, and National Identity*, Berkeley, CA: University of California Press, 2004.
Hughes, Mark Alan, Formation of the impacted ghetto: evidence from large metropolitan areas, 1970–1980, *Urban Geography*, 11(3), 265–284, 1990.
Hughes, Walter, In the empire of the beat: discipline and disco, in *Microphone Fiends: Youth Music and Youth Culture*, Andrew Ross and Tricia Rose, Eds., New York: Routledge, 1994, pp. 147–157.
Jacobs, Jane, *The Death and Life of Great American Cities*, New York: Random House, 1961.
Jameson, Fredric, Postmodernism, or the cultural logic of capitalism, *New Left Review*, 146, 53–92, 1984.
Jameson, Fredric, *The Ideologies of Theory: Essays 1971-1986*, Vol. 2: *Syntax of History*, Minneapolis: University of Minnesota Press, 1988.
Jameson, Fredric, *Postmodernism, Or the Cultural Logic of Late Capitalism*, Durham, NC: Duke University Press, 1991.
Jameson, Fredric, *Signatures of the Visible*, New York: Routledge, 1992.
Jameson, Fredric, *The Seeds of Time*, New York: Columbia University Press, 1994.
Jay, Martin, *Adorno*, Cambridge, MA: Harvard University Press, 1994.
Jones, Steve, Music that moves: popular music, distribution, and network technologies, *Cultural Studies*, 16(2), 212–232, 2003.
Judd, Dennis and Susan Fainstein, Eds., *The Tourist City*, New Haven, CT: Yale University Press, 1999.
Julier, Guy, *The Culture of Design*, Thousand Oaks, CA: Sage, 2000.
Kaiser, Charles, *The Gay Metropolis: 1940-1996*, Boston, MA: Houghton Mifflin, 1997.

Kasarda, John, Structural factors affecting the location and timing of urban underclass growth, *Urban Geography,* 11(3), 234–264, 1990.

Kassabian, Anahid, Ubiquitous listening, in *Popular Music Studies,* David Hesmondhalgh and Keith Negus, Eds., London: Arnold, 2002, pp. 131–142.

Kelley, Robin, *Yo' Mama's Disfunktional!: Fighting the Culture Wars in Urban America*, Boston, MA: Beacon Press, 1998.

Kim, Nancy J. House blends: like its coffee, Starbucks picks and mixes its own music, *Puget Sound Business Journal*, December 8, 1997.

Klumpenhouwer, Henry, Commodity-form, disavowal, and practices of music theory, in *Music and Marx: Ideas, Practice, Politics*, Regula Qureshi, Ed., New York: Routledge, 2002, pp. 23–44.

Kramer, Lawrence, *Music as Cultural Practice, 1800-1900*, Berkeley, CA: University of California Press, 1990.

Kramer, Lawrence, *Musical Meaning: Toward a Critical History*, Berkeley, CA: University of California Press, 2001.

Kramer, Lawrence, *Franz Schubert: Sexuality, Subjectivity, Song*, Cambridge: Cambridge University Press, 2003.

Krims, Adam, *Rap Music and the Poetics of Identity*, Cambridge: Cambridge University Press, 2000.

Krims, Adam, Marxism, urban geography, and classical recording: an alternative to cultural studies, *Music Analysis,* 20(3), 347–363, 2001.

Krims, Adam, The hip-hop sublime as a form of commodification, in *Music and Marx: Ideas, Practice, Politics*, Regula Qureshi, Ed., New York: Routledge, 2002, pp. 63–80.

Kubrin, Charles, Gangstas, thugs, and hustlas: identity and the code of the street in rap music, *Social Problems,* 52(3), 360–378, 2005.

Lanza, Joseph, *Elevator Music: A Surreal History of Muzak, Easy Listening, and Other Moodsong*, London: Picador, 1995.

Lash, Scott and John Urry, *The End of Organized Capitalism*, Cambridge, MA: Polity, 1987.

Lash, Scott and John Urry, *Economies of Signs and Space*, Thousand Oaks, CA: Sage Publications, 1994.

Lee, Stephen, Re-examining the concept of the 'independent' record company: the case of *wax-trax!* records, *Popular Music,* 14(1), 13–31, 1995.

Lenin, Vladimir Ilyich, *Imperialism: The Highest Stage of Capitalism*, trans. Norman Lewis and James Malone, 1916; London: Pluto, 1996.

Leppert, Richard, Introduction, in Theodor Adorno, *Essays on Music*, Richard Leppert, Ed., trans. Susan H. Gillespie, Berkeley, CA: University of California Press, 2002, pp. 1–84.

Levine, Lawrence, *Highbrow/Lowbrow: The Emergence of Cultural Hierarchy in America*, Cambridge, MA: Harvard University Press, 1988.

Lewis, Lisa, *Gender, Politics and MTV: Voicing the Difference*, Philadelphia, PA: Temple University Press, 1990.

Leyshon, Andrew, David Matless, and George Revill, Eds., *The Place of Music*, New York: Guilford, 1998.

Lipsitz, George, *Dangerous Crossroads: Popular Music, Postmodernism and the Poetics of Place,* London: Verso, 1994.

Loukaitou-Sideris, Anastasia and Tridib Banerjee, *Urban Design Downtown: Poetics and Politics of Form*, Berkeley, CA: University of California Press, 1998.

Mahler, Jonathan, *Ladies and Gentlemen, the Bronx is Burning: 1977, Baseball, Politics, and the Battle for the Soul of a City*, New York: Farrar, Straus and Giroux, 2005.

Manuel, Peter, *Cassette Culture: Popular Music and Technology in North India,* Chicago, IL: University of Chicago Press, 1993.

Marcu, Valeriu, *Lenin: 30 Jahre Russland*, Leipzig: List, 1927.

Marx, Karl, *A Contribution to the Critique of Political Economy,* 1859; London: Lawrence and Wishart, 1975.

Marx, Karl, *Grundrisse: Foundations of the Critique of Political Economy*, 1858; Harmondsworth: Penguin Books, 1993.

Marx, Karl, *The Communist Manifesto*, 1848; London: Verso, 1998.

Marx, Karl and Friedrich Engels, *The German Ideology*, Amherst, NY: Prometheus Books, 1998.

McClary, Susan, *Feminine Endings: Music, Gender, and Sexuality*, Minneapolis, MN: University of Minnesota Press, 1991.

Mele, Christopher, Globalization, culture, and neighborhood change: reinventing the lower east side of New York, *Urban Affairs Review,* 32(1), 3–22, 1996.

Merrifield, Andy, *Metromarxism: A Marxist Tale of the City,* New York: Routledge, 2002.

Ministerio di Asuntonan Economico ta organiza un mision entrepresarial pa Antiyas Hulandes y Aruba, *La Prensa*, August 12, 2005.

Mitchell, Tony, *Popular Music and Local Identity: Rock, Pop, and Rap in Europe and Oceania*, London: Leicester, University Press, 1996.

Morissette, Alanis, Interview with Carson Daly, www.mtv.com (accessed February 15, 2002).

Morley, David, Active audience theory: pendulums and pitfalls, *Journal of Communication,* 43(4), 13–19, 1993.

Negus, Keith, *Popular Music in Theory: An Introduction,* Middletown, CT: Wesleyan University Press, 1996.

Negus, Keith, *Music Genres and Corporate Cultures*, London: Routledge, 1999.

O'Connor, Justin, Left loafing: cultural consumption and production in the postmodern city, in *From the Margins to the Centre: Cultural Production and Consumption in the Post-Industrial City*, Justin O'Connor and Derek Wynne, Eds., Aldershot: Ashgate, 1996, pp. 49–90.

O'Connor, Justin, Adam Brown, and Sara Cohen, Local music policies within a global music industry: cultural quarters in Manchester and Sheffield, *Geoforum,* 31, 437–451, 2000.

Paddison, Max, *Adorno's Aesthetics of Music*, Cambridge: Cambridge University Press, 1993.

Paoletta, Michael, Bjork paints from new palette, *Billboard*, July 23, 2001, pp. 19–22.

Parry, Caroline, Classic FM set to woo musical youth: Britain's most popular commercial radio station is rebranding to attract a younger audience, *Marketing Week*, 43(49), 32–33, 19.

Peterson, Richard, Understanding audience segmentation: from elite and mass to omnivore and univore, *Poetics*, 21, 243–258, 1992.

Peterson, Richard and Albert Simkus, How musical tastes mark occupational status groups, in *Cultivating Differences: Symbolic Boundaries and the Making of Inequality*, Michele Lamont and Marcel Fournier, Eds., Chicago, IL: University of Chicago Press, 1992, pp. 152–186.

Piore, Michael and Charles Sabel, *The Second Industrial Divide: Possibilities for Prosperity*, New York: Basic Books, 1984.

PNP na Megapir a atraé kantidat grandi di hende, *La Prensa*, March 27, 2005.

Population Reference Bureau, Human Population: Fundamentals of Growth Patterns of World Urbanization, at http://www.prb.org/Content/NavigationMenu/PRB/Educators/Human_Population/Urbanization2/Patterns_of_World_Urbanization1.htm (accessed November 8, 2005).

Pottullo, Polly, *Last Resorts: The Cost of Tourism in the Caribbean*, London: Cassell, 1996.

Raban, Jonathan, *Soft City*, London: Hamilton Press, 1974.

Record Industry Association of America, http://www.riaa.com/news/marketingdata/facts.asp (accessed June 5, 2003).

Rink, John, Ed., *The Practice of Performance: Studies in Musical Interpretation*, Cambridge: Cambridge University Press, 1995.

Ritter, Kelly, Spectacle at the disco: *Boogie Nights*, soundtrack, and the New American musical, *Journal of Popular Film and TV*, 28(4), 166–175, 2001.

Robotham, Don, *Culture, Society, and Economy: Bringing Production Back In*, New York: Routledge, 2005.

Rose, Tricia, *Black Noise: Rap Music and Black Culture in Contemporary America*, Middletown, CT: Wesleyan University Press, 1994.

Rosen, Charles, *The Classical Style: Haydn, Mozart, Beethoven*, New York: Norton, 1972.

Rumph, Stephen, *Beethoven after Napoleon: Political Romanticism in the Late Works*, Berkeley, CA: University of California Press, 2004.

Sassen, Saskia, *The Global City: New York, London, Tokyo*, Princeton, NJ: Princeton University Press, 1991.

Sassen, Saskia and Frank Roost, The city: strategic site for the global entertainment industry, in *The Tourist City*, Dennis Judd and Susan Fainstein, Eds., New Haven, CT: Yale University Press, 1999, pp. 143–154.

Sayer, Derek, *The Violence of Abstraction: The Analytic Foundations of Historical Materialism*, Oxford: Blackwell, 1987.

Schloss, Joseph, *Making Beats: The Art of Sample-Based Hip-Hop*, Middletown, CT: Wesleyan University Press, 2004.

Scott, Allen, *Regions and the World Economy: The Coming Shape of Global Production, Competition, and Political Order*, Oxford: Oxford University Press, 1998.

Scott, Allen, *The Cultural Economy of Cities*, Thousand Oaks, CA: Sage, 2000.

Sickels, Robert C. 1970s disco daze: Paul Thomas Anderson's *Boogie Nights* and the last golden age of irresponsibility, *Journal of Popular Culture,* 35(4), 49–60, 2002.

Smith, Neil, *The New Urban Frontier: Gentrification and the Revanchist City*, New York: Routledge, 1996.

Soja, Edward, *Thirdspace: Journeys to Los Angeles and Other Real-and-Imagined Places*, Cambridge: Blackwell, 1996.

Sorkin, Michael, *Variations on a Theme Park: The New American City and the End of Public Space*, New York: Hill and Wang, 1992.

Spivak, Gayatri Chakravorty, Can the subaltern speak?, in *Marxism and the Interpretation of Culture*, Cary Nelson and Lawrence Grossberg, Eds., Urbana and Chicago, IL: University of Illinois Press, 1988, pp. 271–313.

Starr, Peter, *Logics of Failed Revolt: French Theory after May '68*, Stanford, CA: Stanford University Press, 1995.

Sterne, Jonathan, Sounds like the mall of America: programmed music and the architectonics of commercial space, *Ethnomusicology,* 41(1), 22–50, 1997.

Strinati, Dominic, *An Introduction to Theories of Popular Culture*, New York: Routledge, 1995.

Swiss, Thomas, John Sloop, and Andrew Herman, Eds., *Mapping the Beat: Popular Music and Contemporary Theory*, Malden, MA: Blackwell, 1998.

Taylor, Timothy, Music and musical practices in postmodernity, in *Postmodern Music/Postmodern Thought*, Judy Lochhead and Joseph Auner, Eds., New York: Routledge, 2000, pp. 93–118.

Tomaney, John, A new paradigm of work organisation and technology?, in *Post-Fordism: A Reader*, Ash Amin, Ed., Oxford: Blackwell, 1994, pp. 157–194.

Turner, Sarah and Phuong An Nguyen, Young entrepreneurs, social capital and *Doi moi* in Hanoi, Vietnam, *Urban Studies,* 42(10), 1693–1710, 2005.

Wallis, Roger, Business as Usual or a Real Paradigm Shift? The Music Industry's Response to E-Commerce Technology and Ideology, Paper presented at the Key Action II annual conference, 2001.

Wallis, Roger and Krister Malm, *Big Sounds from Small Peoples: The Music Industry in Small Countries*, Stuyvesant, NY: Pendragon, 1984.

Walser, Robert, *Running With the Devil: Power, Gender, and Madness in Heavy Metal Music*, Hanover, NH: Wesleyan University Press, 1993.

Warwick, Jacqueline, Review of Theodore Gracyk's rock music and the politics of identity and Lori Burns and Mélisse Lafrance's disruptive divas: feminism, identity, and popular music, in *Journal of the American Musicological Society,* 57(3), 702–712, 2003.

Whiteley, Sheila, Andy Benett, and Stan Hawkins, Eds., *Music, Space, and Place: Popular Music and Cultural Identity*, Aldershot: Ashgate, 2004.

Williams, Alistair, *New Music and the Claims of Modernity*, Aldershot: Ashgate, 1997.
Wilson, William Julius, *The Truly Disadvantaged: The Inner City, the Underclass, and Public Policy*, Chicago, IL: University of Chicago Press, 1987.
Wilson, William Julius, *When Work Disappears: The World of the New Urban Poor*, New York: Random House, 1996.
Wolfe, Tom, *The Bonfire of the Vanities*, New York: Farrar, Straus and Giroux, 1987.
Wood, Ellen Meiksins, *Democracy against Capitalism: Renewing Historical Materialism*, Cambridge: Cambridge University Press, 1995.
Wood, Peter, Flexible accumulation and the rise of business services, *Transactions of the Institute of British Geographers*, 16, 160–172, 1991.
Wynne, Derek, *The Culture Industry: The Arts in Urban Regeneration*, Aldershot: Ashgate, 1992.
Wynne, Derek and Justin O'Connor, Consumption and the postmodern city, *Urban Studies*, 35(5–6), 841–864, 1998.
Zukin, Sharon, *Loft Living: Culture and Capital in Urban Change*, Baltimore, MD: Johns Hopkins University Press, 1982.

Discography

50 Cent, *Get Rich or Die Tryin'*, Interscope 493544, 2003.
50 Cent,*The Massacre*, Shady/Aftermath/Interscope 4092, 2005.
Anonymous 4, *An English Ladymass*, Harmonia Mundi 907080, 1993.
Anonymous 4, *Voices of Light*, Sony 62006, 1995.
Anonymous 4, *Darkness into Light*, Harmonia Mundi 907274, 2000.
Anonymous 4, *American Angels*, Harmonia Mundi 907326, 2004.
Anonymous 4, *The Origin of Fire*, Harmonia Mundi 907327, 2005.
The Association, *Insight Out*, Warner Brothers 1966, 1967.
The Beach Boys, *Pet Sounds*, Capitol 2458, 1966.
The Beach Boys, *Wouldn't It Be Nice/God Only Knows*, Capitol 5706, 1966.
The Beatles, *Sgt. Pepper's Lonely Hearts Club Band*, Parlophone 46442, 1967.
Beck, *Devil's Haircut*, Geffen 22222, 1996.
The Benedictine Monks of Santo Domingo de Silas, *Chant: The Anniversary Edition*, EMI/Angel 62943, 2004.
Bishop, Elvin, *Fooled Around and Fell in Love*, Capricorn 39635, 1976.
Bjork, *Big Time Sensuality*, Elektra 66244, 1994.
Bjork, *Homogenic*, Elektra 62061, 1997.
Bjork, *Hunter*, Polygram 567199, 1998.
Bjork, *Vespertine*, Elektra 62653, 2001.
Black Star, *Black Star*, Rawkus 11581, 1998.
BMG Special Products, *Starbucks Jazz CD*, no serial number given, 1999.
Brandy and Monica, *The Boy Is Mine*, Atlantic 84118, 1998.
Brightman, Sarah, *Time to Say Goodbye*, Angel 56511, 1997.

Brightman, Sarah, *Eden*, Angel 67692, 1998.
Brightman, Sarah, *La Luna*, Angel 56968, 2000.
Burdon, Eric, and War, *Spill the Wine*, MGM K144118, 1970.
The Chakachas, *Jungle Fever*, Polydor 2480 084, 1972.
Charles, Ray, *Genius Loves Company*, Concord/Hear Music 1033, 2004.
Church, Charlotte, *Charlotte Church*, Sony Classical 64356, 1999.
Church, Charlotte, *Just Wave Hello*, Sony Classical 6685312, 1999.
Church, Charlotte, *Voice of an Angel*, Sony Classical 60957, 1999.
Clark, Petula, *Downtown/You'd Better Love Me*, Warner Brothers 5494, 1964.
Clark, Petula, *Who Am I?/Love Is a Long Journey*, Warner Brothers 5863, 1966.
The Commodores, *Machine Gun*, Motown M1307F, 1974.
The Corrs, *So Young*, Atlantic 00571, 1998.
Costello, Elvis, with Burt Bacharach, *Painted from Memory*, Mercury 80022, 1998.
Egan, Walter, *Magnet and Steel*, Columbia 3-10719, 1978.
Einhord, Richard et al., *Voices of Light,* Sony 62006.
The Emotions, *The Best of My Love*, Columbia 10544, 1977.
The Four Aces, *Mr. Sandman*, Decca 29344.
Geto Boys, *The Resurrection*, Rap-A-Lot/Noo Trybe 41555, 1996.
Gibson, Dan, *Beethoven: Forever by the Sea*, Solitudes 14135, 1997.
Gold, Andrew, *Lonely Boy*, Elektra-Asylum 13-082, 1976.
Grandmaster Flash and the Furious Five, *The Message*, Sugarhill 584, 1982.
Haselbock, Martin, *CPE Bach: Sonatina II D-Dur; Concerto per l'Organo G-Dur; Concerto doppio*, Novalis 150025, 1994.
Horner, James, *Titanic* soundtrack, Sony 63213, 1997.
Hot Chocolate, *You Sexy Thing*, EMI 5592, 1975.
Jan and Dean, *Dead Man's Curve*, Liberty 55672, 1964.
Jean, Wyclef, *We Tryin' to Stay Alive*, Sony 78602, 1997.
KC and the Sunshine Band, *(Shake, Shake, Shake) Shake Your Booty/Boogie Shoes*, TK 8, 1976.
Khan, Chaka, *I Feel for You*, Warner Brothers 2-25162, 1984.
Kirbach, Klaus, *C. P. E. Bach: Organ Concertos*, Capriccio 10135, 1995.
Knight, Gladys, and the Pips, *I Feel a Song*, Buddah 5612, 1974.
Led Zeppelin, *Led Zeppelin IV*, Atlantic 7208, 1971.
Lynyrd Skynyrd, *Pronounced Leh-Nerd Skin-Nerd*, MCA 363, 1974.
Ma, Yo-Yo, *Simply Baroque*, Sony Classical 60680, 1999.
Ma, Yo-Yo, *Simply Baroque II*, Sony Classical 60681, 2000.
Yo-Yo Ma, Edgar Meyer, and Mark O'Connor, *Appalachian Journey*, Sony 66782, 2000.
McLachlan, Sarah, *Surfacing*, Arista 18970, 1997.
Madonna, *True Blue*, Sire 2-25442, 1986.
Martha and the Vandellas, *Dance Party*, Motown 915, 1965.
Minogue, Kylie, *Can't Get You Out of My Head*, Capitol 77685, 2002.
Mobb Deep, *Hell on Earth*, Loud 66992, 1996.
Mobb Deep, *It's Mine*, Sony 79265, 1999.
Mobb Deep, *Murda Muzik*, Loud 91270, 1999.

Morissette, Alanis, *Supposed Former Infatuation Junkie*, Maverick 47094, 1998.
Nas, *Nostradamus*, Columbia 63930, 1999.
Raekwon, *Ice Cream*, RCA 64426, 1995.
Raekwon, *Only Built 4 Cuban Linx*, Loud 66663, 1995.
Schornsheim, Christine, *C.P.E. Bach: Symphonies, Concerto pour Orgue et Orchestre*, Harmonia Mundi France 901622, 1997.
Snoop Dogg, *Tha Last Meal*, Priority 23225, 2000.
Springsteen, Bruce, *The Ghost of Tom Joad*, Columbia 67484, 1995.
Three Dog Night, *It Ain't Easy*, Dunhill 50078, 1970.
A Tribe Called Quest, *Beats, Rhymes, and Life*, Jive 41587, 1996.
Turner, Tina, *Private Dancer*, Capitol C2-46041, 1984.
Various artists, *Saturday Night Fever* [soundtrack], RSO 2658123, 1977.
Various artists, *Lost in Meditation: Meditative Gregorian Chants*, Laserlight 14157, 1994.
Various artists, *Mozart on the Menu: A Delightful Little Dinner Music*, Philips 46762, 1995.
Various artists, *Boogie Nights* [soundtrack], Capitol 55631, 1997.
Various artists, *Bach for Relaxation*, RCA 68697, 1998.
Various artists, *Boogie Nights, Volume 2* [soundtrack], Capitol 93076, 1998.
Various artists, *The Most Relaxing Classical Album in the World... Ever!*, Virgin 44890, 1999.
Various artists, *Classical Chillout*, Angel 67737, 2002.
Various artists, *More of the Most Relaxing Classical Music in the Universe*, Denon 17266, 2003.
Various artists, *The Most Relaxing Piano Album in the World... Ever!*, EMI 67526, 2003.
Various artists, *The Most Relaxing Classical Music in the Universe*, Denon 17232, 2003.
Various artists, *Classics for Meditation*, Madacy 25289, 2004.
Various artists, *Classics for Relaxation*, Madacy 24349, 2004.
Various artists, *Moonlight Classics*, Madacy 23329, 2004.
Various artists, *The Most Romantic Classical Music in the Universe*, Denon 17334, 2004.

Index

A

B

F

G

H

S